Applied WPF 4 in Context

Raffaele Garofalo

Apress®

Applied WPF 4 in Context

ISBN-13 (pbk): 978-1-4302- 3470-8

ISBN-13 (electronic): 978-1-4302- 3471-5

Printed and bound in the United States of America 9 8 7 6 5 4 3 2 1

President and Publisher: Paul Manning
Lead Editor: Jonathan Hassell
Technical Reviewer: Damien Foggon
Editorial Board: Steve Anglin, Mark Beckner, Ewan Buckingham, Gary Cornell, Jonathan Gennick, Jonathan Hassell, Michelle Lowman, James Markham, Matthew Moodie, Jeff Olson, Jeffrey Pepper, Frank Pohlmann, Douglas Pundick, Ben Renow-Clarke, Dominic Shakeshaft, Matt Wade, Tom Welsh
Coordinating Editor: Jennifer L. Blackwell
Copy Editors: Sharon Terdeman and Kim Wimpsett
Production Support: Patrick Cunningham
Indexer: Julie Grady
Artist: April Milne
Cover Designer: Anna Ishchenko

Distributed to the book trade worldwide by Springer Science+Business Media, LLC., 233 Spring Street, 6th Floor, New York, NY 10013. Phone 1-800-SPRINGER, fax (201) 348-4505, e-mail orders-ny@springer-sbm.com, or visit www.springeronline.com.

For information on translations, please e-mail rights@apress.com, or visit www.apress.com.

Apress and friends of ED books may be purchased in bulk for academic, corporate, or promotional use. eBook versions and licenses are also available for most titles. For more information, reference our Special Bulk Sales–eBook Licensing web page at www.apress.com/bulk-sales.

The source code for this book is available to readers at www.apress.com. You will need to answer questions pertaining to this book in order to successfully download the code.

To my wife Debbie, and to Morgana, the best dog I ever had!!

Contents at a Glance

Contents

About the Author

Raffaele Garofalo is a .NET software architect who builds line-of-business (LOB) applications for a living. He works for a hedge fund in Bermuda, where he and his wife, Debbie, moved three years ago. He is originally from Italy, and in his free time he loves to travel around Europe with his wife.

Raffaele is passionate about .NET and WPF and spends his free time writing articles and blog posts about WPF and the MVVM. He is Microsoft Certified (MCAD, MCSD, MCTS, SQL Server, and SharePoint) and he hosts articles and blog posts about WPF and MVVM on his blog. You can visit his blog at http://blog.raffaeu.com.

This is Raffaele second book. His first one was *Building Enterprise Applications with Windows Presentation Foundation and the Model View ViewModel Pattern*, Microsoft Press 2011, about LOB applications and the MVVM pattern.

About the Technical Reviewer

Damien Foggon is a developer, writer, and technical reviewer specializing in cutting-edge technologies, and has contributed to more than 50 books on .NET, C#, Visual Basic, and ASP.NET. He is the co-founder of the Newcastle-based user group NEBytes (www.nebytes.net), is a multiple MCPD in .NET 2.0, .NET 3.5, and .NET 4.0. Visit him online at http://blog.fasm.co.uk.

Acknowledgments

This is actually my second book and I am really happy and proud to be an Apress writer. I built a substantial portion of my skills reading Apress books, and the idea of being part of the Apress bookshelf thrills me! Of course, writing a book is not an easy task and it takes a team, even if my name is the only one on the cover of this book!

First of all I have to thank my editor, Jonathan Hassell, for trusting me and giving me this opportunity. Without him, this book would probably never have been written. My technical reviewer, Damien Foggon, has been an amazing volcano of ideas and suggestions, and I'm grateful for his help. And my coordinating editor, Jennifer Blackwell, was the one who made sure we got the book done in time! Thanks, Jenny! Finally, I want to thank the entire Apress team—they are true professionals. I hope I will be able to write another book with them sometime soon!

Last but not least, I thank my wife, Debbie, for her support and dedication. She is my personal project manager and if I have completed two books, it is only because I have a wonderful and understanding partner who allows me to spend much of our family time on these projects. Also, I want to thank my sweetie dog, Morgana, who, after ten years, left me just before I finished this book. I'll always remember the nights I spent with her on the sofa, getting the book done.

Introduction

Windows Presentation Foundation (WPF) is a graphical computer platform built and distributed by Microsoft to create rich client applications for Windows systems. With WPF, you can build rich interfaces with animations and amazing graphical effects as easily as you can build minimalist and corporate user interfaces for line-of-business (LOB) applications. Unfortunately, because WPF is such a powerful and complex technology, it requires some initial effort to understand its mechanisms. Moreover, for a newbie, the XAML markup used to create the user interfaces can be tough to come to grips with.

Creating a WPF application and, more generally, creating any type of application with a user interface is a rather convoluted task; it comprises a number of phases and the final result is likely to be of a certain complexity. A standalone application built using WPF is usually made up of various "components" that are used to encapsulate the "modules" of the software. You might have, for instance, a component to access the data, a component to include a logical function, a component to render the user interface, and so on.

In this book, I will show you how to create and implement WPF, using best practices to create a real-world application. At the same time, I'll also show you how to structure and architect a WPF application made up of different components that you'll be able to recycle for future applications. By the end of the book, you should have a working knowledge of WPF and know how to architect a WPF application using the tools provided by Microsoft, such as SQL Server 2008 R2 Express Edition, the Entity Framework, Window Communication Foundation (WCF), and more.

Who This Book is For

This book is for Windows application developers who want to understand the context in which WPF sits and the standards and best practices that can be employed to improve the efficiency and maintainability of their projects.

How This Book is Structured

The book is divided into chapters but the overall structure follows a specific logic, so I suggest you read the chapters sequentially—especially if the topic is new to you. The book explains how to build a WPF application from beginning to end. You will start by analyzing the user's requirements before setting out to create the application, and then you'll learn how to work with Microsoft Expression Blend to lay out the user interface that is the essence of the application. On the way you'll learn about Agile development concepts such as Domain Driven Design, Object-Relational Mappers, the business layer, and Service-Oriented Architecture. There is even one chapter dedicated to multithreading and parallel programming in WPF, and more generally with the .NET Framework, and I have also dedicated a chapter to the reporting tool offered for free with Microsoft SQL Server 2008 R2 Express edition, SQL Server Reporting Services.

At the end of the book, you'll be able to deploy the application using ClickOnce and IIS, and you'll understand how WPF's distribution mechanism works.

Downloading the Code

The source code for this book is available to readers at `www.apress.com` in the Download section of the book's page. Please visit the Apress web site to download all the code. You can also check for errata, and find related Apress titles.

Contacting the Author

You are welcome to contact the author, Raffaele Garofalo (aka Raffaeu), with questions. You can reach him at `raffaeu@raffaeu.com` or you can contact him by visiting `http://blog.raffaeu.com`. Follow him on twitter @Raffaeu.

CHAPTER 1

■ ■ ■

Introducing WPF and XAML

Developed by Microsoft, Windows Presentation Foundation (WPF) is a graphical subsystem for rendering user interfaces in a Windows operating system. WPF is based on a markup language also known as XAML.

XAML, which is an acronym for Extensible Application Markup Language, is a declarative markup language available in the .NET Framework designed to simplify the UI creation. XAML is applied to different technologies; it is available for Windows Presentation Foundation, Silverlight, and Windows Workflow Foundation (WF).

The principal reason of having a markup language for the UI creation is to decouple the UI code from the presentation logic that can still be written in one of the available .NET languages such as C# or VB .NET. Using this approach, you can assign the UI development process to a developer/designer more specialized in the UI creation, who will probably use Expression Blend, and you can leave the core development process to a .NET developer, who will probably accomplish this task using Visual Studio.

Usually, but not always, a XAML file will have an extension of type .xaml and an encoding of type UTF-8; Listing 1-1 shows the XAML code to create a WPF control. This specific code is declaring a StackPanel control that has a ListBox control; inside the ListBox three items are defined, each one using a ListBoxItem element.

Listing 1-1. Sample XAML Code Used to Create a Button Control

```
<StackPanel>
    <ListBox>
        <ListBoxItem Content="One" />
        <ListBoxItem Content="Two" IsSelected="True" />
        <ListBoxItem Content="Three" />
    </ListBox>
</StackPanel>
```

Before starting to learn how WPF works, you should analyze in more detail the XAML syntax, which is part of the WPF technology.

■ **Note** Especially if you have already worked in the past with XAML, you may find this introduction repetitive. This is not because I had the intention of writing a verbose introduction but because the XAML technology and syntax are unique across different technologies; so if you ever worked in the past with a XAML technology like Silverlight or Workflow Foundation, you may already understand the material in the next sections.

The XAML Syntax

The XAML language is a complex and very flexible markup language applied to different technologies by using different *references* in the XAML file so that you can refer to different objects that provide different XAML elements and attributes.

Like any other XML file, a XAML file must have a valid structure and must follow some specific rules; one of these rules is the presence of a valid root element.

Namespaces and Root Elements

In XAML you define a root element as the root of your XAML document; this is a mandatory requirement for the XAML file and for the XML validation. In a WPF context, the root element of a XAML file will be a `Page`, `UserControl`, or `Window` if you are creating a UI container or a simple `ResourceDictionary` if you are creating a collection of resources for your application (which is another valid root element for a WPF application and which is also a standard file created by the Visual Studio project). These root elements are only some of the available options for a WPF XAML file.

■ **Note** If you are creating a XAML file for another technology like Silverlight or Workflow, you will probably use different root elements provided by these technologies.

Listing 1-2 shows the structure of a `Window` object, which constitutes a normal window UI in WPF and is represented by the root element `Window`.

Listing 1-2. XAML Root Namespaces

```
<Window x:Class="Chapter01.MainWindow"
    xmlns="http://schemas.microsoft.com/winfx/2006/xaml/presentation"
    xmlns:x="http://schemas.microsoft.com/winfx/2006/xaml"
    Title="MainWindow" Height="350" Width="525">
    <Grid>
    </Grid>
</Window>
```

The root element in the Listing 1-2 contains the attributes `xmlns` and `xmlns:x`. These attributes indicate to a XAML processor which XAML namespaces contain the type. The `xmlns` attribute specifically indicates the default XAML namespace. The `xmlns:x` attribute indicates an additional XAML namespace, which maps the XAML language namespace (which is `http://schemas.microsoft.com/winfx/2006/xaml`).

The namespace declaration always applies to all the descendant element of a XAML document, just as they do for an XML document; for this reason, you won't need to declare the same namespace twice in a XAML document in order to use its types, but you will need to declare those types preceded by the corresponding element prefix.

You may also need to reference a custom type provided by a namespace that you have previously created and that is already referenced in your XAML application; to do that, you should use the keyword `xmlns` followed by your custom prefix and then add a reference to the namespace containing the classes you want to use.

Listing 1-3. *XAML file with custom references*

```
<Window
    x:Class="Chapter01.MainWindow"
    xmlns="http://schemas.microsoft.com/winfx/2006/xaml/presentation"
    xmlns:x="http://schemas.microsoft.com/winfx/2006/xaml"
    xmlns:custom="clr-namespace:Chapter01.CustomNamespace"
    Title="MainWindow" Height="350" Width="525">
    <Window.DataContext>
        <custom:CustomClass />
    </Window.DataContext>
    <Grid>
    </Grid>
</Window>
```

Listing 1-3 declared a new custom prefix called `custom`, which references a namespace that is referenced in the example project. Inside this namespace is a class called `CustomPrefix` that is available using the prefix `custom`.

Objects and Common Elements

Like when using XML, if you want to declare a new type in XAML, you should encapsulate the type in an element object that is denoted by an opening bracket (`<`) followed by the type name and then a closing bracket (`>`). The element can be closed by an additional element of the same type, starting with the bracket (`</`) or can be simply *self-closed* using the syntax `/>` at the end of the element declaration.

```
<!-- closed with another element -->
<Button name="MyButton">
</Button>
<!-- self-closed -->
<Button name="MyButton" />
```

As soon as you declare a type in XAML, it is like you are creating a new instance of that element; at that point, you can access the properties and other characteristic of that object using the XAML syntax.

The Attribute Syntax

If you create an object with a .NET language like C# or VB .NET, you can access and modify a property or a visible field of that object using the dot syntax, like this one: `myObject.Property = "myValue"`. In the same way, after you declare and instantiate a type in XAML, you can access and modify the properties available for that type but in a different fashion—using the XAML *attributes*. For example, the following code is declaring a `Button` as a XAML type, and then you are modifying its properties using the XAML attributes:

```
<Button Height="40" Width="120" Content="Hello World!" />
```

You are able to accomplish the same task using C#:

```
Button button = new Button();
button.Content = "Save Entity";
button.Width = 100;
button.Height = 100;
```

The first difference you may notice is that in XAML you don't provide a value for a property based on its data type, while you have this distinction in C# and VB .NET. For example, the property `Width` of a `Button` has an `Int32` data type, but in XAML you must specify its value between two quotation marks, so any value is specified as a `String` value type. This is not really a XAML requirement, but it is inherited from the XML structure, which requires a value for an attribute between two quotation marks. The conversion is then applied using a `TypeConverterAttrbute`, which is explained in the next section.

The TypeConverterAttribute

Any value used in an attribute in XAML is of type `String` when it is inserted in the XAML markup; this value needs then to be translated by the XAML processor to the real value used by that element. For example, you can set the `Width` of a `Panel`, which is an integer value, to 200; the XAML processor will need then to convert this string into an integer value.

If the value is a primitive that is understood by the XAML parser, a direct conversion of the string is attempted; if the value is neither a parser-understood primitive nor an enumeration, then the type has to provide a type converter class.

Let's use for this example the `Background` property of a common WPF control like a `Button` control. When you declare the value for the `Background`, you have to pass an acceptable value of type `Brush`, because `Brush` is the value type for the `Background` property and you write a XAML markup like this: `<Button Background="Red" />`. The `TypeConvert` for a `Brush` value type is composed by a `BrushConverter` that is associated to the `Brush` class using syntax like the following:

```
[TypeConverter(typeof(BrushConverter))]
public class Brush
{
    // code used for the conversion
}
```

The XAML markup used to define a background color can then be translated in the following C# code:

```
Button b = new Button();
b.Background = new BrushConverter().ConvertFromString("Red");
```

If you plan to create a custom type converter for your custom types, these are the steps you need to follow:

Create a custom class that represents your new converter; the class must inherit from TypeConvert and must implement the methods CanConvertFrom, CanConvertTo, ConvertFrom, and ConvertTo.

Decorate the class that represents your custom value with your custom converter using the decoration attribute [TypeConvert(TypeOfConvert)].

Property Element Syntax

Sometimes, you may find it difficult to represent a complex type as a String value for an element property value, so the value should be declared using a different technique. For example, a Button has a Content property that represents the content of the Button. In XAML, the content can be simple, like a String, or complex, like a Panel with nested UI controls. If you want to add such a kind of content in a Button, you may need to use the property syntax element definition, where the property of an element is specified as an additional element, a child one.

The following code shows a Button with a complex type for its Content property. In this example, you are representing the content of a Button using a StackPanel that includes two controls: an Image that will display the button's icon and a TextBlock that will display the button's caption.

```
<Button Height="40" Width="120">
    <Button.Content>
        <StackPanel Orientation="Horizontal">
            <Image Source="home_go_32.png" Margin="0,0,5,0" />
            <TextBlock VerticalAlignment="Center" Text="HomePage"/>
        </StackPanel>
    </Button.Content>
</Button>
```

The property element syntax is represented by the name of the parent element, followed by a dot that is followed by the name of the property. In this way, the property element becomes a complete XAML element that can include a child structure.

You can use the same technique to declare a collection of values. If the property element you are working with is of type collection, you can declare a set of sequential child elements inside it, like in the following code, which is declaring a set of child items for a ListBox element:

```
<ListBox>
    <ListBox.Items>
        <ListBoxItem Content="One" />
        <ListBoxItem Content="Two" IsSelected="True" />
        <ListBoxItem Content="Three" />
    </ListBox.Items>
</ListBox>
```

As you can see the `Items` property has a collection of items of type `ListBoxItem` declared sequentially in the property element.

The Content Property

In XAML there is a particular property available for *any element*, which is the default property that is defined by `ContentPropertyAttribute`; if the element represents a class derived from `Controls.ContentControl`, the default property is of type `ContentProperty`; for other elements like the `TextBlock`, the default property is the `Inlines` property, and so on. Any class represented by XAML can have one and only one content property that can be considered as the *default* property for that class. Because this property is the default property of a class, you can totally omit its declaration in XAML; in order to use it in this way, you should simply add content inside the class element. Of course, not every content property is the same; for example, you may have a content property of type `String` and a content property of type `Object`.

Listing 1-4 shows how you can implicitly or explicitly declare the content value of a `TextBlock` in XAML.

Listing 1-4. XAML Implicit and Explicit Content Declaration

```
<StackPanel>
  <!-- IMPLICIT -->
  <Button>I am implicit content</Button>
  <!-- EXPLICIT -->
  <Button>
    <Button.Content>
      I am explicit content
    </Button.Content>
  </Button>
</StackPanel>
```

In the same way, you may need to declare the content of a specific element using the collection syntax because the content property is of type `collection`. This is the case that applies to any container control in WPF, like a `Panel`, a `StackPanel`, and so on, where the default property is of type `Children`. These types of controls have a type converter for their content property that is translated in a collection of child controls.

Listing 1-4 has a root element of type `StackPanel`, and its content property is implicitly populated by two child elements, namely, two buttons.

The Code Behind

Every time you create a new XAML file in Visual Studio, it will create for you a *code-behind* file based on the language of your project; so if you are working on a WPF application using C#, after you create a file called `MainWindow.xaml`, then Visual Studio will add for you a file with the same name but with the `.cs` extension, `MainWindow.xaml.cs`, which contains the corresponding C# of your XAML file.

If you look more in depth in a XAML file created in Visual Studio, you will notice that in the namespace declaration, there is also the declaration `x:Class="ClassName"`, where `ClassName` is the name of your XAML file. When Visual Studio compiles your file, the CLR will put together the XAML file and the code-behind based on the name in the x:Class attribute; in the same way, if your XAML file doesn't have a code-behind file, the x:Class attribute will not be used.

When you work on a WPF application, you will always have a code-behind file for each XAML file created in your solution; in this file you will save the C# code related to the XAML file and all the events and delegate associated with that UserControl.

Events in XAML

If you have ever worked with WPF or with another client technology such as Windows Forms, you already know that for each control there is a specific event raised in order to inform the UI that the user did something. For example, when you click a Button, the UI raises an event Click associated to that button.

In WPF and in XAML in general, you can't write the procedural code for that event in the XAML file, but you need to write the corresponding event handler in a C# file.

Listing 1-5 shows a XAML Button with a method associated to its Click event. The method is registered in the XAML code, but it's declared explicitly in the code-behind file.

Listing 1-5. *C# Event on a Code-Behind File*

```
// XAML File
<Button Click="Click_Event">Hello World</Button>

// C# Code-behind
private void Click_Event(object sender, RoutedEventArgs e)
{
    Console.WriteLine("Hello World");
}
```

▓ **Caution** In XAML you can also include the procedural code in the XAML file by using this syntax:

```
<x:Code><![CDATA[
    // your code here …
]]></x:Code>
```

I suggest you avoid this technique because one of the aims of XAML is to separate the UI markup from the presentation logic.

Events are fundamental in WPF, and you will see in this book how events are handled in WPF using commands and routed events.

Attached Properties

XAML is a powerful language that can be easily extended using the element prefix or the attached properties. You already saw that after you declare an additional namespace in a XAML root element using a prefix alias, you get a set of new elements available in that namespace.

With the attached properties, you attach element additional properties provided by the parent element in the form of real properties.

Usually, some elements provide an attached property to their child elements because they want to know something from them in order to react in the proper way. For example, WPF provides a container control called DockPanel that allows you to pile the child controls of this panel using the dock position. The available dock positions are left, right, top, and bottom. For each child element of a DockPanel, you can and should specify a different dock location; you may have a label at the top, a text box in the middle, and a button at the bottom. To accomplish this task, the DockPanel attaches a property called Dock to each child element.

Because the property is not provided by the child element, you need to use the syntax Parent.Property; Listing 1-6 shows a practical example of an attached property.

Listing 1-6. Attached Property in XAML

```
<DockPanel Width="200">
  <TextBlock DockPanel.Dock="Top">First Name:</TextBlock>
  <TextBox DockPanel.Dock="Top" />
  <Button DockPanel.Dock="Bottom">Save</Button>
</DockPanel>
```

The attached properties are not the only available extension in XAML provided by the parent element; for example, some elements can provide to the children an attached event that has the same logic of an attached property, but it's an event.

■ **Note** In this short introduction, you saw how XAML works and how XAML is structured. In the next chapters, you will learn how XAML is structured and how it can be used for a WPF application. If your intention is to analyze more in-depth specific topics related to the XAML technology or to the XAML syntax, I suggest you visit the following URL: http://msdn.microsoft.com/en-us/library/ms788723.aspx.

Introduction to WPF

WPF is the Microsoft XAML technology for client applications hosted on a Windows operating system.

The current version of WPF is the 4.0, which is delivered with the .NET Framework 4.

WPF is a vectorial UI technology that uses XAML as a markup language to define the UI and uses C# or VB .NET for the presentation logic.

A WPF application can be built with a simple text editor and the C# compiler carried with the NET Framework (it's a tough job, but it can be done); with one of the available versions of Visual Studio 2010 or with Expression Blend which requires both the NET Framework runtime. Visual Studio is for a more development-oriented audience, and Expression Blend is for a more designer-oriented audience.

As you already saw in the previous section, a WPF application and, in general, a XAML file *may* be composed by a XAML markup file that defines the UI structure of a control and a code-behind file in C# or VB .NET that defines the behaviors of the control.

Right now the .NET Framework allows you to build two different types of WPF applications; the first one is identified as a stand-alone application, and it is composed of the classic `.exe` file that contains all the executable code and runs on a Windows operating system. The second one is an in-browser application and has an `.xbap` extension that can be executed in Internet Explorer.

Figure 1-1 shows a schematized version of how WPF can act as a stand-alone application or an in-browser application. The main difference is in the project type and in the containers you will use to display the UI. Although a stand-alone application displays windows, an in-browser application displays pages.

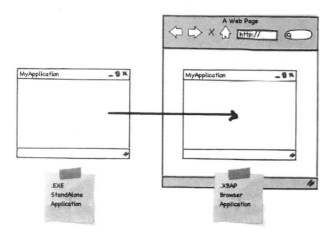

Figure 1-1. Example of StandAlone and Browser application

UI Controls in WPF

Although WPF is a very flexible technology, you may still have the need a default set of controls and containers while you are writing your applications, and WPF comes with a default set of controls and containers that can satisfy most of your needs.

In addition to these controls, you may find it useful to visit the open source community at CodePlex (`www.codeplex.com`), where you can find hundreds of free controls and containers for your WPF applications. In this book, you will use some of these controls to build an Office-style application.

You can add WPF controls to the view using the XAML markup language or at runtime using the code-behind file; you may need to create a particular `UserControl` that will need to create child controls *on the fly* while the application is running, and you may need to accomplish this task using the procedural code (C# or VB .NET).

Controls Containers

The first thing you may need to understand when you write a WPF application or any UI application is how to position you controls in the view (see the following note). WPF is a vectorial technology, which means it is able to adapt the screen resolution without losing quality in the UI.

In WPF the term *framework element* means a theoretical rectangle that represents a portion of the UI. Each component of the UI is a rectangle, and each child component is an additional rectangle. The allocation allowed for a *rectangle* in the UI is affected by the presence of additional controls in the same container; for example, you may have a StackPanel that contains only a TextBox. In this case, the TextBox will cover the entire space provided by the StackPanel; if in the StackPanel you position an additional TextBox, the space will be covered now by the two child controls.

Figure 1-2 shows a practical example.

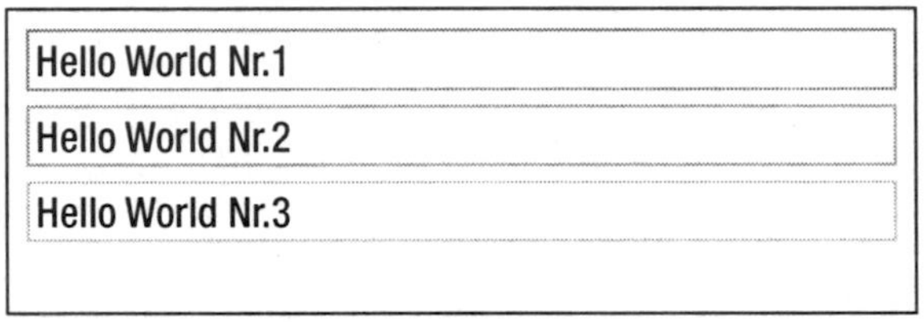

```
Hello World Nr.1
Hello World Nr.2
Hello World Nr.3
```

Figure 1-2. WPF StackPanel with three TextBox controls

As you can see, in this case, each TextBox is occupying the entire width of the parent control container because it is using a vertical flow; with another container, the behavior may result in something different.

■ **Note** With the term *view*, we define any UI container suitable to offer a graphical representation of the data and an interaction between the application and the user. In WPF a view can be a window, a modal dialog, or a simpler user control.

With WPF you have different ways of piling the controls in a container and different ways of resizing the controls in the container when the container size changes or when the screen resolution size changes. The interesting news is that with WPF you don't need anything else to provide the code for the resizing process because the controls container is in charge of that.

Layout containers have different behaviors:

- Canvas: Defines an area where each child control is positioned by providing an absolute coordinates value. This is the same behavior you had in Windows Forms, and it should not be used if you don't have a very specific need for it.

- DockPanel: Defines an area where the position of a control is relative to the position of another child control in the same container. The possible dock positions are <u>Top</u>, <u>Right</u>, <u>Bottom</u>, and <u>Left</u>. In WPF there is not a Fill position like in Windows Forms.

- **Grid**: Defines a table-style container with rows and columns and acts like an HTML table where you can span controls across multiple rows and columns.

- **StackPanel**: A container that stacks the controls vertical or horizontal one after the other one. You can define the space between each control.

- **WrapPanel**: Positions child elements in sequential position from left to right, breaking content to the next line at the edge of the containing box.

In WPF you have the same layout logic described in HTML by the *box model* technique where each control has a **Margin** property and each child has a **Margin** property and a **Padding** property.

Margin defines the space between an element and its child elements. **Padding** defines the space between a child element and its parent container. The main difference between the two properties is that **Margin** gives you space outside the control, and **Padding** gives you space inside the control.

Additional position properties are **HorizontalAlignment** and **VerticalAlignment**, which are used to specify a default position of a control in the container.

Figure 1-3 shows a summary overview of the position techniques in WPF.

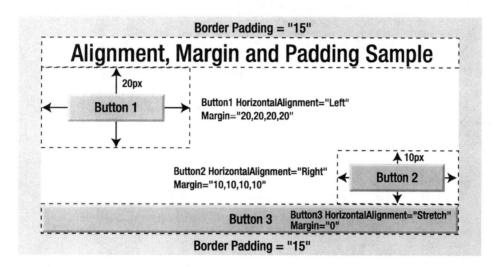

Figure 1-3. WPF controls position overview

Common Controls

WPF offers a set of common controls available in the Visual Studio toolbox that can be used for your daily activities without the need of writing additional code. In some cases, you may need to customize the appearance of a control or to change the behavior of a control using the styles and the templates.

In other cases, you may need to listen for an event of a control in order to execute a specific code; for example, you may need to listen for the **Click** event of a **Button** control in order to execute a specific operation.

All these steps can be accomplished using the XAML markup or by writing code-behind the XAML; it depends on what you are doing and how you are doing it. In this section, you will see the available controls provided by XAML, and in the next chapters, you will see how you can customize the default appearance and the default behaviors of a control.

Control Composition

Each control that inherits from the base class `System.Windows.Controls.Control` is composed by a default set of components that you can customize and change using the `StyleTemplate` or the `DataTemplate`. The class `Control` is composed by a `ControlTemplate`, which represents the default template for the appearance of the control in the UI; when you customize the `DataTemplate` of a control, you change how the `ControlTemplate` should behave.

The `ControlTemplate` may display a single item, a collection of items (like a `ListBox`), or a `Header` of an item; for this reason, in WPF you have controls that are of type `ContentControl`, `ItemsControl`, or `HeaderControl` based on how the `ControlTemplate` should be structured.

Visual Studio and the .NET Framework 4 provide a set of default controls, detailed in the following list. If you want to get a more detailed explanation of each control, refer to http://msdn.microsoft.com/en-us/library/system.windows.controls.aspx, in particular to the section "System.Windows.Controls" where you will find the complete list of available controls.

The following are the categories of available controls in .NET 4; they represent only part of the full set of controls delivered with the .NET Framework 4.

- *Buttons*: This represents a `Button` with a label or complex content.

- *Inputs*: `TextBlock` and `TextBox` are part of the available input controls; the first control can be used as a `Label`, while the second control is used to retrieve or display text in the UI.

- *List*: `GridView`, `ListBox`, `ComboBox`, and `ItemsControl` are controls able to display and select items in a list of items.

- *Layout*: This section consists of all the controls designed to contain and provide layout to child controls, such as `StackPanel`, `DockPanel`, and so on.

- *Documents*: These are controls designed for interacting with documents such as XPS documents.

As I said previously, every one of these controls can be added to the UI using two different approaches: you can declare the control by using XAML or by writing C# code and adding the control to the controls collection of the parent container. Listing 1-7 shows the two methods.

Listing 1-7. *Example of Creating a Control with XAML or with C#*

```
<!-- using XAML -->
<StackPanel Name="pnl">
  <Button Name="btnFirst" Content="First" />
</StackPanel>
```

```
// using C#
StackPanel pnl = new StackPanel();
Button ctrl = new Button();
ctrl.Name = "btnFirst";
ctrl.Content = "First";
this.pnl.Controls.Add(ctrl);
```

WPF Architecture

Windows Presentation Foundation is a complex technology that consists of a set of base assemblies plus a set of additional assemblies used in the UI.

The two primary assemblies that contain most of the WPF code are `PresentationCore` and `PresentationFramework`. `PresentationCore` contains the *core* code for WPF and all the base classes, while the `PresentationFramework` assembly contains all the concrete controls used in the UI. The third component is `milcore`, which stand for *media integration layer* and is the unmanaged part of WPF in charge of orchestrating the UI interaction such as animations, hardware performances, and DirectX.

Figure 1-4 shows the structure of WPF in the .NET Framework (the image is taken from msdn.microsoft.com in the Official WPF section); the PresentationFramework, PresentationCore, and milcore sections are the foundation of WPF.

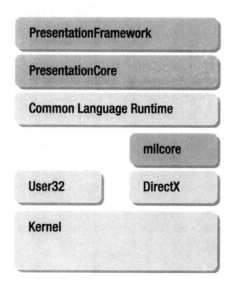

Figure 1-4. WPF architecture

Assemblies and CLR

The first class you are going to analyze is `System.Threading.DispatcherObject`, which provides a mechanism of messaging to communicate between threads from and to the UI. WPF, like Windows Forms, is a UI technology that works using *single-thread* design and *thread affinity*; this means that if you try to update the UI from a different thread, you are in charge of writing the correct code that will redirect the call to the UI thread. The `Dispatcher` provided in this namespace is in charge of solving this problem.

`System.Windows.DependencyObject` is another class fundamental in WPF; it enables the tracking process of the dependencies of a property of a XAML object. For example, when you data bind an object to a view, in XAML `DependencyObject` acts as a mediator between the view and the `Bind` object and notifies the two actors when something changes.

`System.Windows.Media.Visual` is the namespace in charge of controlling the way the UI is designed and the way the pixels are rendered on the screen. This assembly is not used directly by you, but it is used indirectly when you create, for example, a new control in the UI.

In `System.Windows.UIElement`, you can find everything related to layout, input, and events. In the layout, as you saw in the previous section, you will find all the controls in charge of arranging the elements in the UI; in the input and events, you will find all those methods useful to control the user interaction such as `MouseClick` or `SelectionChanged`.

In `System.Windows.FrameworkElement`, you can find part of the UI properties used to manage the layout, such as `HorizontalAlignment` and `VerticalAlignment` for example, or the data binding engine and the styles.

Finally, `System.Windows.Controls` is the namespace in charge of providing everything for the creation of UI controls; it also contains all the UI controls shipped with WPF 4.

These are the namespace available in WPF that provide all the tools and mechanisms to make a consistent and powerful WPF application; in the course of this book, you will see when and how to use most of them.

Technologies

In the previous section, you saw that WPF ships with a set of assemblies, and each one provides one or more WPF-related technologies such as styles, data binding, commanding, and more. In this section, you'll get an overview of the technologies provided with this set of assemblies and how to use them and, more than anything else, why they are useful.

Styles

If you ever worked in the past with any web technology such as ASP.NET, PHP, JSP, or even a simple HTML web page, you may know that every part of a web page can be styled using Cascading Style Sheets (CSS). In this way, you can create a UI style to represent a `TextBox` in a particular way, and this style will be spread all over you web application.

If you ever worked before with a client technology such as Windows Forms or Java Forms, you may know that this is an impossible task to achieve using the basic tools provided by these two frameworks. What I mean is that in Windows Forms, you can't define a style for a UI control; you need to create a specific UI control that has the style hard-coded in the base class. For example, if you want a nice `TextBox` with a specific border color and a specific border shape, in Windows Forms you have to create a custom `TextBox`.

In WPF you have the styles like you have on the Web, but probably with a lot more power and control. In a style you can set static values or dynamic values using triggers; for example, you may have a `TextBox` style that defines the background color to white, but when the `TextBox` gets the focus, the background becomes yellow.

Listing 1-8 shows how you set up some properties on a `TextBox` using the `TextBox` element itself or using an embedded style in the `Resource` property of the parent element.

Listing 1-8. Comparison Between Embedded Setter or Style

```
<StackPanel Name="pnl">
  <StackPanel.Resources>
    <!-- TextBox style -->
    <Style TargetType="TextBox" x:Key="TxtStyle">
      <Setter Property="FontFamily" Value="Verdana" />
      <Setter Property="Background" Value="Yellow" />
      <Setter Property="Width" Value="200" />
    </Style>
  </StackPanel.Resources>

  <!-- TextBox with embedded style  -->
  <TextBox Width="200" Height="25"
   FontFamily="Tahoma" FontSize="12" />

  <!-- TextBox with associated style -->
  <TextBox Style="{StaticResource TxtStyle}" />
</StackPanel>
```

In the second case, you can easily recycle and apply the property Style="{StaticResource TxtStyle}" to any TextBox and spread your style all over the application.

The only constraint you have when you prepare a style for a specific control is that the style must be for a specific control, and to do that, you must provide a value for the property TargetType of the Style element; in this property, you have to specify the control you are styling.

Additional consideration has to be done to the x:Key attached property. If you specify a key, you must provide that key on every control that has to use the style; otherwise, you can avoid specifying a value for the x:Key property so that *any* control of that type will use the style.

Data Templates

Another way to customize the layout of your controls is using the DataTemplates. A DataTemplate is the template that represents the data exposed by your control. Usually you work with a DataTemplate when you want to customize how an ItemsControl displays its items at runtime, but you can use the DataTemplate also to customize a control that displays a single item. Usually, an ItemsControl, like a ListBox, displays the .ToString() method of the items bound to it in the UI, so when you try to bind a list of objects to a List control, you will get a weird result, and the only property available to customize the data you are displaying is the DisplayMemberPath, which allows you to prompt only one property by using a string format. If you customize the DataTemplate of your ListBox, you will be able to visualize the items bound to the control as you want them; for example, you may force the ListBox to display for each row the FirstName and the LastName of a Person class in a StackPanel using two TextBlock controls.

Figure 1-5 shows a screenshot of Visual Studio 2010; in the figure there is a UserControl with two ListBox controls bound to the same data source, which is a List<T> of class Person. As you can see, the first ListBox shows the full name of the object bound to the ListBox, while the second ListBox is using the DataTemplate tocustomize the way the data is displayed in the ListBox.

Figure 1-5. *Differences between ListBox with and without a DataTemplate*

Like with styles, you can add a data template *inside* an element like in the following code:

```
<DataTemplate>
    <StackPanel Margin="3" Orientation="Horizontal">
        <TextBlock
           <!--
              Bind the Firstname property using the String.Format method
              that will display "Name: [FirstName]"
           -->
           Text="{Binding Path=FirstName, StringFormat=Name: {0}}"  Margin="0,0,5,0" />
        <TextBlock
           Text="{Binding Path=LastName}" Margin="0,0,5,0" />
        <TextBlock
           Text="{Binding Path=DateOfBirth, StringFormat=Birth: {0:d}}" />
    </StackPanel>
</DataTemplate>
```

Or you can add the DataTemplate in a resource file (a topic that will be discussed in Chapters 4 and 5 when I talk about the UI composition) and use it all over your application.

■ **Note** Of course, if you believe that the DataTemplate will be used in the future by another control, I kindly suggest you create from the beginning a resource dictionary file in your application with all the DataTemplates you will use. This will save a lot of time!

DataBinding

`DataBinding` is another powerful feature of WPF, and it's probably the most desirable feature of this technology, which makes WPF so powerful and flexible.

In WPF and also in Silverlight, DataBinding is the process that allows the UI to be bound to the application data and make both the UI and the presentation logic aware of changes in the original data or in the UI. In WPF, most of the available UI controls have an in-place binding mechanism that allows you to bind *dynamic* data to the UI.

If you think for a moment about a normal line-of-business (LOB) application, you will find that the main process is composed of three simple steps: retrieve the data from the database, display the data in the UI, and update the data based on actions the user did in the UI. All these steps can be easily accomplished if you write the correct presentation logic and bind it to a WPF control.

This topic in conjunction with the "Styles and Templates" section will be analyzed in depth in this book in Chapters 5 and 7 where you will learn how to create a cool UI and how to apply styles and DataTemplate to the UI.

WPF 4 Tools

WPF is a nice technology, but it is based on a combination of two programming languages—XAML markup and the language you choose for the code-behind file, which C++, C#, or VB .NET. With some effort, you should be able to write and compile an entire WPF application just by using the classic Notepad application and the proper compiler in a Command Prompt window, but at the same time I can guarantee you that it will be a very challenging experience for even the most expert WPF developer.

Fortunately, Microsoft provides a set of tools to develop WPF applications, which will make your life much easier; these tools are targeted to different audiences, so you should find one to write the presentation logic and one that is more feasible for a designer.

Most of these tools are under license, so you will not find them for free on the Internet, but Microsoft offers a basic set of these tools called *express editions*, which are available for free but with a limited set of functionalities.

Finally, there are also free tools available for WPF designers, which can make your life much easier if you need to test your WPF result in the UI without running a WPF application; these tools are usually used to test templates and styles before touching the production code.

Visual Studio 2010

Microsoft Visual Studio 2010 is built on the WPF technology, so it's probably the most feasible tool to build WPF applications. It is delivered in three versions:

- *Professional*: The perfect version if you are starting to develop WPF application and you are still not sure it will be your final choice

- *Premium*: The richer version if you are already working with WPF and you also need to share the code on your team and test it

- *Ultimate*: The richest version of Visual Studio used usually by senior developer, software architects, and QA

- *Test Professional*: An integrated testing toolset version of Visual Studio

You can download each one of these versions on your computer and try it for 90 days without buying the final product.

If you can't afford a license of Visual Studio, there is still the option of downloading and using the express version of Visual Studio available at www.microsoft.com/express/. The express editions of Visual Studio are divided by topic, so you will find an express edition for Visual C#, one for Visual C++, one for VB .NET, one for web development, and one for Windows phone development.

When you open Visual Studio and you choose to create a new WPF application, you will be prompted by Visual Studio to choose from one of the available solutions:

- *WPF Application*: This is the classic stand-alone application that will result in a final .exe file that contains all the code generated in the project; this application can be executed in any Windows OS that has the .NET Framework 4 or NET 3 or 3.5.

- *WPF Browser Application*: This is the web version of WPF, which will produce an .xbap file that contains all the code generated in the project; this application can be executed in Internet Explorer.

- *WPF Custom Controls library*: This is a separate assembly (.dll), which contains custom controls. Customs controls are usually enhancement of existing WPF controls.

- *WPF User Controls Library*: This is a separate assembly (.dll), which contains user-created controls; in this library, you will create controls that do not exist in WPF.

Figure 1-6 shows the New Project dialog box of Visual Studio 2010.

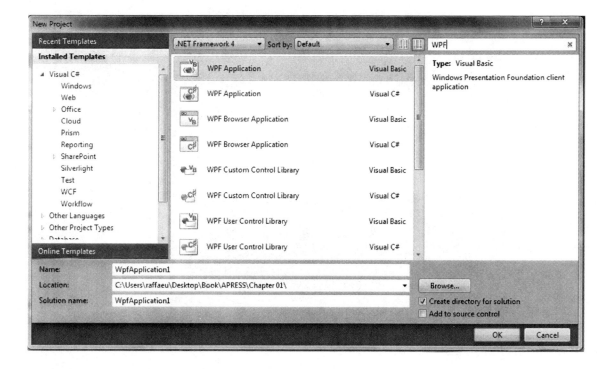

Figure 1-6. *New Project dialog box in Visual Studio 2010*

After you choose which solution you want to create in Visual Studio and select a name and a destination folder, Visual Studio will create for you a folder with the name of your solution, a solution file (.sln) that contains all the code that describes the solution folder structure, and a project file that will describe the current project, in my case a WPF application.

Figure 1-7 shows a WPF application open within an instance of Visual Studio 2010; in this screenshot there some numbered panels that I'll explain.

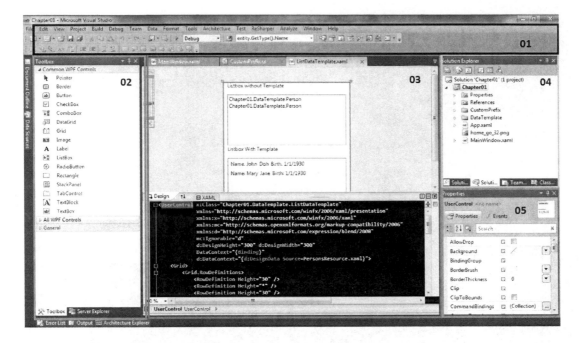

Figure 1-7. WPF application in Visual Studio 2010

Visual Studio is composed by a set of dockable panels; dockable means you can drag and drop any panel of Visual Studio and decide where to stick it in the IDE. If you drag a panel in a section that contains already other panels, the panel becomes a tabbed panel.

Figure 1-7 shows a WPF application open in Visual Studio; there are five major sections, which show you how Visual Studio handles the dockable panels.

- *1, the toolbar and menu bar*: In this section of Visual Studio you will find all the available commands and menus. Using the right-click menu, you can choose which menu to show in the IDE.

- *2, left side*: By default, the left side of Visual Studio shows the Toolbox of available WPF controls and the Server Explorer panel.

- *3, center panel*: The center panel shows the open files in a tabbed-style UI.

- *4, right side*: In the right side of Visual Studio you usually have the Solution Explorer, which displays the structure of your application, and a panel, which shows the properties of the current object selected in the center panel.

- *5, split panel*: In Visual Studio you can use one section of the UI to split panels so that you can have a stack of panels all in one part of the IDE.

The last consideration is how you can interact with your XAML files in a WPF project. Each XAML file is composed by two parts, the code-behind (in our case C#) and the XAML markup. The XAML markup can be viewed in two ways; one is by looking directly at the markup, and the other is by looking at the final UI result (designer). The two views (XAML and designer) can be viewed split or in two separate UIs. These two views can be switched in Visual Studio, and as soon as you make a change in one of them, the other one needs to be *refreshed* in order to show you the final result. If you want to view the code-behind, you simply need to right-click any part of the XAML file and select View Code.

Expression Blend

Expression Blend is one of the products available in set of tools called Expression, and it's available for download at www.microsoft.com/expression/. Expression Blend is delivered in a package that is composed of various tools used by designers to create images, web sites, video, and UIs for WPF or Silverlight. Expression Blend can be considered the Visual Studio for WPF and Silverlight designers; although Expression Blend is still a good tool for coding (because it allows you to edit XAML code and C# or VB .NET code-behind files), its audience is more a designer audience than a developer audience.

You can open and edit an existing Visual Studio 2010 solution using Blend so that you can customize and test your UI styles and then reopen the solution in Visual Studio to focus more on the presentation logic; in the same way, you can open part of your files in Visual Studio (developer) and part in Blend (designer) so that two people can work on the same project and focus on different areas, like the design and the presentation logic.

When you open Expression Blend (Figure 1-8), you are prompted to create a new project (Figure 1-9) or to work with an existing template provided by Microsoft by default in Blend.

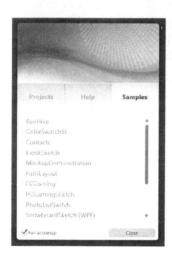

Figure 1-8. *Expression Blend start page*

Expression Blend offers the possibility of working on two major different type of projects that you can call *mockup* projects and *production* projects. The first type of projects can be created using an extension delivered with the Blend Ultimate edition called SketchFlow, which allows you to create powerful and dynamic mockups that can act as a real applications and work with real data; this is useful when the designer is still focusing on the UI structure. The second type of project are the projects available in Visual Studio so you can create applications and controls libraries.

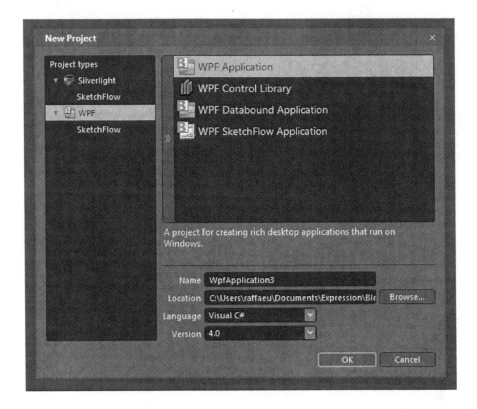

Figure 1-9. Expression Blend's New Project window

The only difference between the projects you can create in Visual Studio and the ones you can create in Blend is the new WPF Databound Application, which is a WPF application that uses the Model View View Model (MVVM) pattern to separate the UI logic from the presentation logic. You will see this pattern in detail in Chapter 12.

Expression Blend is an awesome tool to create and customize rich UIs for WPF, and it is a great tool to learn the XAML syntax; while you drag and drop controls and styles in the Blend IDE, you can switch to the XAML code and take a look on how the styles you are creating work in XAML.

Additional Tools

Sometimes you may need to tweak just a piece of XAML code and you don't want or you can't open and create a new solution in Visual Studio in order to do that. In other situations, you are experimenting with a new setup of a view or user control, but you don't want to screw up the current project, so you need a quick and fast way to create a new WPF application and play with a dummy XAML file.

For these and other reasons, you can find on the Web some pretty cool tools to create and customize XAML files without needing to open Visual Studio. The following is a list of some of the available tools to customize XAML; feel free to download and try them:

- *XAMLPAD*: This XAML editor is delivered with Blend and Visual Studio SDK; it's available for download at `http://msdn.microsoft.com/en-us/library/ms742398(v=vs.90).aspx`. It is a great tool to edit and style XAML files, but it doesn't allow you to edit code-behind files.

- *KAXAML*: This is an alternative XAML editor that you can download for free at `www.kaxaml.com`. It has, more or less, the same characteristics of XAMLPad.

Another interesting tool that comes with the Visual Studio SDK is UISpy.exe, which allows you to *spy* on running applications in order to view whether their structure is conforming to your requirements.

XAML Power Toys are a Visual Studio extension that enables a more context-sensitive XAML IntelliSense while you are working with your WPF applications. It allows you to search and filter specific keywords while you are working in the Visual Studio IDE without interfering with the default IntelliSense.

Summary

XAML is a powerful markup language available in the .NET Framework 4 to create rich interfaces and applications. It is used by three different technologies available in the .NET Framework: Windows Presentation Foundation (WPF), Silverlight (SL), and Workflow Foundation (WF).

It is structured using the XML definition, and it reflects the XML specifics where only one element can define the root element of the file and where you can edit properties using attributes or child elements.

In a code file, you can find the procedural code, which can be VB .NET or C#, in a file called a *code-behind* file that has the same name as your XAML file plus a file extension based on the .NET language the application is done in (such as `.cs` for C# and `.vb` for VB .NET).

WPF is the client-side technology provided by the .NET Framework; it is built on two major assemblies: `PresentationCore` and `PresentationFramework`. It is a vectorial UI technology, which means it is able to adapt to the different screen resolutions without losing quality and can be executed as a stand-alone application or as a browser application within Internet Explorer.

WPF provides two powerful technologies with it; one is the style and template, which allows you to totally customize how your UI behave, and one is the DataBinding, which is a powerful data-binding engine provided in almost every UI control.

Finally, you can edit you WPF applications by using one of the available versions of Visual Studio 2010, by using Expression Blend, or by using one of the available open source tools.

CHAPTER 2

■ ■ ■

Sample Application: Overview and Getting Started

This book is part of the Apress series called In Context; in this specific case, you will see how WPF 4 can be applied in context. But what does *in context* mean? The series focuses on delivering a complete guide to a technology (in this case WPF 4) by building a real-world application via tutorials. I believe that trying a technology is the best way of learning and mastering it.

The application you will develop in this book is a time-tracking application that will be used to track the time spent by ACME Consulting Ltd. employees. ACME Consulting Ltd. is a fake IT consulting company that will be your customer. By the end of the book, you will have a complete time-tracking application developed in WPF 4 that you will be able to deploy and release or that you can use as a road map for any future client application you develop using WPF 4.

In this chapter, you will learn about the requirements for executing the code and samples in this book and what software tools you may need to write a more fashionable UI; everything needed in the book is available through downloads. You'll find the source code at Apress.com; the rest of the downloads links will be provided inside the book.

Requirements

Apress TimeTracker (ATT) is a WPF 4 client application that uses an IIS web server and a SQL Server 2008 R2 Express database server as its datastore. In ATT you will use also some royalty-free UI controls and icons, which you may want to purchase if your final result will be a commercial product.

I have divided the software requirements into two sections. The first one is a list of software and third-party tools used in this book that may not be free, and the second part includes open source projects free of charge that you may want to use in your project.

Tools and Software

The following is a list of software and controls used in this book that are not necessarily free. An evaluation version of each one can be downloaded at the related web link.

- Microsoft Visual Studio 2010: The version of VS 2010 used in this book is the Express version. If you want to be able to open and modify the files that accompany this book, including UML design files and schema, you may consider downloading the Express edition of Visual Studio 2010 for Visual C# at `www.microsoft.com/express/Downloads/#2010-Visual-CS`. You can also download a trial version of Visual Studio 2010 Ultimate or Premium version or purchase a license. A trial version of Visual Studio 2010 is also available at `www.microsoft.com/visualstudio/en-us`.

- Microsoft SQL Server 2008 R2 Express: Microsoft SQL Server 2008 R2 Express edition is available in a lot of different versions; the one used in this book is the Expression Version with Advanced Service, which is available for free at `www.microsoft.com/express/database/`. It includes everything you need to build a robust database including Reporting Services.

Icons and Templates

You can find a lot of free icons and WPF templates on the Web. Just to give you an example, in this application I used icons and images found via the icon search engine `www.iconfinder.com`; if you plan to use graphical images in a commercial application, you must verify the permissions and any potential royalty payments required for the use of those images before including them in your applications.

The themes used on this book are available for free at `www.codeplex.com`, which is the biggest open source portal for .NET applications; the themes are downloadable from `http://wpfthemes.codeplex.com/`.

Third-Party Library and Controls

You can also use some third-party tools and library, which will make your job easier. Parts of these libraries are open source, and they are not the only ones available through the internet. Feel free to use them or to download a different one as suggested in the book.

- Enterprise Library 5.0: The Enterprise Library is a huge .NET application framework that gives you additional capabilities when working with your code. It includes an Inversion of Control framework, validation block, logging, exception handler, and more. It is available at `http://entlib.codeplex.com/`.

- AutoMapper: AutoMapper is an open source framework built on .NET 3.5 that is very useful if you plan to flatter a graph of classes into a single Data Transfer Object class. You will use this framework in the later chapters of the book. It is available for free at `http://automapper.codeplex.com/`.

- Major MVVM Toolkits: In the Chapter 12, you will see some toolkits that allow you to write flexible and reusable code using the MVVM pattern for WPF. In this chapter, you will use also some open source frameworks for MVVM.

- WPF Toolkit: Finally, you should download and install the WPF Toolkit from `http://wpf.codeplex.com`. The toolkit includes additional UI controls, charts, and themes for WPF; this open source project is kept alive by Microsoft, and it's a requirement for any cool WPF application. The version used in this book is the latest as of February 2010.

Application Overview

The application you will build in this book is called Apress TimeTracker. Many consulting companies, especially in IT, need to track the time their employees (consultants) spend every day at a customer's office in order to manage the resources and to invoice the expenses to the customers.

A time-tracking application is a good example for a real-world WPF application; it has specific UI and logical requirements that can be easily designed with WPF and a layered architecture.

The application requirements for Apress TimeTracker are as follows:

- It must provide a rich UI that will expose the data using complex UI controls and dynamic charts.

- It should implement an Office 2010–style UI theme and icons.

- It should persist and retrieve the data to a SQL Server database through a unified web data service.

- It should be easy to maintain and tested.

- It should be easy to deploy, and it should be easy to get a new version when available.

Application Architecture

The process of designing application architecture consists of defining how you will structure and architect the application, how it will be composed and structured, and how you will optimize the code in order to have a secure, maintainable, and manageable application. The biggest risk you can incur if you design an application with a poor architecture is that the application will not be easy to maintain and probably will not be easy to be extended or to be tested.

When you start to architect a new solution, you should focus primarily on three major areas that usually compose any application: the user's requirements, the business's requirements, and the system's requirements. Between these three requirements, there should be always a balance, meaning you should focus on the user's requirements but that they shouldn't affect the infrastructure's requirements.

Other considerations before starting to design the application are more related to the structure of your solution and to the principles you will follow while developing the application. One of the first concepts you should follow is the separation of concerns; in other words, you should find a balanced way of separating features and concepts into different modules so that you will minimize the amount of duplicated code and so you can keep the modules decoupled between each other.

You should also follow basic OOP principles such as single responsibility, where each component is responsible for only a specific task, and the *principle of* last knowledge, where a component or module doesn't know the internal details of other modules.

Saying that, understand that a complex application doesn't mean a well-done application; you should always find the right balance between a complex application and an over-engineered application that may result in a hard-to-maintain application.

Layered Applications

When you architect an application, you will have to decide which type of style you will apply to the architecture; for example, you may find it useful to define a domain model (covered in Chapter 6) that represents your business requirements; you may also find it useful to separate the various modules of the application into different layers and to separate some components of the application into different tiers.

The main principle of a layered architecture is to separate the various functionality of your application into layers that are stacked vertically into the application so that the communication between them is clear and loosely coupled. Usually with this type of architecture, the component of a specific layer is able to communicate only with the component of a lower layer. Sometimes, because of the complexity of the application architecture, the layers may reside on a distributed system (n-tier), which will force you to apply to your architecture the principles of n-tier architecture (covered next).

When you design a layered architecture, you should be firm about some principles that apply to this design:

- Keep the layers abstract while you focus on the primary role of each layer; the main purpose of a layer is to be independent and focused on a specific task.

- Consider the functionality of each layer, how it will communicate with other layers, and where it will be positioned in the application layer's stack.

N-tier Applications

The structure of an n-tier architecture is similar to the structure of a layered application; the n-tier solution can be considered a more complex design of a layered application. In addition, a tier can be considered as a layer placed into different physical machines. Of course, if you plan to move into this type of solution, you may come up with a more complex design and more infrastructure requirements such as high availability, high scalability, and high manageability.

The most used and most known n-tier architecture is the three-tier application architecture, which is composed by the following tiers:

- A presentation tier that executes on the client side made up of the GUI part of the application, which is composed of a graphic interface and a presentation logic layer.

- A business layer distributed through a Service-Oriented Architecture (SOA) that can be a web service or a Windows Communication Foundation (WCF) library.

- A data tier that resides on the database server and that is in charge of distributing the data across the various clients.

An n-tier application is an advanced solution because it requires more code, more complexity, and more tests. Usually this type of architecture is adopted during the refactoring process, when the simplest layered architecture is not able to satisfy the business demand anymore.

A tiered application is any computer software that is composed of more than one logical block or layer distributed over different locations; usually the application is defined by the number of tiers that composed it, so you may have the classic three-tier application, two-tier application, and so on.

The reason you want to separate logical code by affinity in separate layers is because you want to make your logical block more loosely coupled, because you want to make your code easy to maintain and upgrade and you want to cover with tests as much code surface as you can.

If you have ever worked with a stand-alone application or with a web application, you may have already encountered a two-tier application where the first tier was the client application and the second tier was the remote database. If the application was interacting with a middle tier composed by a WCF or a web service, then the application was a three-tier one.

The main difference between these two types of n-tier applications is that the first one is composed by one tier (client application), which includes all the code layers (user interface, business code, data access), while the second one is composed by a client tier that composes the UI (UI layer and presentation layer), a second tier for the business logic (business layer and data layer), and a third tier for the data store (database server). Figure 2-1 shows a schema of a one-tier, two-tier, and three-tier application.

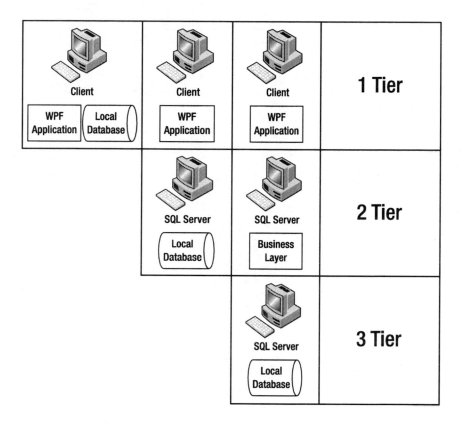

Figure 2-1. *Schema representing the various n-tier applications*

The WPF application you will create will be a three-tier application that will be structured in the following way:

- Database tier: The database tier will be composed of a SQL Server 2008 Express database and reports that you will store on a database server that can be a local instance (development machine) or a remote instance.

- Business tier: In the business tier, you will store the *business logic* of the application; a domain layer that represents the business entities of the application, a data layer that uses .NET Entity Framework to *translate* the business entities in T-SQL object and that will have a reference to the database tier; and finally a WCF service layer that will expose the business logic and the business objects. All these layers will be stored on a Windows web server that can be local or remote.

- Client tier: This is the tier that you will install on the client computer. It will contain the UI and presentation layers (WPF application), and it will have a reference to the business layer.

Figure 2-2 shows the UML layer diagram of Apress TimeTracker; it has been realized with Visual Studio 2010 Modeling project using the Layer Diagram item, a tool able to translate into a layer diagram an existing layered application structure.

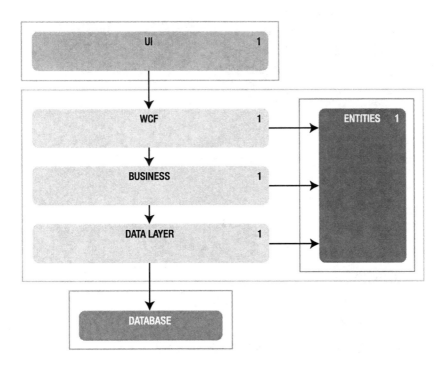

Figure 2-2. *TimeTracker layer diagram*

The square around the layer shapes defines the boundary limit of a tier. Starting from the bottom, you have the database tier, followed by the business tier, exposed through a WCF service, ending with the UI client tier, installed in the user's computer.

The next step is to understand how the application will behave and what the major business processes executed by the application will be.

TimeTracker Architecture

You saw the possible solutions for software architectures and what type of considerations are before adopting a specific architecture. Figure 2-2 shows the overall architecture of the TimeTracker application and how it will be composed.

Before starting to write the code for your WPF application, you should architect the structure of the Visual Studio solution and think about how you will separate the code using different layers.

▓ **Note** An *application layer* is a group of objects, in this case a group of classes and structures, that have a similar meaning or that are reusable in similar circumstances.

When you write an application using an OOP technology like .NET or Java, you have the option of architecting the solution in different ways, based on the complexity you want to add to the solution and based on the customer requirements and the resources available.

Architecting a WPF application can be easy if you know already what the available solutions are and when you should use a specific architecture instead of another one. In this section, you will see what type of layered applications can be built using WPF and the .NET Framework and which one you will use to architect the Apress TimeTracker application.

User Stories

A user story is a sentence that describes a specific business process; it is usually represented by a default sentence like "As an *actor*, I *want/desire* something so that I can get this *benefit*." In the context of the agile methodologies, a use case is the description of an interaction between a system and one or more actors. The main purpose of designing use cases before starting to architect an application is to identify the key scenario that will drive the development process of the application and that will help you make critical decisions about the technology you will use and the techniques you will apply to the application.

With Visual Studio 2010, you can lay out the user stories using the use case diagram, available in the Model project. You can design a macro use case that represents the overall process of TimeTracker plus a more detailed use case that will analyze in depth every single business process described in the main use case.

The following list represents a set of potential use cases you may encounter on the TimeTracker application. Of course, they can be considered as use scenarios and not simply use cases. For example, in a use scenario, you will have a set of use cases that consist of the scenario; for example, the editing process of an employee is a use scenario where you have various use cases such as creating a new employee, editing an existing one, and so on.

- As a manager, I want to be able to manage the existing employees of the company so that I can add, update, or remove employees from the database.

- As a manager, I want to be able to administer the appointments from the employees and the customers.

- As a manager, I want to print and view daily, monthly, and annual reports of the time spent by the employees to the various customers.

- As a manager, I need a dashboard that will give me access to all the available functions of the application in a single UI.

These user stories can be represented in a main use case that can be expanded into four more detailed use cases. Figure 2-3 shows the main use case.

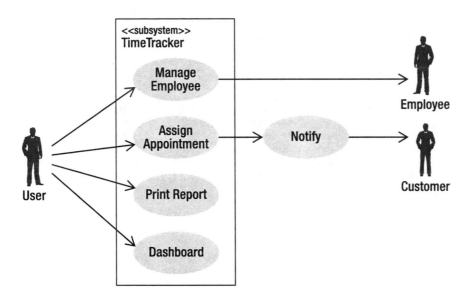

Figure 2-3. *TimeTracker use cases*

Domain Model

In any application you write, you have a domain model that is a conceptual model consisting of domain entities that represent your business objects in the application. The domain objects are usually retrieved from the user stories after you identify the actors of each use case. In the previous section, I marked in bold the actors of each user story (Employee, Customer, Appointment, Address and Contact) so that you can easily identify the five domain objects in the TimeTracker application.

The domain model should be an effective representation of the application domain problems and should be designed as the blueprint of your application; each entity of the domain should have a relation to the other entities of the same domain in order to constitute a complete graph of domain entities that interacts with each other. If the domain model is well designed, it should allow you to understand the overall application just by reading the UML representation of the domain.

In the TimeTracker application, you can identify five major domain objects that are the actors for the application. Let's try to read the user stories and to translate the requirements into domain entities.

The first requirement is that you will have a list of Employees, and this list should be managed only by a Manager, which means you will have an Employee entity with a Role entity associated. The Role entity will define the membership of an Employee to a specific group, like the Manager one.

The second requirement is to have a list of Customers that you can contact so you will have a Customer entity.

You have an Address entity as both, because an Employee and also a Customer may have more than one address.

Finally, you need to schedule appointment between a Custom and an Employee and monitor the time spent during the appointment; so, you will have an Appointment entity that will reference an Employee and a Customer, and that will carry some additional information such as the time, date, and so on.

Figure 2-4 represents the domain model for the TimeTracker application; in this model, I used the Entity Framework class diagram designer because through this designer you can generate the SQL code and the C# code in one shot.

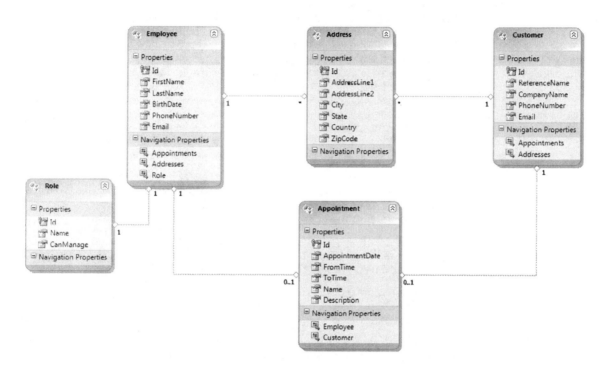

Figure 2-4. *TimeTracker domain model*

Using the domain-driven design approach (DDD), you can make the application *readable* by a non-WPF developer; for example, if you pass the previous UML diagram to an analyst or to a non-IT expert, you are still giving them a *readable* map of your application; in this case, it is very easy to understand that the previous Entity Framework model represent a relationship between Employee, Customer, and Appointments.

■ **Note** This type of development is called *domain-first development* or *domain-driven design*; the domain is in the first place, and the application is developed around the domain UML. The domain is the blueprint of the application and represents the business requirements of the application.

Database Schema

The database is another important component of the application and in our case is a very important component because it represents the data store where you will save and retrieve the data. In this book, you will use SQL Server 2008 R2 Express, which can be administered and developed using SQL Server Management Studio or simple T-SQL code. As you saw in the previous chapter, the application will use the domain-first approach, so you will build the database schema based on the domain design; thanks to the Entity Framework, you can build the domain using C# or VB .NET (depending on the type of language you chose when you created the project) and then leave the arduous task of creating the database schema to the Entity Framework engine.

Another approach may be to have a database-first application where the application will be driven by the database design; this may happen in applications where the database has been created before the application or in architecture where the database already exists and can't be modified.

A database is usually a set of objects that interacts and provides a way of saving, retrieving, and querying data in organized containers. The database is composed by specific objects:

- Table: The table is the container of data in the database. Usually it is organized in rows and columns, where a column describes a data type with a specific name and a row is a set of data. Each row, usually, is a unique combination of values. A table can have a virtually infinite number of rows but a predefined number of columns.

- View: As the name says, the view is a virtual table composed by the result of a query over one or more tables or views. The primary purpose of this object is to provide a specialized virtual container of data.

- Stored procedure: A stored procedure is a set of T-SQL commands executed against one or more database objects. It can be an INSERT statement or a more complex query to filter data.

- Key, constraint: The database contains data in tables in the form of unique rows. A row can be unique because it has a single column that is unique in the entire table (primary key) or because it is composed by a set of column that has a combination of values that is unique in the entire table (composite key). The database may also be forced to contain a specific set of value of a specific type of value in one or more columns (constraint).

The database generated for the TimeTracker application has a simple schema that reflects, in a relationship of one-to-one, the domain model generated with the Entity Framework. In Chapter 6, you will analyze in depth the T-SQL code generated with this tool, and you will analyze also the database structure used by TimeTracker.

Application Configuration

In the first part of this chapter, you saw how to structure an application into different layers, how to transform the customer requirements in user stories that will be then transformed in real code, and how to design and structure the data store used by the application.

In this part of the chapter, you will prepare the Visual Studio 2010 solution for the TimeTracker software, including third-party resources and components.

By the end of the chapter you should have a working Visual Studio 2010 solution that will include a set of projects and a main WPF stand-alone application.

But before starting to write code, you need to prepare the environment for your application.

Visual Studio Solution

The first thing you need to do is to open Visual Studio 2010 and create a new application, in this case a WPF application that will be the repository for the TimeTracker application. The application name is APRESS.TimeTracker, and it will be the startup project of the VS application.

The second step is to separate the code from the resources and the tests; right-click your Visual Studio solution and choose Add   New Solution Folder; this command will create a new folder in the root of your Visual Studio solution. You're creating a repository structure in your solution so that the application code will contained in one folder, the resources in another one, and the tests and the documentation in another.

Create the folders Application, Lib, Test, and Documentation.

These types of folders are also known as *solution folders*, and they are virtual containers that will help you keep the solution tree organized.

At the end, you should have a Visual Studio solution with one WPF Application project named APRESS.TimeTracker inside the folder Application and three additional folders.

Layers in TimeTracker

As I said previously, the TimeTracker application will be composed of some layers that you have already analyzed: the UI layers that are the WPF application, a presentation layer that is a class library project, a business layer, a WCF service, and an Entity Framework data access layer. All these layers will be covered by a unit test project. A modeling project will then be used to analyze the user requirements and to draw the application architecture.

Table 2-1 represents the additional projects you need to add to the WPF solution, including the name of the project, the project type, and the folder that will contain the project.

The code used in this book and in the sample application is C#, so remember that when you refer to any project in the solution, like Class Library, WCF Service Library, and WPF Application, you always refer to the project template under the tree of the Visual C# projects.

Table 2-1. *WPF Application Structure*

Project name	Project Type	Folder	Layer Type
[APRESS.TimeTracker]. BusinessLayer	C# Class Library	Application	BLL
[APRESS.TimeTracker]. DataLayer	C# Class Library	Application	DAL
[APRESS.TimeTracker]. ServiceLayer	WCF Service Library	Application	BLL
[APRESS.TimeTracker]. Test	Test Project	Test	TDD
[APRESS.TimeTracker]. Architecture	Modeling Project	Documentation	UML

Each layer has some specific references to other layers and components. To add a new reference to a project, you should select the source project, right-click the project icon, and choose Add New Reference; Visual Studio will open the Add Reference window that allows you choose a reference: an existing project, a third-party DLL, or a .NET assembly installed on your development machine.

When you choose the context menu item Add Reference, Visual Studio will open a tabbed window with three tabs: Projects, COM, and Assemblies. Based on the type of component you want to reference, you will have to choose one of these tabs. On the first one, Projects, you will add a reference to another project available in the solution, and on the second one, COM, you will add a reference to a COM object. With the third one, Assembly, you will add a reference to a .NET assembly compiled with the same version of the .NET Framework or with a previous version.

Figure 2-5 shows the Add Reference window. On the left side you can choose the location of your reference, while on the right side Visual Studio shows the available references by location. If the reference is a third-party DLL, you can click the Browse button and locate the DLL file.

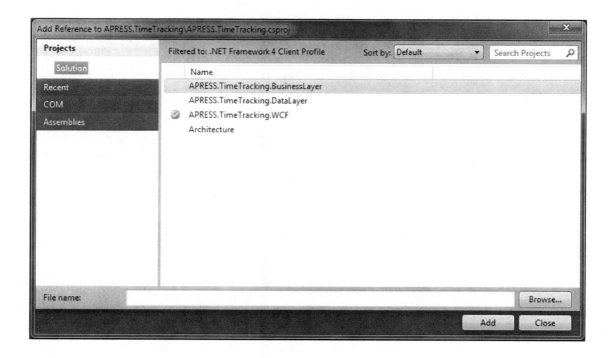

Figure 2-5. *Add Reference window*

The reference map should be created in the following way:

APRESS.TimeTracking (WPF app)
    APRESS.TimeTracking.WCF
    APRESS.TimeTracking.BusinessLayer
    APRESS.TimeTracking.DataLayer
APRESS.TimeTracking.WCF
    APRESS.TimeTracking.BusinessLayer
    APRESS.TimeTracking.DataLayer
APRESS.TimeTracking.DataLayer
    Nothing
APRESS.Test
    APRESS.TimeTracking
    APRESS.TimeTracking.BusinessLayer
    APRESS.TimeTracking.WCF
    APRESS.TimeTracking.DataLayer

Additional third-party references will be added by the developer during the application development life cycle.

Figure 2-6 displays the final solution.

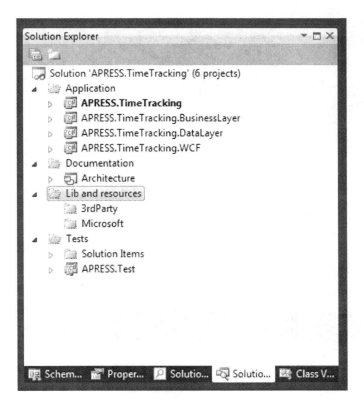

Figure 2-6. *Apress application layers in Visual Studio*

■ **Note** The naming convention used in this book may look a little bit verbose. This naming convention follows the ISO standard where a namespace or a package (Java) should contain three parts divided by a dot: the company name, the application name, and the specific layer name.

This convention is useful if you work in a big project that may have 20 to 30 layers. A name like APRESS.TimeTracking.BusinessLayer is more readable than AP.TT.BLL.

Resources and Third-Party Components

In Visual Studio 2010 you can include in the solution the third-party DLLs or the resources used by the application. This may be really useful, especially if you are going to move the solution to a different location in the file system or if you want to take the solution with you on a removable device.

Adding an existing file to the solution root, using the solution folder, doesn't guarantee you that the file will be included in the solution folder created in the file system. For example, if in the solution in Visual Studio there is a solution folder called lib and in this folder you added an existing item from the file system, you will not find the item in the same location in the solution folder in the file system.

Therefore, you will add the necessary third-party references to your solution, but you will also save a copy of them in the file system so that you will be able to carry with you all the necessary files related to the Visual Studio solution.

Right-click your Visual Studio solution, and choose Open Folder in Windows Explorer; this command will open the root folder in the file system that contains the Visual Studio solution. Add a folder and call it Lib; inside this folder create three additional folders: 3rdParty, Microsoft, and Resources. If you have already downloaded the files mentioned in the "Tools and Software" section, you should already have all the files available in the file system; otherwise, you should download them now or copy them from the Visual Studio solution available at Apress.com (simply search for the book using title, author, or ISBN, then look for the Book Resources tab). Move the Enterprise Library DLLs available in the installation folder you created during the setup of the Enterprise Library to the Microsoft folder, move AutoMapper and WPFToolkit to the 3rdParty folder, and move the icons of your application to the Resources folder. If you open now Visual Studio, you will not find anything in the Lib folder available in your root, because it doesn't point to the same location. To reflect the file system structure, you should use the right-click menu in your Visual Studio solution and use the Add Solution Folder command in order to reflect the same structure you have in the file system. When you are set up with the structure, select one of the created folders, right-click, and choose Add Existing Item; locate the DLL you want to add to your VS folder, and click Add.

At the end of this process, the structure will look like Figure 2-7.

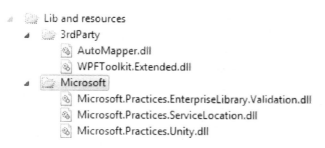

Figure 2-7. *External assemblies used in the TimeTracker application*

How WPF Uses the Resources

Right now you have just added some file to a solution folder, but this doesn't mean you can access these files directly from your WPF application as external resources. In this specific case, because they are an assembly's files, in order to use them, you should add a reference to the Visual Studio project that points to the corresponding physical DLL file.

In other situations, like with the images or with the icons used in a WPF application, you need to use a different approach because you want to be able to localize these graphic files as resources available throughout the entire application.

The first thing to do is to create an images folder in the Visual Studio project called APRESS.TimeTracking, which is the root project of the application and which is also the WPF stand-alone project. After you create the folder, you need to drag all the desired images and icons inside this folder from the file system, right-click each one, select Properties, and mark them as Resources. The images used in the application are composed by a set of free icons called woofunction, available at `www.woothemes.com/2009/09/woofunction-178-amazing-web-design-icons/`; they are just one of the hundreds of available icons set on the Web. Starting from now, your WPF application will be able to locate them using the unique path convention `[folder]/[image name]`.

Figure 2-8 shows the two steps described previously.

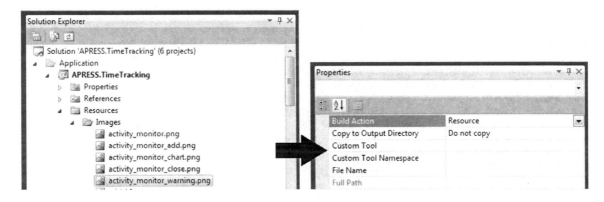

Figure 2-8. *Adding resources images to the WPF application*

At this point, you may be wondering why you created a file in the file system, added the file in the root folder of your application when you created the third-party assembly folder, and then dragged the images to a project folder and marked them as resources.

Well, the procedure is slightly different from the previous one; when you add a file to a root folder, which means to a solution folder, the file will not deployed with the application just because that file doesn't really exist; it's just a shortcut to the physical one. In the other method, when you add a file to a WPF project and you mark the file as resource, the file will be included in the final compiled DLL or EXE file. This approach is useful especially when you deploy your application because you don't have to worry about how to move the external resources such as images and animation used by your WPF application.

These types of resources can be accessed using both XAML or C# file. You can use the code in Listing 2-1 to access resources and images from the same assembly or from a referenced assembly.

Listing 2-1. *How to Use Referenced Resources in WPF*

```
<-- From XAML in the same project -->
<Image Source="Images/MyImage.png" />

// from C# in the same project
var source = (BitmapSource)Application.LoadComponent(
            new Uri("Images/MyImage.png", UriKind.Relative));
```

```
<-- From XAML in an external project -->
<Image Source="ReferencedAssembly;v1.0.0.1;component/Images/MyImage.png" />

// from C# in an external project
var source = (BitmapSource)Application.LoadComponent(
                new Uri("ReferencedAssembly;v1.0.0.1;component/Images/MyImage.png",
                UriKind.Relative));
```

■ **Note** Resources management in WPF is a complex topic that will be covered in later chapters. You can use resources for different purposes, and one of them is to reference physical resources such as images and videos. There is not really a best practice on how to use the resources; usually it is preferred to use the resources in a separate assembly so that the style of the application can be easily exchanged with another one.

Summary

Before starting to build a WPF application, you should consider some fundamental requirements such as application architectures, customer requirements, additional resources needed in the application, and so on. You can easily accomplish this task using the UML tools integrated with Visual Studio 2010.

The TimeTracker application will be designed as a three-tier application; the front-end tier is composed of the presentation logic and the UI in WPF; the middle tier is composed of a business layer, a WCF Service layer, and a data layer with the Entity Framework; and the data tier is composed of a SQL Server database.

CHAPTER 3

■ ■ ■

Microsoft Expression Blend

Microsoft Expression Blend is an application provided by Microsoft to overcome the shortcomings of WPF and the Silverlight designer integrated in Visual Studio. The current version of Visual Studio, 2010, has a well-done WPF integrated designer, but the previous version, 2008, lacked a lot of functionality.

Another reason we have an additional WPF designer in Blend is because Visual Studio's audience is more *development* oriented, while Blend's audience is more *designer* oriented; in fact, the target audience of Blend is not the application developer but the application designer.

WPF is composed of two languages: the XAML markup code, which is used to create the UI graphics and effects; and the code-behind code, which can be C# or VB .NET. The UI and tools available in Visual Studio are more designed for developers, while the UI and the way Blend works makes for a better experience with XAML. With Visual Studio, it is easier to mess up the XAML markup if you start to drag controls here and there in the UI—mainly because in Visual Studio the WPF designer is just one of the available tools, while in Blend, the WPF is the main tool and has more functionalities from a designer standpoint.

In this chapter, you will see how Blend is structured, how you can switch a project from Blend to Visual Studio and vice versa, and what Blend offers to provide a better development experience for a WPF application.

Overview

Microsoft Expression Blend 4 is available at `www.microsoft.com/expression/products/blend_overview.aspx`; you can download the trial version and use it for 60 days for free, or you can buy it through the Microsoft web site. Expression Blend is available in the Ultimate version of Microsoft Expression Studio, which also includes the SketchFlow plug-in; it is not sold separately anymore, and it is not available in the Professional edition. It is also part of the MSDN Ultimate subscription, which gives you an awful lot of extra stuff.

Expression Blend is a graphical tool that uses the PC hardware resources such as the memory and graphic card extensively; for this reason, it comes with certain hardware requirements, as described in Table 3-1.

Table 3-1. *Expression Blend Hardware Requirements*

Hardware	Minimum
OS	Windows XP SP3
CPU	1GHz
RAM	2Gb
GPU	Direct-x 9 128Mb

Expression Blend 4 has been released with a lot of new features that make it the perfect tool for XAML designers who want to learn quickly how to make cool XAML UI effects or how to build complex XAML UI layouts.

The following list highlights some of the major improvements of Blend 4, as per the Blend web site:

- **SketchFlow**: This is a plug-in for Blend that allows you to build dynamic mock-up applications for WPF and Silverlight that look like they're hand-drawn.

- **Import**: Blend 4 can import files from graphic software such as Adobe Photoshop or Adobe Illustrator without losing the structure of the original file (in other words, the layers and styles).

- **Behaviors**: These are a new concept in Blend; behaviors represent graphic animation and behaviors that are easy to use but that bring cool features to your UI.

- **Sample data**: Blend 4 is able to provide sample data to your UI, which will reflect the structure of the final `DataContext`; in this way, the designer is able to view the final result at design time without needing to execute the UI controls through a WPF application.

- **Transitions**: Blend allows you to build cool transitions to move from one view to another with an integrated set of default transitions.

- **IntelliSense**: Both XAML and C# can be edited in Blend with the help of the well-crafted IntelliSense feature.

- **Styling and templates**: You can navigate through the control template and change its layout by creating new templates and styles without writing any XAML markup.

Expression Blend would need an entire book just to explain how it works and how many things you can accomplish with it; in this chapter, you will get an overview of the WPF features available in this tool, and you will learn how to start using its IDE; I suggest you take a look at the tons of online tutorials available on the Internet and check out the Apress book *Pro Expression Blend 4* if you plan on learning more about this amazing tool.

Blend Workspace

Expression Blend has an interesting dark gray IDE that is entirely built in WPF; behind the scenes, all the panels, toolboxes, and tab controls available in Blend are nothing more than WPF controls orchestrated with the Managed Extensibility Framework (MEF) bind using the Model View ViewModel MVVM pattern.

As soon as you open Expression Blend for the first time, you will be prompt by a small start page with three tabs: Projects, Help, and Samples, as shown in Figure 3-1.

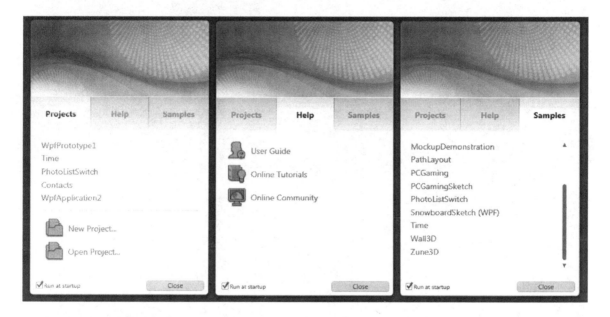

Figure 3-1. *Expression Blend startup page*

The Project tab contains the latest projects you worked on plus two shortcuts—one to open a new project and one to open an existing project not listed in the recent items list.

On the Help tab, you can find shortcuts to the help system integrated in Blend and links to the online tutorials and community (MSDN).

Finally, the Samples tab has a list of links to the sample projects installed on your development machine and built using SketchFlow, WPF, and Silverlight. These projects show you most of the cool features available in Blend; you can open any sample and run it by simply clicking F5.

If you choose to create a new project, Blend will open a New Project window that allows you to choose from a variety of WPF and Silverlight projects; depending on the plug-in or SDK installed on your development machine, you may or may not able to see some specific project templates, such as the WPF Ribbon project template or the Windows Phone 7 project template.

Figure 3-2 shows the New Project window.

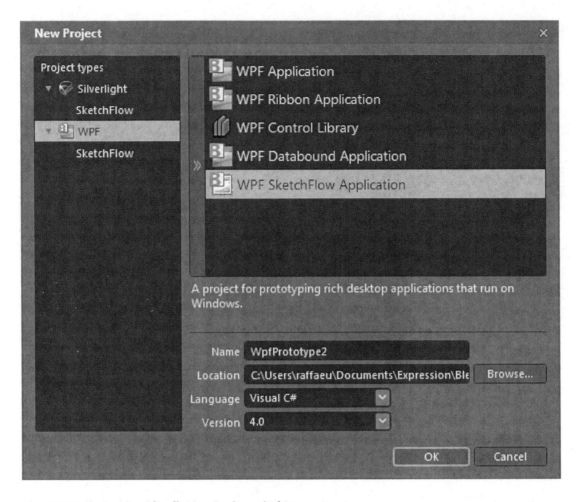

Figure 3-2. Expression Blend's New Project window

Workspace Panels

The workspace area of Blend is composed of panels, toolbars, design areas, and storyboards. These entire panels can moved around the workspace, closed, or temporary hidden based on the work you are doing, such as designing a component or writing custom XAML markup.

The Blend workspace also has four major regions that can be resized and hidden independently. As soon as you resize a specific region, all the panels inside the region will be resized too. Figure 3-3 shows how this concept works in the Blend workspace.

Figure 3-3. Blend workspace's resizable regions

When a panel is dragged or added to a specific region, the panel's shape changes and becomes a *tabbed* panel shape. A tabbed panel differs from a floating panel because the header of the panel is displayed in a different way by hiding the pin icon. If you drag a panel outside the region it is contained in, it will take on a rectangular shape and still include the tabbed header, but it will have the close and pin icons in the right corner instead of having them on the tab header.

As shown in Figure 3-4, there is a region of Blend that has a panel group containing a set of panels; the second rectangle shows a *region group*, which is floating in the Blend's workspace. You can make a group or panel float by simply dragging it somewhere outside the containing region.

Figure 3-4. Tabbed panel and floating panel with panel group

You can move and change the Blend panels using some simple IDE shortcuts:

- Double-click a panel's header to make the panel floating or tabbed depending on its position in the workspace.

- Turn off/on the autohide option of a panel by clicking the pin icon.

- Press F4 to show or hide all the panels loaded in the workspace.

- Drag panels around the workspace until a blue border is visible; that blue border represents the region or panel group that will include your current panel.

- Drag the tabs within the same panel group to re-order the tabs.

■ **Note** The workspace of Expression Blend is composed of a very rich set of toolboxes and panels that will not be examined in this chapter because they are not the primary topic of this book. You can see a more detailed explanation of each of these panels by reading the articles at the Expression Blend web site (http://expression.microsoft.com/library/).

Drawing

When you build a new WPF application, you may need to draw custom shapes or import existing art that will make up the final UI of your application. Expression Blend is the graphic software for XAML UI applications such as WPF, Silverlight, or Windows Phone 7; for this reason, it makes it easier for you to design XAML elements in those applications.

You should keep in mind that Blend is not for vector graphic images, so if you have to create complex graphic images using vector graphics, you may consider using software such as Adobe Illustrator or Expression Design.

■ **Note** Vector graphics are images composed of a set of lines, points, and curves, while raster images are images composed of square pixels. A classic raster type is the bitmap, for example. The main difference between these two types of image is in how they are displayed on the screen. A vector image will appear the same, without losing quality, at any screen resolution, while a raster image will lose quality as soon as you try to resize it.

In Expression Blend you have two options to design a new shape; you can use one of the available predefined shapes, or you can create your own shape by defining its path or modifying the path of a predefined shape.

Shapes and Objects

To draw a shape or predefined object in Blend, you need to open the Asset panel and find the Shape node. After you select this node, on the right side of the panel, Blend will show you a predefined set of shapes, among which you can find common geometrical shapes such as arrows, squares, rectangles, and lines. Starting from this set of basic shapes, you can easily create any geometrical object. Figure 3-5 shows a session of Blend with the Hexagon shape that has been transformed into a 3D cube in three easy steps.

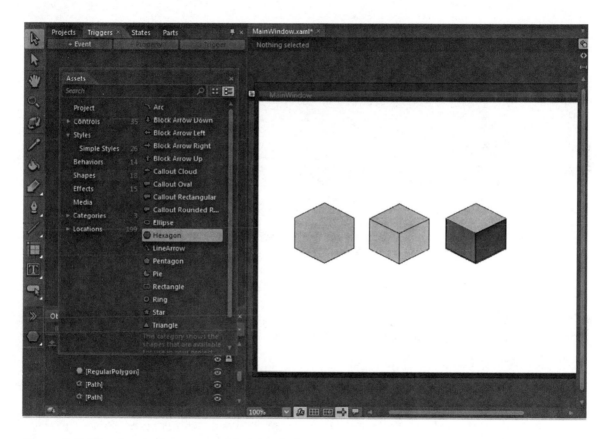

Figure 3-5. 3D cube creation process using simple shapes

If the shape you are working with doesn't satisfy your requirements, you can transform the shape by modifying the points of the path in order to create a new shape. The path can be considered part of the shape or a new shape.

When you play with the paths, you can obtain different results depending on what you do with the paths; the following list represents the available results you can obtain by combining two or more paths:

- **Unite**: The resulting shape is the union of the two original shapes.

- **Divide**: The resulting shape is a set of shapes composed of the common part of the shapes and the remaining parts.

- **Intersect**: The resulting shape is composed only of the overlapping area of the original shapes.

- **Exclude Overlap**: This shape is the opposite result of an Intersect operation.

- **Extract**: This operation cuts out the last selected shape from the first selected shape.

To execute one of these commands, you must select one or more object in the designer surface; then select Object ➤ Combine and select the command you want to execute.

Text and Text Effects

Expression Blend offers a set of predefined controls to display text in a WPF application; these controls are available in the XAML markup and are composed of read-only controls, editable controls, and other type of text controls.

The most commonly used controls are `TextBox` for editing text, `TextBlock` and `Label` to display read-only text, and `RichTextBox` and `DocumentPageView` to display complex formatted text.

If you are not satisfied with an existing control layout or style, you can always edit the control and change the current template, or you can create a new control that will display the text in a fashion closer to your design needs.

■ **Note** In the IDE of Expression Blend, you can modify the text content of any control on the fly by simply pressing F2 when the control is selected. The same shortcut applied in Windows to a selected file or folder will allow you to rename that object.

Some controls such as the `TextBox` or `PasswordBox` control can be modified at runtime by user interaction; in Expression Blend you can avoid this behavior by changing the read-only property of the control to `true`.

With Expression Blend, you can control how the text is displayed in your WPF application and also how it will behave and react to the user activity. The following are some of the most common operations you can do with a text object using Blend:

- You can embed fonts and style. Blend can help you include a custom font in your WPF application.

- You can format text in various styles. For example, you can format a paragraph, create bulleted and numbered lists, and make the text bold, italics, underlined, and more. However, this depends on the control type; for instance, you can't underline a `PasswordBox` control.

- You can choose two solutions with paths. You can transform your text as a vector path or make your text go around an existing path.

As you can see, Blend allows you to easily customize your text in a variety of ways without needing to write custom XAML.

Animations

An object animation is composed of a sequence of images, with each interpolated to the next one, that when played sequentially creates the illusion of animation. Expression Blend uses the concept of *storyboard*, which is a predefined sequence of steps. Each step can be identified as a *keyframe*. To execute an animation, you will need at least two keyframes on your timeline and will need to define what is going to change on an object between these two keyframes; then Blend will interpolate the changes in the timeline in order to make the animation more realistic.

Expression Blend, in order to save memory and keep the animation small in size, doesn't save an interpolated image of the change in every frame. Unlike other complex animation software, Blend simply asks you for the keyframes where the animation will happen and what properties will be changed; it will then smooth the changes by spreading the change over all the affected frames.

In Blend you can create an animation by using a storyboard (as shown in Figure 3-6), by using the XAML code, or by simply using the new concept of *behaviors* with a predefined animation.

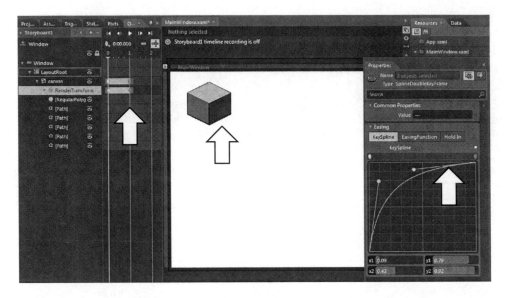

Figure 3-6. *Expression Blend storyboard editor*

In Figure 3-6, I have pointed out three key points of the storyboard editor available in Blend 4; the first arrow on the left indicates the storyboard that represents the timeline and the keyframe being edited in the timeline. The middle arrow indicates the object involved in the animation available in the application. Finally, the right arrow indicates how you are going to create the animation; you can set the keyspline of the animation or choose from a predefined set of curves (acceleration, bounce, elastic, and more).

When you are set with the animation, you need to decide how you will activate it. For example, Listing 3-1 shows the resulting XAML of a simple moving animation; the code defines the animation, but it doesn't define when the animation will happen. What you are specifying in the XAML code is a double animation to modify the value of the X property by translating the canvas.

Listing 3-1. *Animation Created in Blend*

```
<Storyboard x:Key="Storyboard1">
    <DoubleAnimationUsingKeyFrames
Storyboard.TargetProperty="(UIElement.RenderTransform).(TransformGroup.Children)[3].(Transla
teTransform.X)" Storyboard.TargetName="canvas">
        <SplineDoubleKeyFrame KeyTime="0" Value="-273"/>
        <SplineDoubleKeyFrame KeyTime="0:0:1" Value="29" KeySpline="0.2,0.55,0.57,0.06"/>
    </DoubleAnimationUsingKeyFrames>
</Storyboard>
```

If you want to execute the previous animation in Blend, you have to define the trigger that will fire the Play command, or you need to tackle the C# code-behind and fire the Play command somewhere during the application execution.

In Figure 3-7, I have associated the animation's Play command to the Click event of a button; this combination of actions and behaviors is a trigger.

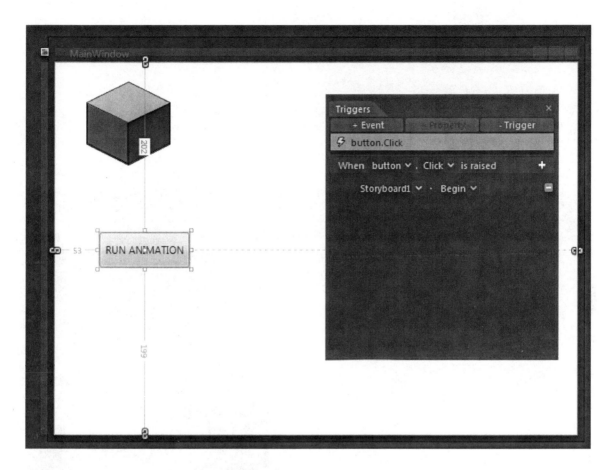

Figure 3-7. *Trigger created in Expression Blend*

If you plan to use animations in your WPF application, you may need to consider some design factors. For example, it may not look professional to have an accounting application that exposes button with fancy animations, or it may be weird to have a classic data entry application that executes custom animations.

Before creating a custom animation, you should look at transitions. You can play transitions between screens by using the visual state manager.

Styling and Templating Controls

In WPF you have different ways of changing the way a control looks; you can start by modifying the properties of a control, but the problem with this solution is that you would have to repeat the same steps for every control of the same type. The next way would be to create a style and apply it to a specific control, but that may still not be enough yet for you to create the look you want. The final and most advanced solution of creating a custom control is to modify the template of an existing one. You can easily accomplish each of these steps using the Expression Blend UI.

Modifying Properties

Every time you select an object in Expression Blend, the Properties panel adapts to the current selected item in the designer. In the Properties panel, you have access to the most common properties of the selected object; you can modify these properties to change how the selected object looks. Figure 3-8 shows the Properties panel for a Button control selected in the designer.

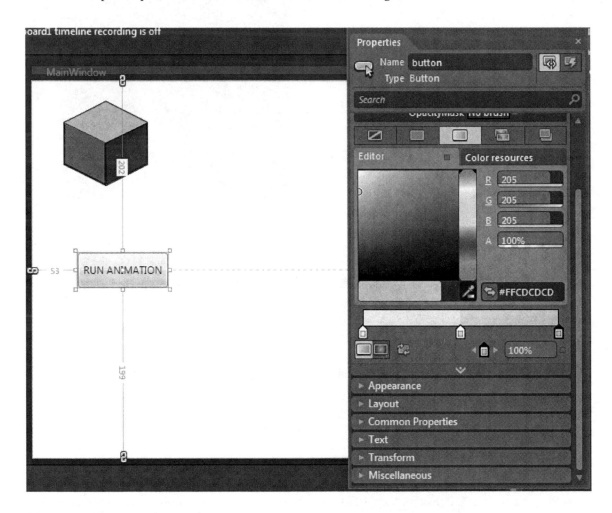

Figure 3-8. The Properties panel

The Properties panel is context sensitive. In other words, based on the control you select, the panel will display a specific set of group panels, each one containing a specific set of visual properties, grouped by category. In the Properties panel you can modify almost every property of an object. The following are the most common properties that can be modified in this panel:

- The name of the control

- Brushes, color, border color, filling, gradient filling, and pattern filling

- Appearance, border, and various effects (shadow, blur, and more)

- Layout, position on the screen, and alignment

- Text

- Transform, scale, and rotation

- Miscellaneous

- Common properties

All the properties exposed in the Properties panel can be also modified using XAML.

Creating Styles

The process of creating a custom control can be very complex; it can require a lot of steps, which can be time-consuming if you have to apply all these changes to another control of the same type. Let's assume, for example, that you want to customize the classic Button control of a WPF application by adding a custom shadow, a custom font, a custom border, and a custom background color. After you figure out what the control will look like, you have to apply the same style to all the Button controls available in your application.

So, the first you need to do to create a style for a specific control type is to drag the control you want to edit, such as a Button, into the designer. After you place the control in the designer, you need to modify the control template by creating your custom control template and then decide where to store it; the best place is usually a custom dictionary or the application resources so that you can easily grab the new style to use in another control. At this point, as shown in Figure 3-9, you can start creating your custom style.

Figure 3-9. Standard Button and Button with a custom template

The figure shows that the custom template is not included in the current XAML window because you have told Blend to save it in a global resource dictionary that will be used across the WPF application.

Finally, if you want to apply the same style to the second control, you can use the code displayed in Figure 3-9: `Template={DynamicResource ButtonStyle}`, where `ButtonStyle` is the name of the newly created style. Alternatively, you can select the new control, choose Edit Template ➤ Apply Resource from the Blend menu, and select the newly created style.

Creating new styles or new control templates is a very useful task in Blend because you can easily create a set of custom styles for you controls, save them in a custom dictionary, and have a new theme for your application. You can then switch to a different theme (resource dictionary) and change the whole UI look in a few lines of code.

■ **Note** Creating styles and control templates can be time-consuming, and it requires a deep knowledge of how the controls are structured in WPF; if you don't have time or you haven't mastered the WPF controls set, you can always go to the Blend community web site and download one of the available styles for WPF (`http://gallery.expression.microsoft.com/`).

Design-Time Data

One of the most challenging aspects of working with WPF and other UI technologies such as Silverlight, Windows Forms, and ASP.NET is getting a preview of how the data will appear at runtime by the application. Well, if you draw a set of predefined UI controls in a panel, such as `TextBox` and `Label` controls, the final result will be pretty obvious, but as soon as you start to work with templates and custom visual styles, the task will became more challenging.

Expression Blend has a feature called *blendability* and that allows you to create a custom `DataContext`, specifically a design `DataContext`, which reflects the real data but can be displayed by Blend or Visual Studio while you are designing your UI so that you can view right away how the final UI will look.

If you want to create a custom data source, the panel you are interested in is the Data panel, displayed in Figure 3-10. With this panel, you can create three different types of data sources that will be available in the current user control, window, or application.

- **XML data source**: You can create this type of data source by binding the UI to an existing XML file that contains structure data.

- **Object data source**: An object data source is a data source that exposes an existing object available from a C# or VB .NET class.

- **Sample data source**: A sample data source is an object that you create on the fly within the Blend application and that will be populated with dummy data by Blend for you in a custom file attached to the application.

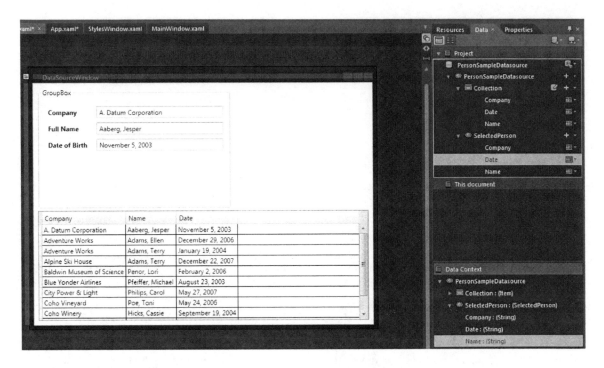

Figure 3-10. *Custom sample data source with design-time rendering*

After you create your custom data source with the Data panel, you can start dragging the data into the designer surface of your WPF application, and like magic, Expression Blend will do the rest for you.

Blend allows you to define specific types of dummy data such as a set of predefined strings (Company, Name, Address, Email) or a set of other data types (Prices, Amount, Percentage); that way, you don't need to struggle by generating custom data just to design your controls.

■ **Note** Design data is a very cool feature of Expression Blend; if you are working with other developers on a WPF application and your primary role is to develop the UI of the application, you will not need to wait for other developers until the real data is available in order to test your UI; the only constraint you will have is that your sample data structure must match the final data structure provided by the presentation layer.

SketchFlow and the Mockups

Building a UI application is a time-consuming task, and often you don't have the time to prototype your entire application before meeting with the customer who requested the application. At the same time, creating the entire UI *before* meeting the customer can be a big risk, especially if the creation will keep you busy for while. Other times you may not know yet how the UI will look, but you still need to present the customer with a mock-up UI that represents the skeleton of the real application.

When you purchase the full package of Expression Studio Ultimate, you will get Microsoft Expression Blend with an additional plug-in called SketchFlow, which allows you to create a fully functional WPF or Silverlight application with mock-ups that look pencil-drawn.

Figure 3-11 shows a sample WPF application built in SketchFlow that is available in one of the sample applications delivered with Blend 4.

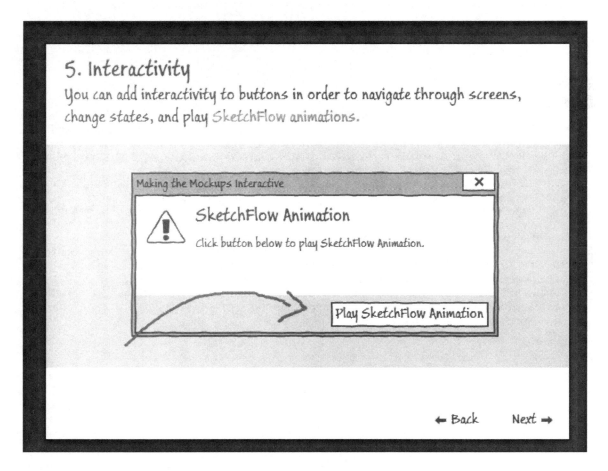

Figure 3-11. Mock-up WPF application with SketchFlow

With SketchFlow you can do almost everything you do in a normal WPF/Silverlight application. You will be able to deliver a mock-up of your application in a few hours to the customer and receive dynamic feedback from the customer's interaction with the SketchFlow mock-up.

SketchFlow 4 allows you to do the following:

- You can create an application flow composed of a set of views that interact with each other using custom triggers or other types of interactions.

- You can add almost any of the available WPF controls but with a fancy draw style applied to them, which will result in a mocked-up UI application.

- You can display in the mock-up real data or dummy data using the sample data creation process you would use for a normal WPF application.

- You can provide a sample player to the customer that will add feedback, notes, and edits over your mock-up.

- You can export and transform in a few clicks the created mock-up into a real WPF application.

Summary

In this chapter, you got an overview of how Blend works and how it can help you produce faster and more reliable XAML code just by dragging controls into a designer surface. Microsoft Blend is composed of a pluggable IDE that can be easily customized depending on what you are doing, such as designing controls, customizing UI, writing XAML, and creating animations.

Expression Blend is a vector tool that translates whatever you are able to accomplish with its designer into XAML code compatible for WPF, Silverlight, and Windows Phone 7 applications.

With Expression Blend, you can create custom control styles, change properties and the graphical aspect of an existing control, or create a new custom control. It allows you to draw vector paths and text, and it also allows you to treat graphical objects like text.

You can also create custom animation by working with a storyboard, keyframe, and timeline like you would in any other animation software. The interface for creating animations is easy to understand; it also plugs easily into existing controls by using triggers and behaviors.

Finally, Microsoft added a mock-up plug-in to Expression Blend for WPF and Silverlight that allows you to create dynamic and prototyped UI application. This tool is called SketchFlow and is available only with the Expression Studio Ultimate edition.

CHAPTER 4

∎∎∎

Creating the Views

The process of creating the views of a WPF application may look simple, but it is probably the most important part of the development process; you can't simply drag controls onto a window or user control, add some fancy styles on it, and pretend that the user will learn how to use the UI.

There are some concepts in the UI design process that are fundamental for a successful product. For example, it doesn't matter if the product is a complex enterprise resources planning (ERP) application or a simple time tracker; it has to satisfy the user requirements, and it has to be effective and easy to use.

In this chapter, you will see how you can create dynamic prototypes in WPF using Expression Blend and how you can move forward from these prototypes and create the skeleton of your application that consists of the views, the view models, and the navigation between the views. At the end of the chapter, you will be ready to add custom controls to the views in the TimeTracker application.

Overview

When you start to define the graphical aspect of an application, the first consideration is about the user who will buy or use your application. You should ask yourself questions such as the following: Why would a user buy my application instead of another one? How will my application be different from other applications of the same kind? What are the daily steps that the user will take with the application? How can my application make the user's daily tasks easier and faster?

Of course, it is not easy to provide an answer for each of these questions. First, you must know the user type, the target, or the audience of your application. Second, you need to focus on the tasks that will be accomplished in your application's UI.

For example, in the TimeTracker application, you will need a big main screen that I will call the **dashboard**. This will provide to the user an overview of what is going on with the application. Then, moving forward, you should provide the user with an easy way of editing and monitoring the available data by being able to open additional views from the dashboard.

The following are the potential tasks that a user will do with a time-tracker application:

- After logging in, the *user* would like to have a main *overview* of the whole situation.

- With few clicks, the *user* should be able to *modify, create,* or *delete* new appointments.

- With few clicks, the *user* should be able to *print* invoices related to a specific *customer.*

- Finally, with a few clicks, the *user* should be able to *edit customers* and *employees* data.

Now that you know what the basic requirements for the UI are, you can start to prototype the UI using Expression Blend's SketchFlow and propose the prototyped UI to the client.

By doing that, you will not block the development process of the core layers because the prototype application doesn't need them. In addition, you can offer the customer the opportunity of customizing and commenting on the prototyped UI before you start the hard work of developing the application.

Creating a Mock-up and Prototyping

In the sample provided with this book, the Expression Blend prototype application is a project created and managed in Blend; you may have it inside the production solution, which will include two different project types for WPF—the production UI and the SketchFlow UI application. I prefer to keep these two types of projects separate because I don't like to mix the prototype with the production application.

First you need to open Expression Blend and create a new application of type WPF *SketchFlow Application*; this is available in the WPF application templates list if you have the Ultimate version of Blend; if you haven't already, you can still download the 60-day trial version of Blend.

When you create a new WPF prototype application, Blend will create two projects for you in one solution. The first project is of type WPF application, and it is just a bootstrapper for a SketchFlow player. The second project is a class library that contains all the available views that will be displayed by the SketchFlow player; in our case, you will give it the name of `TimeTrackerPrototype`.

The bootstrapper project has only one class, the `App.xaml` class, which is available in any WPF application and is used to bootstrap the UI. In the code of the `Application.xaml.cs` file, you will find a simple call to the SketchFlow WPF player, as shown in Listing 4-1.

Listing 4-1. Application.xaml.cs in a SketchFlow Application

```
[assembly: Microsoft.Expression.Prototyping.Services.SketchFlowLibraries↩
("TimeTrackerPrototype.Screens")]

namespace TimeTrackerPrototy_e
{
    /// <summary>
    /// Interaction logic for App.xaml
    /// </summary>
```

```
public partial class App : Application
{
    public App()
    {
        this.Startup += this.App_Startup;
    }

    private void App_Startup(object sender, StartupEventArgs e)
    {
        this.StartupUri = new Uri(@"pack://application:,,,/Microsoft.Expression↵
.Prototyping.Runtime;Component/WPF/Workspace/PlayerWindow.xaml");
    }
}
}
```

As you can see, the application has a reference to the class library project that I called TimeTrackerPrototype, and the rest is done by calling the SketchFlow player available in the Microsoft.Expression.Prototyping namespace.

Now, for the rest of your time, you will work in the SketchFlow Map panel, which you can open by choosing it from the menu or by pressing Shift+F12. Figure 4-1 shows the final result of the prototype application, which will have six views.

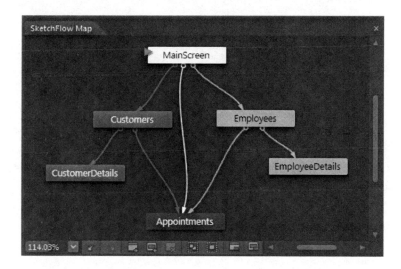

Figure 4-1. *SketchFlow Map panel*

Right now just delete all the views provided by the solution template of Blend so that the surface of the SketchFlow map is empty. You can also right-click each view in the SketchFlow Map panel and select the Delete command. You will then create the views and the animation to interact between the views.

The Main Screen

The first screen you are going to create is the main screen. This is the screen that the user will see when running the TimeTracker application. On this screen you want to give to users an overview of what is going on and give them the ability to access the Customers or Employees view or to manage the appointments. You also want to show users a couple of charts so that they can see who is busy and who is not.

To add a new screen, you can simply go to the SketchFlow Map panel, right-click the designer, and select *Create a Screen*; as soon as you do that, Blend will add a new label in the SketchFlow Map panel plus a corresponding .xaml file in the screens project for you, which represents the new view (screen). You can rename the label in the SketchFlow Map panel, and the corresponding .xaml file will have its label renamed, but pay attention because it won't rename the .xaml file and you have to do it manually.

Now, to drag elements onto the screen, or *view*, you need to keep the **Assets panel** open and point to the SketchFlow controls; this set of controls is nothing more than a WPF control library with some *special UI styles* applied on it.

Figure 4-2 shows the final result of this view.

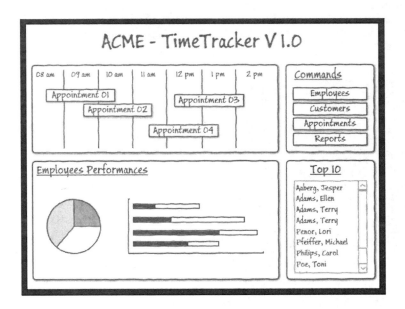

Figure 4-2. *Dashboard view prototype*

You create the four panels by dragging a simple `Rectangle-Sketch` control (which can be found in SketchFlow ➤ Sketch Shapers or Shapes ➤ Sketch Shapes) into the UI, which is nothing more than a `Border` XAML element with a Sketch style applied on it. The real XAML element is called `SketchRectangleUC`. Over this element you apply a new effect by adding it through the Properties panel of the `Rectangle` control and by choosing the `DropShadow` effect; I've changed the shadow a little bit by choosing a gray color instead of the default black and by decreasing the shadow size and opacity. Listing 4-2 shows the final XAML.

Listing 4-2. SketchFlow Rectangle with Drop Shadow

```
<pc:SketchRectangleUC
    Style="{DynamicResource Rectangle-Sketch}"
    Radius="5"
    Background="White">
    <pc:SketchRectangleUC.Effect>
        <DropShadowEffect Color="#FF8B8B8B" ShadowDepth="2" Opacity="0.7"/>
    </pc:SketchRectangleUC.Effect>
</pc:SketchRectangleUC>
```

You can make this a new style so that you don't have to remember the settings for each rectangle you will draw on the UI.

The remaining controls are a combination of Button, TextBlock, ListBox, and Pie shape provided with the default set of controls for SketchFlow in Blend under SketchFlow ➤ Styles ➤ Sketch Style or Styles ➤ Sketch Styles.

All the available controls provided by SketchFlow are the WPF controls available in WPF but with a different style (the Sketch style) applied to them so that they look hand-drawn.

The Top 10 panel represents a hypothetical list of top customers; as you can see in Figure 4-2, the list is filled with dummy data, which is provided by Blend.

Dummy Data

Creating dummy data with Blend is very easy. Follow these steps to create a dummy data list in your view:

1. Locate the Data panel, and click the Project node.

2. Click the plus button on the Database icon, and choose to add new *sample data*. Type a name for the sample data like SampleDataSource.

3. In the data source, click the plus button, and add a new *collection property*. Call it Top10List.

4. Now, in the collection property, delete the two properties added by default by Blend, add a new sample property, and rename it to Name property. Select the little arrow on the right of the property, and in the second field choose *"Name template data"* in the Format drop-down list; this will inform Blend to create a list of sample objects so the property you called Name will be populated by a set of dummy names.

5. Now, drag the collection Top10 over the ListBox, and Blend will populate the DataContext of the ListBox with the dummy data.

Now you can move forward to the Lists screens. Later you will return to this view and connect the Button controls to the corresponding views by using the Blend behaviors, but for now let's just focus on the next views.

The List Views

When the user clicks the Employees or Customers button, the application will load a view containing a list of existing objects, a search `TextBox` to filter the results, and a set of commands in a command bar's style panel. If the user selects an existing object in the grid or creates a new one, an additional Details view will be loaded by the application.

Locate the *SketchFlow Map* panel, and click the first small icon on the left at the bottom of the main screen (dashboard) label; this command will create a new screen in the project and link it to the main screen. Figure 4-3 shows the final result of the Employees List view; the same layout and concepts will be applied for the Customers List view.

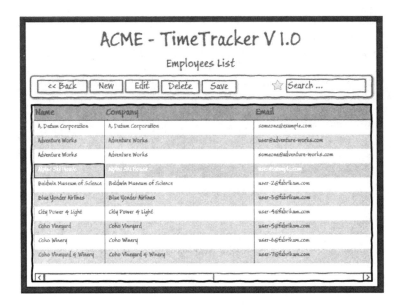

Figure 4-3. Employees List prototype screen

In this screen, you have a top SketchFlow `Rectangle` with the same style used in the main screen (shadow and border width), which is your toolbar; in WPF you will use a common toolbar and style it in order to get a nice, bold style. You also include in the toolbar a `TextBox`, which is used to search for specific employees; if the user types a value inside the search `TextBox`, you will filter the content of the grid.

The second part of the prototype is composed by a `DataGrid` styled for SketchFlow; the data is a collection of dummy data created using the same technique explained in the previous section but just with some more properties (Name, Company, and E-mail).

■ **Note** By default Expression Blend 4 doesn't provide a SketchFlow style for the `DataGrid` control in WPF, but you can easily circumvent this issue by downloading the Sketchable controls toolkit from the blog of its creator, Philipp Sumi (`www.hardcodet.net/2010/05/announcing-sketchables`). An additional solution that's more complicated would be to create your own SketchFlow style for those controls, such as the WPF `DataGrid`, which don't have a mock-up style in Blend.

Now that the view is ready, you need to enable the navigation; in fact, one of the amazing features of SketchFlow that makes it different from any other UI mock-up software is the possibility of integrating animations and navigation features in the application. These features are available in Blend and are known as behaviors.

Behaviors for SketchFlow

Behaviors are a kind of object, available in Blend, that can be attached to any element of the UI; a behavior can be a WPF element or a Silverlight element. These objects (behaviors) can provide additional properties and methods to the element and make it interactive. For example, you can use a behavior that will enable drag-and-drop on a `Button`, or you can add a behavior on a `Button` that when clicked will open a different view.

The behaviors in Blend are interactive behaviors in the form of an object that can be attached to an object by simply dragging them from the Expression Blend toolbox or by using XAML. With Blend you can use a set of behaviors that are shipped with the software, or you can create your own behaviors and display them inside the Expression Blend UI; you can also download behaviors from the Expression Gallery web site.

The concept of the behaviors is the same of the attached property because they work using the attached property technology of WPF. When you drag a behavior to the UI, it simply creates an attached property to the corresponding element that is composed by the behavior object itself.

Behaviors in Blend are of two types: action behaviors and full behaviors. The main difference between these two types of behaviors is that with the action behavior you simply associate an action to a trigger that can be fired by an element event. The action can be a simple step like playing a sound. With the full behavior, you can attach to an element a more complex behavior, such as the `MouseDragElementBehavior` that provides drag-and-drop functionalities to any element of the UI.

Adding a behavior on an element in Blend is very easy. Follow these steps to add a navigation behavior on a `Button` in the UI (Figure 4-4 shows the behavior Properties panel):

1. Open the *main view (dashboard)* screen, and locate the `Button` labeled with *Employees*.

2. Click the *Assets* panel in Blend, and locate the *Behaviors* node. You will see that this node has an additional child node called *SketchFlow*, which contains behaviors specific for a SketchFlow prototype application.

3. Locate the `NavigateToScreenAction`, and drag it over the Employees `Button`.

4. Now, the Properties panel has changed to be a Behavior property panel. Locate the `TargetScreen` group box, and select the Employees view as your target.

Figure 4-4. *Behavior-contextual Properties panel*

A behavior can be triggered by any type of event; in this case, you associated the Click event of the Employees Button with the open view behavior. You can also add conditions to the behavior before it can be executed. (You will learn more about this topic later in this chapter and in Chapter 5.)

At this point, you should be able to press F5 (Debug and Run) or Ctrl+F5 (Run without Debug) in Blend and execute your prototyped application. As soon as you click the Employees button, it should open the Employees view for you.

Remember also that whatever you do in Blend is always translated into XAML code, so a NavigateToScreen behavior in XAML corresponds to the code in Listing 4-3.

Listing 4-3. *NavigateToView Behavior in XAML*

```
<Button Content="Employees" Style="{DynamicResource Button-Sketch}">
    <i:Interaction.Triggers>
        <i:EventTrigger EventName="Click">
            <pi:NavigateToScreenAction↩
TargetScreen="TimeTrackerPrototypeScreens.Employees"/>
        </i:EventTrigger>
    </i:Interaction.Triggers>
</Button>
```

■ **Note** Behaviors are not available, when added to the UI, in the owner's property panel; for example, the previous behavior is not visible by default in the property panel of the Employees button. To access it later, you have to open the **Objects and Timeline panel** and locate the behavior in the UI tree. As soon as you select it in the tree view, the property panel context will change and reflect the corresponding behavior properties.

You should apply the same concept to the Back button in the Employees view; in this case, the behavior should link you back to the MainScreen view.

Repeat these steps for the Customers view by adding a new screen, linking the view to the dashboard and vice versa using the navigation behaviors, and creating a Customers dummy data list that will be bound to the `DataGrid` control.

The Details Views

The last task the user will execute with the prototyped application will be to edit a specific object, such as a customer, an employee, or an appointment, or to add a new one. Of course, based on a contextual property that you will add to the Details view, if the item passed to the view is an existing one, you will show the view in Edit mode. Otherwise, you will show the view in Create New mode.

These two options of the Details view are not part of the prototype requirements, so you will not see right now how to add this interactivity; but let's see how a Details view is composed for the Employees List view, represented by Figure 4-5.

A Details view will display all the available properties of the object selected in the List view, so for an employee selected in the Employees view, you will show a Details view with all the available properties of the Employee object.

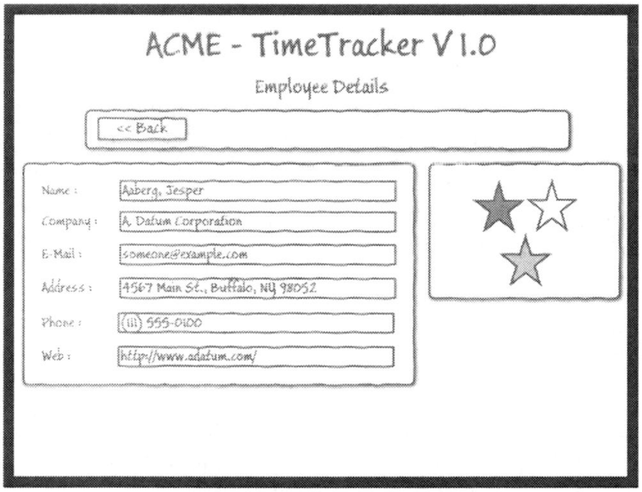

Figure 4-5. Employee prototype Details view

In this case, the dummy data has been created by using a complex property instead of using a collection property. The difference for Blend is that when you create a collection property, you choose the size of the collection, and Blend will randomly generate data for you by filling up the collection. The complex property represents just a single object in the UI, like a selected employee.

When you are done with the generated data, you can simply drag each property of the complex object to the corresponding control in the UI; for example, supposing that the Employee object will have a Name property, you will drag this property to the corresponding TextBox in the view.

When you are done with this step, you have to assign the behaviors for the navigation also in this view, in the Back button, and in the Employees view in the New and Edit buttons.

Now you can create the same views also for the Customer object, and at the end you will have a navigation tree similar to the one in Figure 4-1 earlier in this chapter.

The View Models

When you create an application in WPF like the TimeTracker application, you will have a project that has some views, and each view will display some data. You can decide to display this data in a lot of different ways; some of them will require more effort than others.

In any case, you will need to present to each view a specific set of values to be displayed and a specific presentation logic that will be applied to the UI. In WPF you provide this information to the view by using an object that takes the name of DataContext. In WPF you can think of the DataContext dependency property of an element as a container of data; more precisely, it is the container for the data bound to that specific element. Because the DataContext property is a dependency property, when you set it to a specific object (such as an Employee object) in the root element of your view XAML tree, all the descendants elements will refer automatically to that object.

You will build a specific view model for each view in the TimeTracker application starting from the main screen and going deep into the List and Details views. You will then complete the view model later in this book; for now, you will just see what the base concepts of these view models are and how you can then bind the ViewModel to the views.

Base ViewModel Implementation

For this part of the chapter, you need to close the prototype application built with SketchFlow and re-open the Visual Studio solution you created in Chapter 2. You will work inside the UI layer on the WPF application called APRESS.TimeTracker, which contains the views, the view models, and the resources used by the UI.

If you don't have one yet, create a new project folder and call it ViewModels; then create another folder in the root and call it Views. Finally, create another folder and call it Utilities. At this point, you should have a WPF application project composed of four folders and an App.xaml file and the MainWindow.xaml file.

The INotifyPropertyChanged

When you bind a view model to a DataContext, the view model must implement the INotifyPropertyChanged interface provided by the .NET Framework. You will see in Chapter 7 why and how this interface is used by the WPF binding engine. For now just add a new class called ObservableObject in your ViewModels folder, and mark it as abstract; by using generics as explained in Listing 4-4, you will implement INotifyPropertyChanged in this object.

Listing 4-4. ObservableObject<T>

```
Using System.ComponentModel;
Using System.Linq.Expression;
Using System.Reflection;

namespace APRESS.TimeTracker.ViewModels
{
    public abstract class ObservableObject<T> : INotifyPropertyChanged
    {
        #region Implementation of INotifyPropertyChanged

        /// <summary>
        /// Occurs when a property value changes.
        /// </summary>
        public event PropertyChangedEventHandler PropertyChanged;

        #endregion
        /// <summary>
        /// Called when [property changed].
        /// </summary>
        /// <param name="property">The property.</param>
        public void OnPropertyChanged(Expression<Func<T, object>> property)
        {
            var propertyName = GetPropertyName(property);
            if (PropertyChanged != null)
            {
                var handler = PropertyChanged;
                handler(this, new PropertyChangedEventArgs(propertyName));
            }
        }


        /// <summary>
        /// Gets the name of the property.
        /// </summary>
        /// <param name="expression">The expression.</param>
        /// <returns></returns>
        private string GetPropertyName(Expression<Func<T, object >> expression)
        {
            if (expression == null)
            {
                throw new ArgumentNullException("propertyExpresssion");
            }
```

```
            var memberExpression = expression.Body as MemberExpression;
            if (memberExpression == null)
            {
                throw new ArgumentException("The expression is not a member access↵
    expression.", "expression");
            }

            var property = memberExpression.Member as PropertyInfo;
            if (property == null)
            {
                throw new ArgumentException("The member access expression does not access↵
    a property.", "expression");
            }

            var getMethod = property.GetGetMethod(true);
            if (getMethod.IsStatic)
            {
                throw new ArgumentException("The referenced property is a static property.",↵
    "expression");
            }

            return memberExpression.Member.Name;
        }
    }
}
```

The usage is very simple. You pass with the Lambda expression the property of the object, and by using reflection, you try to translate the property into a string by reading the name of the property itself. You can inherit from this class and notify the listener with an event when the value of a specific property has changed. Let's assume for a moment that you have a view model that exposes a `ViewTitle` property; using the previous code, you will raise the `PropertyChanged` event with this pseudocode: `OnPropertyChange(() => this.ViewTitle)`.

BaseViewModel

Now that you have a base class to implement `INotifyPropertyChanged`, you need the base class for the view model; in this chapter, you will not implement all the features for this class, but you need it in order to prepare the base presentation model.

Locate the ViewModels folder in the Presentation project. Add a new abstract class, and call it `BaseViewModel`; this class will represent the base object for any view model you have in the application. Listing 4-5 contains the full code of this class.

Listing 4-5. *BaseViewModel<T> Class*

```
Using System.ComponentModel;
Using System.Linq.Expression;
Using System.Reflection;
```

```
namespace APRESS.TimeTracker.ViewModels
{
    public abstract class BaseViewModel<T> : ObservableObject<T>
    {
        /// <summary>
        /// ViewTitle private accessor
        /// </summary>
        private string viewTitle;

        /// <summary>
        /// Gets or sets the view title.
        /// </summary>
        /// <value>The view title.</value>
        public string ViewTitle
        {
            get { return viewTitle; }
            set
            {
                if (viewTitle == value)
                {
                    return;
                }
                viewTitle = value;
                OnPropertyChanged(vm => this.ViewTitle);
            }
        }
    }
}
```

The BaseViewModel is a very simple object; it inherits ObservableObject<T> and exposes just one property, the title of the view.

For now this is enough for you to create a base ViewModel graph that you will decorate and complete in the next chapters with more properties and methods.

Details ViewModel

In the application TimeTracker, except for the dashboard (MainScreen) view, you have two different type of views in the application—a List view that implements a classic master-details view where there are a list of objects and a current object, and a Details view that exposes only one object, usually the selected one of a List view. You will have three different types of base view model that you will use to create the concrete view models; one is the base view model that you created previously, and the second one is the view model for a Details view that you are going to create now. The third one is the List view model.

The Details view model is a view model that exposes an object through some properties. Listing 4-6 shows the final class used for BaseDetailsViewModel.

Listing 4-6. BaseDetailsViewModel Code

```
namespace APRESS.TimeTracker.ViewModels
{
    public abstract class BaseDetailsViewModel<TEntity> : BaseViewModel<TEntity>
    {
        /// <summary>
        /// Initializes a new instance of the class.
        /// </summary>
        /// <param name="currentEntity">The current entity.</param>
        protected BaseDetailsViewModel(TEntity currentEntity)
        {
            CurrentEntity = currentEntity;
        }

        /// <summary>
        /// Gets the current entity.
        /// </summary>
        /// <value>The current entity.</value>
        public TEntity CurrentEntity { get; private set; }

        /// <summary>
        /// Froms the model to view.
        /// </summary>
        protected abstract void FromModelToView();

        /// <summary>
        /// Froms the view to model.
        /// </summary>
        protected abstract void FromViewToModel();
    }
}
```

As you can see from the previous code, for now in the Details view model you will expose an *entity* that you didn't define yet but that could be a ***domain entity*** (such as an employee or a customer) or another view model (think about a composed view model). Each concrete implementation of this view model will have to provide two methods that are marked as abstract, `FromViewToModel` *and* `FromModelToView`, which will be used to move the information back and forward from the UI to the domain entity bind into the view model.

You will see in Chapter 7 why you should not expose directly the model in the view model; you should expose only the information you need to use in the UI.

List ViewModel

The last class you are going to create in the base view model set is the one in charge of displaying a set of objects. This type of view model exposes a list of Details view model and a current Details view model, which is the one selected in the grid. This approach reflects the classic logic of the master-details view where you have a list of objects and a selected one. Listing 4-7 contains the code of the `BaseListViewModel` class.

Listing 4-7. *BaseListViewModel Class*

```
System.Collections.ObjectModel
namespace APRESS.TimeTracker.ViewModels
{
    public abstract class BaseListViewModel<TEntity> : BaseViewModel<TEntity>
    {
        /// <summary>
        /// Gets or sets the collection.
        /// </summary>
        /// <value>The collection.</value>
        public ObservableCollection<BaseDetailsViewModel<TEntity>> Collection { get;
 private set; }

        /// <summary>
        /// Gets or sets the selected.
        /// </summary>
        /// <value>The selected.</value>
        public BaseDetailsViewModel<TEntity> Selected { get; set; }

        /// <summary>
        /// Initializes a new instance of the <see
cref="BaseListViewModel&lt;TEntity&gt;"/>
class.
        /// </summary>
        /// <param name="collection">The collection.</param>
        protected BaseListViewModel(List<BaseDetailsViewModel<TEntity>> collection)
        {
            Collection = new
ObservableCollection<BaseDetailsViewModel<TEntity>>(collection);
        }
    }
}
```

The following are a couple of notes for this class:

- The view model exposes a `Selected` property, which represents a `SelectItem` in the view; it doesn't matter if the view will expose these items using a `ListBox` or a `DataGrid`; using the binding engine of WPF, you will be able to bind this object to the `SelectedItem` of the UI control.

- The list of view models is encapsulated inside `ObservableCollection<T>`, which is a specific collection provided by .NET for the WPF binding engine.

■ **Note** The ObservableCollection<T> is a specialized collection available in the namespace
System.Collections.ObjectModel, which represents a dynamic data collection that provides notifications when
items get added, when items get removed, or when the whole list is refreshed. It is specific for the binding engine
of WPF, and it works perfectly with it.

Now that you are done with your base view model objects, you should have in your Visual Studio
project a small graph like the one in Figure 4-6.

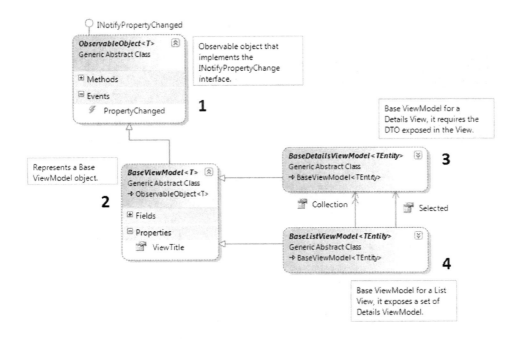

Figure 4-6. Complete graph for the base view model classes

The dashboard will have a view model that inherits from the BaseViewModel class because of its
complexity, while the List and Details views will inherit, respectively, from BaseDetailsViewModel and
BaseListViewModel.

You will add more information to these classes in the next chapter, when you start to add controls to
the views that you have prototyped with SketchFlow. You will also create the specific view models for
each view.

Navigation Between the Views

Some important aspects of a WPF application are how you will navigate from one view to another one, how you will communicate between the views, and how you will keep track of the changes and propagate them to the other views. For example, you may need to create a new customer, and when you are done, you update the Customers List view, which is behind the New Customer view that you just used.

To accomplish this and more complex tasks in a stand-alone WPF application, the Microsoft community has released some specific design patterns for WPF that you will analyze in Chapter 12; there are also some useful tools and third-party frameworks that will make your work easier. The point I want to focus now is how you can easily orchestrate a navigation between the views of a WPF application and how this process should be accomplished without having a third-party framework or a specific design pattern; you will see later that using a framework or a specific design pattern will make the work easier.

The App.xaml File

When you create a new WPF stand-alone application, by default Visual Studio creates a new WPF project, which contains a WPF window called Window1.xaml and an application file called App.xaml. If you look inside the code-behind file of the App.xaml file, you will find the code in Listing 4-8.

Listing 4-8. App.xaml Code-Behind File Content

```
/// <summary>
/// Interaction logic for App.xaml
/// </summary>
public partial class App : Application
{
}
```

If you take a look inside the XAML markup of the App.xaml file, you will discover that the application startup process is all there, as shown in Listing 4-9.

Listing 4-9. App.xaml Markup Code

```
<Application x:Class="APRESS.TimeTracker.App"
             xmlns="http://schemas.microsoft.com/winfx/2006/xaml/presentation"
             xmlns:x="http://schemas.microsoft.com/winfx/2006/xaml"
             StartupUri="MainWindow.xaml">
    <Application.Resources>

    </Application.Resources>
</Application>
```

That is pretty easy, right? But what about if you wanted to customize the application startup, for example, by adding a log, by using an authentication service, or simply by running the application using a splash screen? To do that, you need to remove the StartupUri attribute from the Application element in the App.xaml file and customize its code-behind file.

Custom Startup Process

The `App.xaml.cs` file exposes a class called `App` that inherits from the `System.Windows.Application` object that represents a WPF application object. With this object (application), you can easily control the startup and customization of the TimeTracker application. In this object you can define a navigation engine, which is an application controller that will drive the flow of the views or a simple splash screen.

The application object exposes some methods that you can override in order to customize the startup process. The first one you are going to analyze is the `Startup` method, which is called every time the user runs a new instance of the application (see Listing 4-10). Inside this method you may want, for example, to show a new view that will be the MainScreen view of the application.

Listing 4-10. Display a View in the Application_StartUp Method

```
public partial class App : Application
{
    /// <summary>
    /// Raises the <see cref="E:System.Windows.Application.Startup"/> event.
    /// </summary>
    /// <param name="e">A <see cref="T:System.Windows.StartupEventArgs"/> that contains the
 event data.</param>
    protected override void OnStartup(StartupEventArgs e)
    {
        base.OnStartup(e);
        // init the NavigationService class
        var mainView = new MainWindow();
        mainView.Show();
    }
}
```

The argument `StartupEventArgs` available in this method is filled up by all the arguments you, the user, or the operating system passes to the application startup process; for example, you may want to start the application using a command line like this one: `TimeTracker.exe -l - d`. Then check for these command-line parameters in the `StartUp` method.

Another interesting thing you may need to do before the application main screen is loaded is to open a temporary splash screen that will keep the user informed of what is going on during the bootstrapping process. To add a new splash screen in Visual Studio, you can simply create a `transparent.png` file that represents your splash screen UI and add it to the Visual Studio solution in two ways:

- Drag the image from a folder into the Visual Studio solution tree.

- Click the WPF project, choose "Add existing item," and locate the PNG file on your file system.

At this point, you have to set the file to `SplashScreen` in the Build action field of the Properties panel; this will inform the WPF engine to display this image before the `Application.Run()` method is called by the StackTrace , in this case, until you call the `mainView.Show()` method.

The following are other interesting methods in the `App.xaml` file:

- *Application.Activated* **and** *Application.Deactivated:* These methods are called every time the application is activated or deactivated by the user or by another process that will take the focus in the operating system. You can, for example, refresh the UI every time the application is activated and close the connections to the database every time the application is deactivated.

- *Application.ShutDown:* This method is called when the user closes the application using the Close button located in the top-right corner of a Windows application or when the method `Shutdown` is called. You can control how to shut down WPF applications by using the `ShutdownMode` *property* of the `Application` object.

Wrapping Up with IoC

Integrating an inversion of control (IoC) container inside the WPF application will provide more power and control over the application flow. Before showing how to integrate IoC in the TimeTracker application, I'll give you an overview of what the IoC pattern is, how it works, and how it can be implemented.

Inversion of Control

The concept of inversion of control, also known as *dependency injection* (DI) was introduced by Martin Fowler in 2004 while discussing enterprise patterns and architectures for the Java technology. The same concept applied later to the .NET world because the two systems are very close and use the same concept: a base framework implemented using an object-oriented programming (OOP) language.

There are a lot of discussions about what inversion of control and dependency injection are and how you should implement them. I will use the concepts mentioned by Fowler in his book *Patterns of Enterprise Application Architectures.*

The term IoC refers to the more generic implementation; you apply IoC to your code when you invert the flow of the control of the application. In other words, rather than a caller deciding how to use an object, in this technique the object called decides when and how to answer the caller, so the caller is not in charge of controlling the main flow of the application. According to Fowler, you can implement this pattern using two different and more specific techniques, ***dependency injection*** or a ***service locator***. With ***dependency injection***, you leave the task of populating the dependencies to a container, which knows how to resolve these dependencies; with a service locator, a global container (usually a container that implements the Singleton pattern) is able to resolve dependencies globally. The main difference is that with DI you hard-code the dependency as a property or in the constructor of the called object, while with the service locator you resolve the dependency using the locator when it's needed. The result is the same.

A Classic Implementation, Navigation Service

In this section, I will dive a little bit into the IoC technique; it forms the base of a good WPF implementation because it provides a good way of chaining all the pieces together. You saw already in the section "The App.xaml File" that the entire application life cycle in WPF is managed by this file; unfortunately, by default WPF doesn't provide a great navigation service that can help you display views or messages to the user. Another issue you can solve using the IoC approach is to provide a specific flow for the application.

First download the latest version of Microsoft Unity (version 2), which is available from the CodePlex web site at http://unity.codeplex.com. Unity is a DI container provided by the Microsoft Patterns and Practices team, and it's an open source, stable project.

Unity comes with a lot of features that you will not see in this book because they are not the primary topic of the book; I kindly suggest you take a look at the project and how it works by reading the documentation associated with it; you will discover that Unity is not only an IoC container.

Before starting to play with the IoC container, you need some sample code; you will use two services for this example. The first service is called IDialogService and provides utility methods to open a dialogue between the UI and the user (MessageBox, FileExplorer, and so on). The second object is INavigationService, which requires IDialogService as a dependency. Listing 4-11 shows the two service contracts (Interface). If you want to see the concrete implementation, refer to the TimeTracker application found on the Book Resources section of the Apress.com website for this book. You can search for the book website by title, isbn or author name, then click the "Book Resources" button.

Listing 4-11. IDialogService Contract

```
public interface IDialogService
{
    void ShowInfo(string title, string message);

    void ShowError(string title, string message);

    void ShowAlert(string title, string message);

    bool AskConfirmation(string title, string message);
}
```

The previous code is pretty simple; you are just providing a common service to display the various types of dialog boxes in the UI.

Listing 4-12 shows part of the NavigationService you will use in the TimeTracker application. In this case, the target of this example is to show you how IoC works.

Listing 4-12. INavigationService Partial Code and Partial Implementation

```
// the contract of the Navigation Service
public interface INavigationService
{
    bool ConfirmClose();
}

// the concrete implementation
public sealed class NavigationService : INavigationService
{
    [Dependency]
    public IDialogService DialogService { get; set; }

    #region Implementation of INavigationService
```

```
    public bool ConfirmClose()
    {
        return DialogService
            .AskConfirmation("Close TimeTracker.", "Do you want to close TimeTracker?");
    }

    #endregion
}
```

The code in Listing 4-11 creates a `IDialogService` interface that can be used anywhere in the application; in Listing 4-12, I added a dependency to the navigation service by creating a public property and by decorating the property with the `[Dependency]` attribute. (In order to do that, you need to reference `Unity.dll` in your application; it is located in the Microsoft Unity installation folder. You also need to add a reference in your code to the `Microsoft.Practices.Unity` namespace.) Now, because you used this attribute, you have informed Unity that when a new instance of the navigation service is created, Unity is in charge of resolving the `IDialogService` dependency.

■ **Note** DI can be achieved in different ways using Unity. One way is to mark a public property with the `[Dependency]` attribute. Another way is to pass the dependency in the constructor of the called object, and a third way is to decorate a method that resolves the dependencies using the `[DependencyMethod]` attribute. I prefer leaving the constructor of my objects parameterless and creating the dependencies using public properties; this approach leaves me more space for testing and more flexibility for future changes.

Now that you have set up the chain in the project, you should come up with a simple graph like the one in Figure 4-7. As you can see, because I deliberately left the dependencies open using a public property, the dependencies are clear in the UML.

■ **Note** In Visual Studio you can create a simple graph in the solution explorer by choosing the command Add New Item and selecting the Class Diagram item. This will create, by default, a new file called `ClassDiagram1.cd`. You can drag and drop classes, enumeration, interfaces, and other objects from the solution explorer to the class diagram designer, or vice versa. If you create a new object in the class diagram, it will be also created in the solution tree.

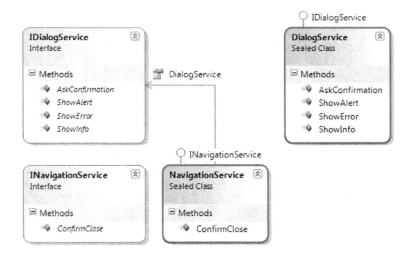

Figure 4-7. Final dependencies graph

The final step is to configure the Unity container. You can do this by changing the code in the App.xaml.cs file, which is the bootstrapper.

The following is the code to create DialogService:

```
using System;
using System.Windows;

namespace APRESS.TimeTracking.Services
{
    public sealed class DialogService : IDialogService
    {
        #region Implementation of IDialogService

        /// <summary>
        /// Shows the info.
        /// </summary>
        /// <param name="title">The title.</param>
        /// <param name="message">The message.</param>
        public void ShowInfo(string title, string message)
        {
            MessageBox.Show(title, message, MessageBoxButton.OK,
MessageBoxImage.Exclamation);
        }
```

```
        /// <summary>
        /// Shows the error.
        /// </summary>
        /// <param name="title">The title.</param>
        /// <param name="message">The message.</param>
        public void ShowError(string title, string message)
        {
            MessageBox.Show(title, message, MessageBoxButton.OK, MessageBoxImage.Error);
        }

        /// <summary>
        /// Shows the alert.
        /// </summary>
        /// <param name="title">The title.</param>
        /// <param name="message">The message.</param>
        public void ShowAlert(string title, string message)
        {
            MessageBox.Show(title, message, MessageBoxButton.OK, MessageBoxImage.Asterisk);
        }

        /// <summary>
        /// Asks the confirmation.
        /// </summary>
        /// <param name="title">The title.</param>
        /// <param name="message">The message.</param>
        /// <returns></returns>
        public bool AskConfirmation(string title, string message)
        {
            return
                MessageBox.Show(title, message, MessageBoxButton.YesNo,
MessageBoxImage.Question)
                == MessageBoxResult.Yes;
        }

        #endregion
    }
}
```

■ **Note** The code presented in the following sample is a more complex solution of the navigation service presented previously. For reasons of space I am not presenting all the code of the navigation service in this chapter; you will jump back to this service in the next chapter.

The first thing you need to do is to configure the IoC container; you will do this in the constructor of the App.xaml file:

```
public partial class App : Application
{
    // need a reference to Microsoft.Practice.Unity
    private IUnityContainer container;

    private INavigationService navigation;

    public App()
    {
        ConfigureContainer();
    }

    private void ConfigureContainer()
    {
        container = new UnityContainer();
        container.RegisterType<IDialogService, DialogService>();
        container.RegisterType<INavigationService, NavigationService>();
        container.RegisterType<MainWindow>();
        navigation = container.Resolve<INavigationService>();
    }
}
```

In the ConfigureContainer method, you informed Unity how it should resolve the various services you created previously. As you can see, you are telling Unity how to resolve dependencies to create classes, which is the objective of using the IoC framework.

Now, in the App_Start method, you can simply call the method on the navigation service:

```
protected override void OnStartup(StartupEventArgs e)
{
    base.OnStartup(e);
    // add a timer for the splash screen
    Thread.Sleep(2000);
    // init the NavigationService class
    var mainWindow = navigation.ShowMainWindow();
}
```

The same thing can be done on the Session_Exit method; in this case, you want a confirmation before exiting the session:

```
protected override void OnSessionEnding(SessionEndingCancelEventArgs e)
{
    base.OnSessionEnding(e);
    e.Cancel = navigation.ConfirmClose();
}
```

That was pretty easy, wasn't it?

In the next chapter, you will see how to build the production views by following the prototypes you designed with Blend and the suggestions you received from the customer. After that, you will plug all the views into the navigation service, and you will build a controller class that will help you keep a logical flow in the application and also manage the life cycle of objects and views.

Summary

In this chapter, you saw how important the prototyping process of the UI is. It can save a lot of time and make the customer more interactive with the project. Of course, a prototype UI has to be dynamic, and it has to include some dummy data that simulates the real final data. With SketchFlow, you can accomplish this task easily; in fact, with the behaviors, effects, and other cool features delivered with Blend 4, you can accomplish the task with just a few steps.

The binding engine of WPF is the core of this UI technology, and it will allow you to bind very complex objects to the UI. I'll talk about the data binding engine of WPF in Chapter 7 and the MVVM pattern in Chapter 12, but it is really important to understand that the view model, the data that you will display in the UI, is the most important aspect of a WPF application.

Finally, you saw how a WPF application is bootstrapped and controlled using a single file called `App.xaml`; this object by default doesn't provide a rich navigation framework; however, with a custom service and an IoC container like Microsoft Unity, you can accomplish this task and make the application more controllable.

CHAPTER 5

■ ■ ■

Adding Controls to the Views

At this point in your application development process, you should have already received some feedback from the customer on the prototyped UI you created by using the SketchFlow application in the previous chapter. You probably received feedback in the form of annotations and suggestions.

In this chapter, you will see how to put together all of this information, how to define a common style for the application, and how to make a composite UI by using user controls and views.

By the end of the chapter, you will apply to the UI some cool navigation effects so that it will be ready to receive the real data from the business tier.

Resources and Styles

WPF is able to store custom resources such as strings, images, styles, and custom data templates using a resource dictionary; by using this approach, you can store a custom style or an image in one place in the application that is visible and accessible from all the UI components.

The resources in WPF can be used, created, and modified by using either C# or the XAML markup; because the resource dictionary is nothing more than a XAML file, you can access this special container using the XAML markup. This choice is just a design choice and doesn't mean you should not access a resource using C# code.

The resources are an attached property of every XAML framework element, starting from the root element. Even if you can define the resource property in any element of the UI, you would usually define it in the root container element, such as the `Page`, `Window`, or `UserControl` element of a WPF application.

Resources are usually identified by using a unique key that is available by the XAML attribute `x:Key`; it is used by the controls that will use the resource to identify that specific resource. For example, Listing 5-1 is applying a specific style to a button by using the `x:Key` attribute of that style.

Listing 5-1. Button Static Style

```
<!-- Define the Style -->
<Window.Resources>
    <Style x:Key="ButtonStyle" TargetType="Button">
        <Setter Property="Background" Value="AliceBlue" />
    </Style>
</Window.Resources>
```

```
<!-- Apply the Style -->
<Button
    Height="100" Width="100"
    Style="{StaticResource ButtonStyle}"/>
```

After you define (bind) the value of a property to a specific resource, the WPF engine will go over the XAML tree and see whether that resource (x:Key) is available in the calling element; if the resource is not available, the engine will traverse the entire XAML tree until it does find the resource. If the resource is not available, WPF will throw an error in the trace stack, but *it will not raise an exception!*

Differences Between Static and Dynamic Resources

In Listing 5-1, you associated the style to the Button using the StaticResource value before the x:Key attribute value; this is a new XAML value that you haven't seen before. In WPF, you need to know when and how to use a StaticResource and when to use a DynamicResource; the performances of the application are slightly different based on the type of resource in your XAML markup, so it is better to understand when you should use one instead of the other one.

The following is the major difference between these two types of resources:

- A *static resource* is accessed and evaluated by the WPF engine only one time— before the application starts. That said, if you change the value of a static resource at runtime, the change will not affect the UI because a static resource *is evaluated once* and only once in the entire life cycle of the application.

- A *dynamic resource* is a resource that is evaluated by WPF every time it requires evaluating that resource.

The amount of resources used by a static resource is pretty different from the amount used by a dynamic one, which is reevaluated by the UI many times.

So, you may now be asking, "When should I use a dynamic resource?" Well, you should use a dynamic resource only if you believe that the resource will change at runtime and the change will affect the UI. Let's look at the example of a UI that has multiple styles applied to it (a skinnable UI); if you plan to allow the user to change the style (skin) on the fly without rebooting the application, the UI would have to use dynamic resources because they will change at runtime. On the other hand, if the application will not allow the user to change the skin on the fly, it would make more sense to leave the resources as static because they will be less heavy for the client machine, since they are evaluated only one time.

The Resource Dictionary

Resources can be contained within the Resource property of a container element or can be stored in a separate file called a *resource dictionary*. A resource dictionary can contain or refer to other dictionaries, and this design can make your UI structure pretty flexible but at the same time very complicated to debug, especially when you are trying to figure out why a control is not getting the specific UI style you have defined.

To create a new dictionary, you have to open the TimeTracker application and add a new resource dictionary in the WPF project, more precisely, in the Resources folder that you created earlier. In this project, you will have four dictionaries: two for the icons you will provide to the application, one for the basic controls' styles, and one for the UI customization (effects, brushes, and more).

The available dictionaries in the TimeTracker application are as follows:

- *SmallImagesDictionary.xaml:* This refers to 16×16 pixel images.

- *BigImagesDictionary.xaml:* This refers to 32×32 pixel images.

- *BasicControlsDictionary.xaml:* This refers to the basic styles applied to common controls such as `TextBox` controls, `Button` controls, and more.

- *CustomControlsDictionary.xaml:* This refers to custom controls, data templates, and particular styles.

Embed Images in a Dictionary

The first thing you are going to do is to download a set of icons on your local development machine and include these images in the WPF project. You will embed the images as a local resource in the application so that you will not need to refer directly to the images; instead, you will be able to refer just to the `x:Key` attribute used in the dictionary to refer to a specific image.

In my example, I am including two images; one is 16×16, and it will be included in the `SmallImagesDictionary.xaml` file, while the other one is a 32×32 pixel image, and it will be included in the `BigImagesDictionary.xaml`.

Before starting to work in the dictionary, you have to create a new folder (Images) in your Resources folder and add two additional child folders: Small and Big. Now that you have the full structure available on your WPF project, you have to drag one image into the specific folder (Small or Big based on the image size)and change its properties as shown here:

- *Build Action:* Resource

- *Copy to output:* Do not copy

If you configure the image in this way, it will be directly embedded into the assembly so that you don't have to worry about that when you release the application.

Now you can open `SmallImagesDictionary` and start referring to the images you have added to the project by using an `ImageSource` element, as shown in Listing 5-2.

Listing 5-2. ImageSource in a Dictionary File

```
<ResourceDictionary
    xmlns="http://schemas.microsoft.com/winfx/2006/xaml/presentation"
    xmlns:x="http://schemas.microsoft.com/winfx/2006/xaml">
    <!--
        BEGIN IMAGES
    -->
    <ImageSource
        x:Key="AddSmall">
        /Resources/Images/Small/add_16.png
    </ImageSource>
    <ImageSource
        x:Key="SearchSmall">
        /Resources/Images/Small/search_button_16.png
```

```
    </ImageSource>
    <!--
        END IMAGES
    -->
</ResourceDictionary>
```

The second step is to refer to the dictionary in the application or in the framework element that will use it. For example, you can refer to this dictionary every time you need it by merging it into an element resource like the code in Listing 5-3.

Listing 5-3. Dictionary Referenced in a Framework Element Resource

```
<!-- Dictionary embedded in a Framework element -->
<Window>
    <Window.Resources>
        <ResourceDictionary
            Source="/Resources/SmallImagesDictionary.xaml" />
    </Window.Resources>
    <Grid>
        <Image
            Source="{StaticResource AddSmall}"
            Height="16"
            Width="16" />
    </Grid>
</Window>

<!-- Dictionary in the App.xaml -->
<Application>
    <Application.Resources>
        <ResourceDictionary>
            <ResourceDictionary.MergedDictionaries>
                <ResourceDictionary Source="/Resources/SmallImagesDictionary.xaml" />
                <ResourceDictionary Source="/Resources/BigImagesDictionary.xaml" />
                <ResourceDictionary Source="/Resources/BasicControlsDictionary.xaml" />
                <ResourceDictionary Source="/Resources/CustomEffectsDictionary.xaml" />
            </ResourceDictionary.MergedDictionaries>
        </ResourceDictionary>
    </Application.Resources>
</Application>
```

The second option is to mention the dictionary in the `App.xaml` Resource element using the `MergedDictionaries` element so that the resource will be shared throughout the application UI without needing to embed the dictionary in every framework element.

■ **Note** When you embed images in an assembly, you have to be careful about their size. If you embed 100MB of images in your assembly, the assembly will be at least 100MB, which could be a very big problem. Consider also that you may able to create an additional Class Library project only to contain resources such as images and videos; you may then be able to reference the resources using the syntax in Table 5-1.

Table 5-1 shows the shortcuts you should keep on your desktop to refer to a resource in a dictionary from the same file, from a different file, and from a different assembly.

Table 5-1. *Different Ways of Accessing a Dictionary Resource*

Location	Syntax	Example
Local	/[path]/[dictionary	/Resources/MyDictionary.xaml
Different assembly	/[assembly];component/[dictionary]	/MyExternalAssembly;component/MyResources.xaml

Controls' Styles

In the same way you refer to a resource, you can refer and use a style that is defined in a resource dictionary or in a resource element of any framework element. Of course, like you do in a web application with Cascading Style Sheets (CSS), in a WPF application it is highly recommended that you keep styles in a common dictionary so that you can refer the styles throughout the UI. In WPF, the styles that are closest win. For example, if an element says it is red and the style says it is blue, then the element wins.

In the following sections, I will give you an overview of how styles work in WPF. Unfortunately, this topic is pretty complex; I highly recommend you study it in more detail by referring to
http://msdn.microsoft.com/library/bb613570.aspx.

Basic Style Concepts

When you start to use the styles in WPF and more in general in XAML (WPF, Silverlight, and Windows Phone 7), you should consider a style as a shortcut to customize the properties and the content of a specific control. In fact, when you write a style for a control, you don't do anything more than apply changes to properties' values.

In the example application, you have a dictionary that you called `BasicControlsDictionary`; in this dictionary, you will define all those styles that will affect basic controls such as the `TextBox`, `Label`, `Button`, and more. You will also define in this dictionary some additional styles such as Title, Subtitle, and so on. At the end, the `BasicControlsDictionary` should look like a theme or skin for the TimeTracker application.

When you start to define a style, the first attribute you have to use is the `TargetType` attribute, which will specify for which control you are writing the style. This attribute is mandatory because the WPF designer needs to figure out how to resolve the setters and triggers you are defining in the style.

If you do not define an `x:Key` attribute for the style, it will be applied to all the controls of that type available in your application in those views that are referencing the style. In this way, you can define a base style for a specific type of control, like a `Label`, and then override it with some specific customizations. You can inherit from another style by using the attribute `BasedOn`.

Listing 5-4 defines three different types of style for a `Label` control, while two of them inherit from the base one.

The setter property element is a special property of object that inherits from the `System.Windows.SetterBase` class and is used to apply a property value. It requires two properties: the property name and the value applied to the property.

Listing 5-4. Styles for a WPF Label

```
<!-- Classic Label -->
<Style TargetType="Label">
    <Setter Property="FontFamily" Value="Segoe UI" />
    <Setter Property="Foreground" Value="SteelBlue" />
</Style>
<!-- Error Label -->
<Style TargetType="Label" x:Key="ErrorLabel"
        BasedOn="{StaticResource {x:Type Label}}">
    <Setter Property="Foreground" Value="Red" />
    <Setter Property="FontWeight" Value="Bold" />
</Style>
<!-- Label for a Control -->
<Style TargetType="Label" x:Key="ControlLabel"
        BasedOn="{StaticResource {x:Type Label}}">
    <Setter Property="Foreground" Value="Black" />
    <Setter Property="FontWeight" Value="Bold" />
</Style>
```

Figure 5-1 shows the final result available at design time in Visual Studio.

Figure 5-1. Label styles applied on a WPF window

■ **Note** When you start to define a set of styles for a specific skin you are building for your WPF application, it is better that you create a test window that contains all the available controls and that you apply the styles to these controls. When you are ready, the window will act as a blueprint for you and for the other developers who will need a reference for the application UI styles. This is how Microsoft presents the WPF themes on CodePlex, by using a big window that includes all the available styles for a specific theme.

Triggers

Triggers are another interesting and powerful object available in the WPF style. They are a sort of method that is able to change one or more properties of a control based on when something happens in the UI: a property is changed, an event is fired, or a combination of both happens. The two different types of trigger are as follows:

- A *property trigger* gets or sets the property that returns the value that is compared with the Value property of the trigger. The comparison is a reference equality check.

- An *event trigger* represents a trigger that applies a set of actions in response to an event.

For example, the TextBox control in WPF doesn't have a disabled UI style by default, so you may want to create a custom style that will change the background color of a TextBox when its IsEnabled property is set to false. Another task you may want to accomplish with a trigger would be to change the background color of a TextBox when it has focus or display a watermark if the TextBox content is empty.

Listing 5-5 shows this type of style, and Figure 5-2 shows the final result at runtime.

Listing 5-5. Property Trigger for a TextBox

```
<!-- Standard Textbox -->
<Style TargetType="TextBox">
    <Setter Property="FontFamily" Value="Segoe UI" />
    <Setter Property="Foreground" Value="Black" />
    <Style.Triggers>
        <Trigger Property="IsFocused" Value="true">
            <Setter Property="Background" Value="LightYellow" />
        </Trigger>
        <Trigger Property="IsReadOnly" Value="true">
            <Setter Property="Background" Value="#EFEFEF" />
        </Trigger>
    </Style.Triggers>
</Style>
```

Figure 5-2. *Style triggers applied to a TextBox*

In this chapter, you will see how to customize the UI and the UI behaviors using styles and triggers; one important thing you need to keep in mind is that the triggers (and in general the styles) should be used to customize the UI appearance or the UI behaviors; they should never be used to customize business behaviors such as validation logic, for example.

Image Button

Something that I really miss in WPF is a simple button that is able to display an image and some text, maybe with the ability of retrieving the image and the text using some binding references.

When you try to create a new control template that has a complex UI, it is always better to try to accomplish the same result by using a combination of basic WPF controls; then when you get the desired result, you can start to translate it in a WPF style or control template. For example, for an image button, you need a `StackPanel` with a horizontal orientation that includes a `TextBlock` and an `Image` element. The code should be something like Listing 5-6.

Listing 5-6. *Image Button Without Styles*

```
<Button>
    <StackPanel
        Height="30" Width="80"
        Orientation="Horizontal">
        <Image Source="{StaticResource AddSmall}" Height="16" Width="16" />
        <TextBlock Margin="5,0,0,0" VerticalAlignment="Center">Add New</TextBlock>
    </StackPanel>
</Button>
```

Here you have defined a StackPanel with a fixed size (30×80) so that the content will not overflow and so the button will have the right size; then you assigned a horizontal orientation to the button so that you will have the Image and the TextBlock stacked horizontally. Then you added an image and a text block. The TextBlock has the left margin set to 5 pixels so that it will not be attached to the image.

At this point, it's pretty clear that the Content property of the element is the tricky part of the style/template control you want to build. In this case, you have two different content properties: one that defines the text displayed in the TextBlock and one that defines the image displayed in the Image element.

To accomplish this task, there are probably four or five solutions; what I will do is create a simple *user control* that will expose two ***dependency properties*** that will be available through the XAML markup; the properties are Text and Image. The control should be stored in a Controls folder in the WPF project (you should create this folder before creating the control). Listing 5-7 shows the final result.

Listing 5-7. *ImageButton UserControl's XAML and C# Code-Behind*

```
<!-- XAML -->
<UserControl
    x:Class="APRESS.TimeTracker.ImageButton"
    x:Name="ImageButtonControl"
    Height="auto" Width="auto">
    <Button>
        <StackPanel HorizontalAlignment="Stretch" Orientation="Horizontal">
            <Image
                Source="{Binding ElementName=ImageButtonControl, Path=Image}"
                Width="16" Height="16"
                Margin="3,0,0,0" VerticalAlignment="Center" />
            <TextBlock
                Text="{Binding ElementName=ImageButtonControl, Path=Text}"
                Margin="5,0,0,0" VerticalAlignment="Center" />
        </StackPanel>
    </Button>
</UserControl>

// code-behind file
public partial class ImageButton : UserControl
{
    public ImageButton()
    {
        InitializeComponent();
    }

    public string Text
    {
        get { return (string)GetValue(TextProperty); }
        set { SetValue(TextProperty, value); }
    }
```

```
public static readonly DependencyProperty TextProperty =
    DependencyProperty
        .Register("Text", typeof(string),
        typeof(ImageButton), new UIPropertyMetadata(""));

public ImageSource Image
{
    get { return (ImageSource)GetValue(ImageProperty); }
    set { SetValue(ImageProperty, value); }
}

public static readonly DependencyProperty ImageProperty =
    DependencyProperty
        .Register("Image", typeof(ImageSource),
        typeof(ImageButton), new UIPropertyMetadata(null));
}
```

In the second part of Listing 5-7, you have created two dependency properties on the code-behind file of the user control ImageButton; these two properties can be created in Visual Studio 2010 by typing **propdp** and pressing Tab twice. In the first part, you have added a reference to the user control ImageButton, and you simply bind the Image and Text properties. Figure 5-3 shows the final result.

Figure 5-3. UserControl ImageButton on a WPF window

Note The most important thing when you define a style for a specific control, like a button, for example, is to know exactly how to structure the control template. If you already know the XAML structure of the control you are going to style, consider that 80 percent of the job is already done. My suggestion is to locate the XAML default control template at http://msdn.microsoft.com/library/aa970773.aspx and start from there. You can also do this by editing the control template in Blend and looking at the XAML produced by Blend.

WPF Themes

A good alternative of customizing each control provided by WPF, in order to satisfy your customer's requirements, is to create a theme. A theme or skin is a set of styles, triggers, and customization applied to the entire WPF application; as soon as you apply a custom theme on a WPF application, the entire UI will change to using the new UI style.

In WPF there is no real theme file, so the easiest way to create a theme is by adding a new `ResourceDictionary.xaml` file that encapsulates all the required styles, triggers, and data template to customize the UI of your application.

On the Internet there are hundreds of WPF themes ready to be used; some of them are produced by third-party companies, and some of them are available for free. You can try, for example, the set of themes available for WPF at `http://wpf.codeplex.com`. This is the official open source project, maintained by Microsoft, for supporting WPF; on this web site you will find many themes and custom controls updated every month, and you will find many other utilities useful for your WPF application.

As you can see in Figure 5-4, I have created a simple window with a `GroupBox` and some basic controls. Just by changing the theme of the window, the entire UI takes on the new UI style. This solution can save you time, especially if you are planning to build a set of plug-ins for a specific WPF application.

Figure 5-4. *Same window with different theme applied*

Creating the Views

Now that you know how you can easily customize the UI of TimeTracker, you need to add the views to the application by using the prototyped SketchFlow application and the suggestions received from the customer. You will start from the Details view because it is the simplest one, and then you will move forward by creating the List views and the dashboard.

Login View

Before starting to create the views of the TimeTracker application, you need to define the entry point of the application, and that is a Login view. As soon as the application starts, you want to display a Login screen; based on the user accessing the application, you will display some controls in the dashboard. In this chapter, you will only design the views; then in the next chapters, you will retrieve the data from the database, and you will bind the data to the views.

First you have to locate the Views folder in the WPF project, right-click it, and add a new window. Table 5-2 shows the set of specific properties you will define for the Login view window.

Table 5-2. *Login View Window Properties*

Property	Value	Description
WindowStyle	Tool Window	This window style doesn't provide the Minimize and Resize buttons.
WindowStartupLocation	CenterScreen	The window is displayed in the center of the screen.
ResizeMode	NoResize	The window can't be resized.
TopMost	True	The window is the topmost visible widget on the screen.

By setting these properties, you can guarantee that the Login window will stay on top of any other open application and that it is not resizable; however, you easily use a canvas panel and place the controls using an absolute position.

For this window, you need the following:

- A Label with a special style for the window title

- A TextBox for the user name

- A PasswordBox for the password

- A Label with a special style to display errors during the authentication

- Two ImageButton controls: a Cancel button and a Login button

The final result should look like Figure 5-5.

Figure 5-5. *Login view final result*

The last step you need to do is to change the bootstrap process; you want that at the startup of the TimeTracker, so you display a Login screen, and you wait until the login is executed properly (see Listing 5-8).

Listing 5-8. *Login Bootstrap*

```
// App.xaml.cs

// import the APRESS.TimeTracker.Views

private void ConfigureContainer()
{
    container = new UnityContainer();
    container.RegisterType<IDialogService, DialogService>();
    container.RegisterType<INavigationService, NavigationService>();
    container.RegisterType<LoginView>();
    container.RegisterType<MainWindow>();
    navigation = container.Resolve<INavigationService>();
}
// Bootstrap
protected override void OnStartup(StartupEventArgs e)
{
    base.OnStartup(e);
    navigation.ShowLoginWindow();
}
// Navigation service
public Window ShowLoginWindow()
{
    var window = Container.Resolve<LoginView>();
    window.ShowDialog();
    return window;
}
```

When you add the view model for this view, you will also include the business logic to load the application or to close it if the user can't be authenticated.

To be consistent with what you wrote in the previous chapter, you need to modify the `INavigationService` interface by declaring a new method called `ShowLoginWindow`.

Regarding the `Container` property you exposed in Listing 5-8, this property is available in the `NavigationService` concrete class by using the dependency injection technique. When you create a new instance of a `NavigationService` object using the Unity IoC container, it will inject the corresponding instance of the container in the service. You can accomplish this task by adding a property of type `IUnityContainer` decorated with the `[Dependency]` attribute, like so:

```
[Dependency]
public IUnityContainer Container { get; set; }
```

Details View

The Details view contains the detailed information of a selected view model. You will have two different Details views—one for a selected employee and one for a selected customer. In the TimeTracker application, the view is a simple container for information and doesn't have any presentation logic. For this reason, the views don't really know anything about the presentation logic provided by the view models; they are only in charge of displaying the information.

For this type of view, I prefer to use a `Grid` container instead of using a `StackPanel` or a `Dock` container because with the `Grid` I have more control over the layout but also can still have my controls resizable.

If you do not define a `MaxHeight` on your controls' styles, the control will extend its height in the entire height of the grid cell that contains it.

The first view you will build is the employee Details view; then you can easily follow the same instructions to build the customer one or simply look the code of the TimeTracker application. The first important note about this view is that you have too much information to be displayed all in one view. When you open the Details view for a selected employee, you need to read the employee's information (such as the first name, last name, and so on). Then you need also to read the available contacts and addresses of the employee, and finally you need to view the list of appointments assigned to the employee. To accomplish this task, you need to use a `TabControl`, which will be able to separate this information into different tabs.

The trick then is to create three different user controls: one for each tab so that you will keep the XAML markup clean in the employee Details view and be able to recycle the markup for a future reuse.

The `TabControl` is pretty easy to use; you have to declare a `TabControl` element as the root element that will act as a container for a number of tab items. Each `TabItem` has an `Header` property that will display simple text or more complex content in the tab header, as well as a `Content` property that can have anything inside it. Listing 5-9 shows the XAML markup of Figure 5-6.

Figure 5-6. *Employee Details view with a TabControl*

Listing 5-9. *Base XAML Markup for the Employee Details View*

```
<Window>
    <DockPanel LastChildFill="True">
        <TextBlock DockPanel.Dock="Top" Style="{StaticResource TitleBlock}">TimeTracker
Employee Details</TextBlock>
        <StackPanel
                DockPanel.Dock="Bottom"
                MaxHeight="30"
                Orientation="Horizontal" HorizontalAlignment="Right"
                Grid.Column="1" Grid.Row="3" Grid.ColumnSpan="3">
            <Controls:ImageButton
                    Padding="3"
                    Text="Save"
                    Image="{DynamicResource SaveSmall}"/>
            <Controls:ImageButton
                    Padding="3"
                    Text="Cancel"
                    Image="{DynamicResource CloseSmall}" />
        </StackPanel>
        <TabControl DockPanel.Dock="Bottom" Margin="5">
            <TabItem Header="Employee">

            </TabItem>
            <TabItem Header="Contacts">

            </TabItem>
            <TabItem Header="Appointments">
```

```
            </TabItem>
        </TabControl>
    </DockPanel>
</Window>
```

User Controls

You can consider a `UserControl` control like a window or page framework element; it can contain any control and can act like a WPF window or page. It has a `DataContext` property and can be reused in other controls, pages, and windows. To create a new `UserControl` control, right-click the Views folder of the WPF application, select the command *Add New UserControl*, and give it a name of *EmployeeDetailsUserControl*.

By default, when you add a new control, page, or window in a WPF application, the main container (root element) added to the view is of type `Grid`; this type of container is composed by a set of `RowDefinition` and `ColumnDefinition` properties, like an HTML table. You can set up the row height or the column width to be a specific size *(such as 30px)* or automatic *(auto)* or to fill up the remaining space *(*)*. Another easy way to accomplish this task (creating new row and columns on a grid) in Visual Studio or Blend is to right-click the `Grid` container in the designer and select the property Grid Row or Grid Column. Within these commands you can choose to add, remove, or resize the rows and columns.

After you have set up all the rows and columns in the `Grid` container, you can simply drag a control such as a `Label` or a `TextBox` in the design surface of the user control and specify the attached properties `Grid.Row` and `Grid.Column`.

When your user control is done, you can reference it in any other view or control using the code in Listing 5-10 or simply drag it from the toolbox so that the WPF designer will create a new reference to the corresponding namespace in your XAML code.

Listing 5-10. Details UserControl Referenced in the Details View

```
<!-- In the root element -->
xmlns:my="clr-namespace:APRESS.TimeTracker.Views"

<TabControl DockPanel.Dock="Bottom" Margin="5">
    <TabItem Header="Employee">
            <my:EmployeeDetailsUserControl Padding="5" />
    </TabItem>
</TabControl>
```

Using this approach, you will build a main view model that will be able to carry all the data needed by the Details view and by every single tab (Details, Contacts, and Appointments); then using the IoC container and the data binding engine of WPF, you will bind the data in the XAML tree structure of the Details view.

Figure 5-7 shows the final result of the Details view including the user controls; in the figure you can see how each part of the UI is carrying its own `DataContext` (view model).

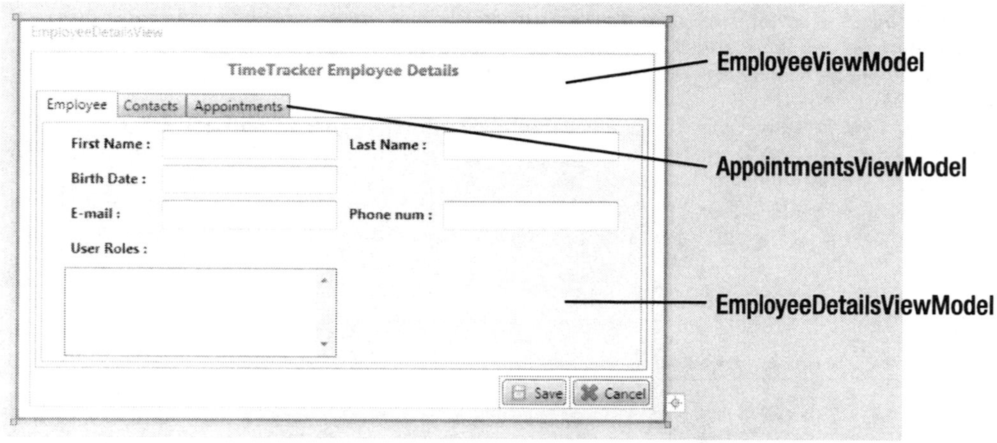

Figure 5-7. *Final structure of the employee Details view*

The same process can be easily accomplished for the customer Details view; of course, the information is different, but the procedure is the same. You need to identify and group the information by topic and create a user control for each group; then you have to aggregate all this information inside a view (window) that will pass the `DataContext` down to the child containers.

■ **Note** If you want to follow the Inversion of Control technique, the method used to call a Details view should get injected in the caller with a parameter of type `Object` that represents the current `DataContext` of the Details view. In this way, you can guarantee that a Details view can't really exist if a corresponding view model is not associated with it. For example, a good way of opening a Details view is to use something like the following pseudocode:

```
var ViewModel = repository.GetEmployee("Raffaele Garofalo");
var View = navigation.OpenEmployeeDetailsView(ViewModel);
```

Data Validation

The process of validating the data in WPF is accomplished in two steps. The first step is to create a specific style with UI elements and triggers that can show the user that the data inserted in a specific control (`TextBox`, `DatePicker`, and so on) is invalid and reflect some specific validation rules. The second step is to define and implement the IDataErrorInfo interface in your WPF view, and suddenly in your WPF ViewModel, in order to provide to the WPF binding engine a proper mechanism to validate the input inserted by the user and notify it to the UI engine that will apply the proper UI style.

The validation process of a value inserted in a control, in WPF, is strictly related to the binding engine of WPF, a topic you will learn about in Chapter 7; in this section, you will see how the ErrorTemplate works and how it can be set up in a TextBox by displaying a ToolTip and by marking with a red border the TextBox control.

The property that you are looking for in WPF is called Validation.HasError, and it is an attached property; the property is triggered by the validation process of the view, and it will be covered in depth in Chapter 7.

Figure 5-8 shows an example of how you can style a TextBox to display a red border and a ToolTip with an error message that says the date of a specific object being invalid.

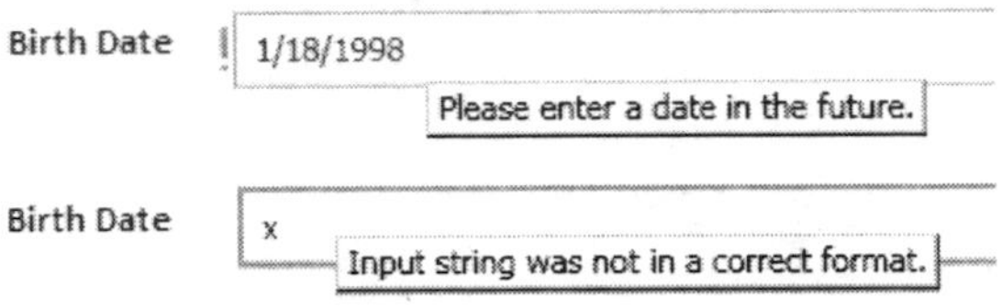

Figure 5-8. *Validation errors in WPF*

Listing 5-11 shows the XAML style applied to the TextBox control.

Listing 5-11. *XAML Validation Error Style*

```
<Trigger Property="Validation.HasError" Value="true">
   <Setter Property="BorderBrush" Value="Red" />
   <Setter Property="ToolTip"
      Value="{Binding RelativeSource={x:Static RelativeSource.Self},
      Path=(Validation.Errors)[0].ErrorContent}"/>
</Trigger>
```

List View

The List view is a simple view. It doesn't really expose a lot of controls. In this case, it exposes a bar at the top of the view that contains a set of ImageButton controls and a WPF DataGrid control that contains the available employees/customers object retrieved from the database.

First you need to create a new view; this time the name is EmployeesListView, and it will be placed inside the Views folder. This view is composed of a DockPanel container that has the following sequence: a title TextBlock, a StackPanel with a search TextBox, a DataGrid, and another panel with the Create, Read, Update, and Delete (CRUD) buttons.

Figure 5-9 shows the final result, and Listing 5-12 shows the XAML markup.

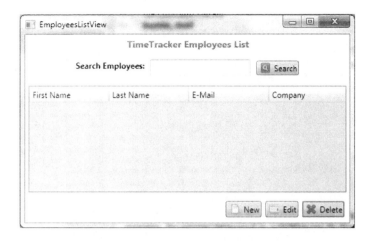

Figure 5-9. *Employees List view*

Listing 5-12. *XAML Markup Used for the Employees List View*

```
<Window>
    <DockPanel>
        <TextBlock
            DockPanel.Dock="Top"
            Style="{StaticResource TitleBlock}">TimeTracker Employees List</TextBlock>
        <StackPanel
            Margin="5" MinHeight="30"
            HorizontalAlignment="Center" Orientation="Horizontal" DockPanel.Dock="Top">
            <Label Style="{StaticResource ControlLabel}">Search Employees: </Label>
            <TextBox Margin="3"></TextBox>
            <Controls:ImageButton
                    Text="Search"
                    Image="{DynamicResource SearchSmall}" />
        </StackPanel>
        <StackPanel
            Margin="5" MinHeight="30"
            HorizontalAlignment="Right" Orientation="Horizontal" DockPanel.Dock="Bottom">
            <Controls:ImageButton
                    Text="New"
                    Image="{DynamicResource NewSmall}"/>
            <Controls:ImageButton
                    Text="Edit"
                    Image="{DynamicResource EditSmall}" />
            <Controls:ImageButton
                    Text="Delete"
                    Image="{DynamicResource CloseSmall}" />
        </StackPanel>
```

```
        <DataGrid Margin="5" DockPanel.Dock="Bottom">
            <DataGrid.Columns>
                <DataGridTextColumn Header="First Name" Width="120" />
                <DataGridTextColumn Header="Last Name" Width="120" />
                <DataGridTextColumn Header="E-Mail" Width="120" />
                <DataGridTextColumn Header="Company" Width="120" />
            </DataGrid.Columns>
        </DataGrid>
    </DockPanel>
</Window>
```

The code doesn't need a lot of attention; in this case, the only new control you encountered is the DataGrid.

The DataGrid

The WPF DataGrid was introduced in the default set of WPF controls in Visual Studio 2010 and NET 4. Before, in order to use this control, you were forced to download the *WPF Toolkit*, an open source project hosted on www.codeplex.com and supported by Microsoft in order to fill the gaps left by the default set of controls provided with Visual Studio 2008.

The DataGrid control in WPF is a very powerful control and can be used as is just by dragging a grid on a WPF surface and by assigning its ItemsSource to a bindable collection of object or manually setting the bind and styles.

If you plan to manually set the columns of your DataGrid, first set the AutoGenerateColumns property of the Grid to false; otherwise, the column will automatically generate a column for each available property of the object bound to it.

The current version of the WPF DataGrid offers four basic column types:

- TextBoxColumn used to display string values

- CheckBoxColumn used to display Boolean values

- ComboBoxColumn used to display selectable or enumerable values

- HyperlinkColumn used to display hyperlinks values

- TemplateColumn used to display custom styles

The columns can be added and created by using the XAML markup or the WPF designer provided within Visual Studio.

■ **Note** The DataGrid control in WPF 4.0 has a lot of features; for example, it allows you to group columns by using specific group criteria. It also allows you to execute specific custom cell and row selection and to define complex UI styles. The DataGrid is not a control that you will analyze in detail in this chapter, but it will be used in the TimeTracker application. You will see in the next chapters how to bind data to this control and how you can customize selection and sorting. For details, please refer to http://msdn.microsoft.com/library/ system.windows.controls.datagrid.aspx.

User Controls for the Dashboard

In WPF you can create different types of views; for example, if you are building a navigation application that will be displayed on Internet Explorer (.xbap), you will create some page containers; on the other hand, if you are building a stand-alone (.exe) application like TimeTracker, you will have to use the window containers. There is then a third type of control container that is called UserControl, which cannot be hosted by itself but has to be included in a Page or Window control. You have already created a couple of UserControl controls when you created the Details views for the employee and customer objects.

The trick of using UserControl controls is that you can totally recycle the UI of your views, and the only thing you need to do is to pass a valid view model to the DataContext of the UserControl control.

Charts with WPF

The main window of the TimeTracker application is composed of a set of panels that consist of nothing more than four different UserControl controls arranged on the dashboard UI using a Grid control container. To each UserControl you simply apply an additional shadow effect in order to make the UI cooler.

In the WPF project, locate the Views folder, and create a new UserControl that you will call EmployeeStatisticsUserControl; it will contain a couple of custom charts that will display general performances of the employees of the ACME Ltd Company.

To use charts in WPF, if you haven't purchased a third-party chart component, you can download the WPF Toolkit from http://wpf.codeplex.com/releases/view/29117. This provides a rich set of WPF controls including bar charts, graphs, pie charts, and more.

In Figure 5-10, I am showing two different charts, so I have divided the layout of the UserControl using a Grid layout container by creating two columns and five rows in order to separate the charts and view titles.

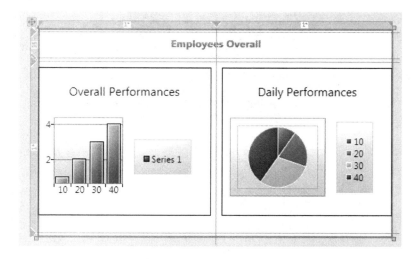

Figure 5-10. *Employees overall UserControl*

You can start to design your UI by dragging a couple of Chart controls from the Toolkit toolbar to your UI application. The toolkit will provide some fake data that is displayed at design time. You will then bind the charts with some real data, discussed in Chapter 7. In this way, you can view the final result right away without needing to provide real data to the chart.

■ **Note** The WPF Toolkit is a third-party control library for WPF containing a set of controls included in one or more assembly (.dll file). You can use these controls in two ways; the first way, which is the easiest, is to create a new tab in your Visual Studio Toolbox and select the controls by using the right-click command "Add controls." After you have added the controls to the Toolbox, you have to simply drag and drop the controls into the UI. The second option is to emulate what the Visual Studio designer will do for you when you drag something from the Toolbox, and that is to add a reference to the project that points to WPFtoolkit.dll and reference the namespace in the XAML markup using the following syntax: xmlns:chartingToolkit="clr-namespace:System.Windows. Controls.DataVisualization.Charting;assembly=System.Windows.Controls.DataVisualization. Toolkit". Then use the new element prefix chartingTookit in your XAML markup.

Drag and Drop (Appointments Control)

Another interesting control in the dashboard is the appointment calendar control, which displays the appointments available for today and allows you to drag and drop these appointments around the UI. There are a lot of solution to accomplish this task, and I believe that the most functional is still what is done in the Office Outlook software, which is called the Daily Scheduler. It is nothing more than a grid with a set of rows (one for each hour of the day) where you can drag over shapes that represent appointments.

I have found some schedule controls provided by third-party companies such as Infragistics, Telerick, and DevExpress; in this demo, I have included an open source control, the WPF Schedule Control, created by Rudi Glober and available at www.rudigrobler.net/Blog/timeslotpanel. It allows you to accomplish the task, but you may also consider purchasing a professional one or customizing the open source one provided with this book. The open source control is a basic daily schedule control and can be downloaded from http://wpfschedule.codeplex.com.

Figure 5-11 shows the final result; in this case, I have just included the schedule control inside a StackPanel so that the control will fill the entire space of the container.

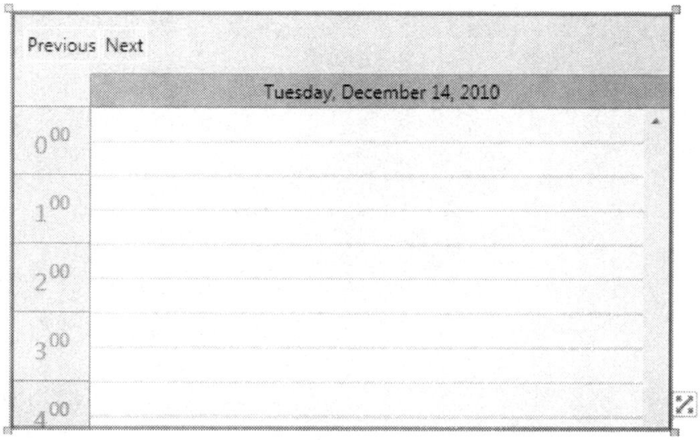

Figure 5-11. *Daily schedule control*

The Dashboard (MainView)

The last component of the dashboard is the ListBox that contains a set of employees. In this case, you will query from the database the top ten employees based on the performance they have every month. (You will see this control in Chapter 7 when you bind the data retrieved from the database.)

The dashboard control has a very simple layout. It is a grid layout that splits the screen in four sections, like you did in Chapter 2 with SketchFlow; in each cell of the grid, you have a ScrollViewer control so that you can easily display a scrollbar if the content in the cell overflow the size of the container.

If you press Ctrl+Shift+B, Visual Studio will rebuild the entire application for you; after you rebuild the application, you can find in the Toolbox a new tab that contains all the user controls available from your application. You don't have to do anything more than dragging the controls inside the UI.

Figure 5-12 represents the result, a WPF window composed of four WPF user controls ready to be customized by a theme and to be bound with some real data.

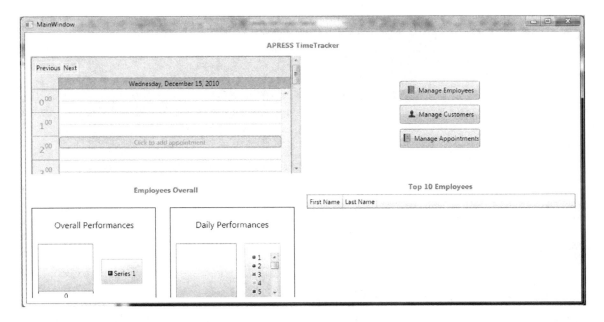

Figure 5-12. *Final draft of the dashboard*

Add Features to the Application

You can leave the UI as is for now because you already have a nice UI style that can be easily customized. Or you can start to look at the amazing effects you can obtain on any WPF controls by using few simple lines of XAML markup or by playing a little bit with Expression Blend.

My personal choice is to use the XAML markup because I want to learn and understand exactly how a specific effect or behavior works; however, feel free to open the TimeTracker application in Expression Blend and do some experiments on the UI in order to obtain a custom style that you can apply to your version of the TimeTracker.

Custom Effects

When you want to open a view, because you chose to use the Inversion of Control, you do not have a lot of power over how to open it. For example, you don't have a framework that allows you, within the DI container, to open a view with some kind of animation.

If you remember at the beginning of this chapter you saw that the WPF styles provide a powerful object called a *trigger* that is a set of evaluation rules applied to a style.

Any framework element in WPF has a `Triggers` property element that can be used by simply declaring the element using the syntax `[frameworkelement].[triggers]` and writing the implementation of the trigger inside this element. In this case, you want to create an event trigger, in other words, a trigger that is fired when a specific event occurs. So, you may wonder which event when fired will trigger an animation in the view? Well, the animation should occur when the window is open, so the event should be the OnLoad event. Listing 5-13 shows how you can open a window and use a simple animation with a storyboard to change the opacity of the window. It's like creating a fade effect.

Listing 5-13. *Window Load Event with Animation*

```
<Window.Triggers>
    <EventTrigger RoutedEvent="Window.Loaded">
        <EventTrigger.Actions>
            <BeginStoryboard>
                <Storyboard>
                    <DoubleAnimation Storyboard.TargetName="TransparentStop"
                        Storyboard.TargetProperty="Offset" By="1"  Duration="0:0:1"    />
                    <DoubleAnimation Storyboard.TargetName="BlackStop"
                        Storyboard.TargetProperty="Offset" By="1" Duration="0:0:1"
                        BeginTime="0:0:0.05" />
                </Storyboard>
            </BeginStoryboard>
        </EventTrigger.Actions>
    </EventTrigger>
</Window.Triggers>
```

In this example, you are using a DoubleAnimation element to create an interpolation between to values of a property; in this case, the TransparentStop property is used to re-create a fade effect.

As you saw in the Chapter 3, you can easily accomplish this task by using one of the predefined animations available in Blend, or you can create your custom animation.

The base concept with the animation is to create a storyboard and then attach the storyboard to a trigger that will play it when it's required by the application.

A few notes on using animation with WPF are necessary:

- WPF animation requires certain hardware. The more complex the animation is, the more power the GDI engine will require.

- Having the power of running stand-alone applications using a storyboard doesn't mean that every single component of the application should be animated.

- Having a window that takes 20 seconds to be animated and opened is probably not really user-friendly.

During the next chapters, you will add some more animations to the TimeTracker application, but they will not be analyzed in depth because they are beyond the scope of this book. If you are interested in learning WPF animation, I suggest you refer to http://msdn.microsoft.com/library/ms752312.aspx. Also, look at Expression Blend, which can be a very useful tool to learn in a *visual way* how to write XAML animations.

Summary

One of the more important concepts in WPF is how you can style the UI of the application and where you can store these customizations. Thanks to the structure of WPF, you can create various XAML files that can be used as a *resource dictionary*, which is a dictionary of information stored using the XAML markup.

Within a *resource dictionary*, you can store the location (path) of a graphical resource such as an image or an animation, or you can store a UI style that will be used to customize the graphical appearance of a UI control.

Using styles, you can revolutionize the UI appearance of a control, starting from modifying basic properties such as the border color or the font family. Then you can go down to the core template control and drastically change the appearance and behavior of any control. Using this approach, you can embed a set of styles in a resource dictionary and share it across the WPF application like it is an application theme or skin.

The process of creating a view with Visual Studio is pretty simple; after you have identified the layout that will compose the view, you can choose from writing the XAML markup or simply drag the control into the designer from the Toolbox. You can use and drag the predefined set of controls provided by WPF, or you can add custom controls downloaded from open source communities such as www.codeplex.com or purchased from third-party companies.

You also saw how you can create a UI with a complex view composed of several little views; this task can be achieved by creating user controls.

Finally, you got a brief overview of how to attach an animation to a component of a view or to the view events such as the view load process.

■■■

CHAPTER 6

The Entity Framework

Software is typically developed to solve a particular problem set that arises from and comprises various business requirements. You can group those requirements together into something known as a *domain*, and in this domain model, the business requirements are called *domain entities*. Each domain entity is a unique business object in the domain space, and it is able to interact and to have relationships with the other domain entities of the same domain model. A domain entity represents a specific problem of the domain model.

These concepts are the basis of Domain Driven Design (DDD), introduced by Martin Fowler in his book *Patterns for Enterprise Application Architectures* (Addison-Wesley, 2002). With DDD, you try to rationalize the solutions for common problems by building a framework composed of objects and their behaviors. The DDD approach allows the team (analysts, architects, developers, and so on) to build a shared language—a domain-specific language (DSL). This is a unified language understandable by all members of the team, which eases collaboration among team members and helps them find gaps and errors in the domain.

Of course, this adds another layer of abstraction to the system: by keeping the business logic of the application loosely coupled from the rest of the application code, it forces the developers to add an additional level of isolation to the domain, and this requires more effort and more code. However, there are also advantages. One of the advantages is the amount of testable surface you can cover. The loosely coupled approach produces layered applications, and each layer can be tested separately from the other layers, so the testable surface is much higher than with an application composed of a single layer. An additional advantage is the extensibility of the application; if the business logic is totally separate, far less code is required to implement a new feature in the business tier than in a single-layer application.

Using this approach also means the way you persist and retrieve the data from the database will be different—you want to keep the domain unaware of the particular persistence technique. Applying this concept can be tough, especially if you are a junior developer and have never worked on a layered application before.

In this chapter we are going to take a look at how to persist a domain model on a database without spending a lot of time writing complex stored procedures or creating classes to map the domain entities against the database tables. We will also explore the various DDD techniques and how to tie everything together using the Microsoft Entity Framework.

Object Relational Mappers

The first challenge when you're working with a set of objects that need to be persisted on a database is creating specific database code, using a particular database language like T-SQL for SQL Server that will tell the database how to persist or retrieve the objects. You may, for example, need to inform SQL Server that a specific object called `Customer` should be persisted in a database table called `tbl_Customers`, and that the property `FirstName` should be persisted in a field of the table called `fld_first_name`, and so on.

Another challenging task may be to persist or retrieve a complex graph composed of a set of objects tied together by some relationships. For example, the `Customer` object may have a collection of child `Address` objects that are persisted in a different table in the database and linked by a foreign key; how would you persist and retrieve them using procedural T-SQL code? Probably you'd come up with a complex, hard-to-maintain stored procedure that would execute a specific `INSERT` or `UPDATE` commands for each object that has to be saved or, much better, a separate stored procedure for each object that needs to be saved or updated. Usually, all the code and procedures are tied together and orchestrated by a set of components and classes exposed by the Data Access Layer (DAL).

An object-relational mapper (O/RM) is a framework that can map and persist a domain model, or more generally, a graph of objects, into a relational database. The task is accomplished via a set of instructions and mapping files that tell the O/RM how to persist a specific object of the model on a specific object (table) of the database.

One of the very useful features of most O/RMs is the capacity to either autogenerate a database schema or adapt to an existing database schema. In the first case, the O/RM lets you autogenerate the Data Definition Language (DDL) scripts that will create or update the corresponding database schema; in the second case, the O/RM will adapt (map) the structure of the domain model to an existing schema that can't be modified because of some business requirement (the database is legacy; the database contains production data; the schema is used by other applications; and so on). The first approach is known as Code First development—the domain model drives the application development. The second approach is known as Database First—when the domain model design is based on a pre-existing database schema where, usually, the relationship between database tables and domain entities is one to one.

At the time of this writing, the .NET community mostly uses two O/RMs, Entity Framework and NHibernate. Entity Framework is the O/RM provided with the .NET Framework 3.5 and later. Depending on the .NET Framework version you're using, you will able to work with one of the available CTPs. You can download CTP 5, released at the end of 2010, at `www.microsoft.com/downloads/en/details .aspx?FamilyID=35adb688-f8a7-4d28-86b1-b6235385389d`.

NHibernate is an open source O/RM that is a porting of the well-known Java O/RM, Hibernate, for the .NET Framework. The NHibernate community is very active and in December 2010 released a major new version, 3.0, which you can download from `http://nhforge.org/Default.aspx`. NHibernate is open source, and it's a more mature and complex O/RM than the Entity Framework. Unfortunately, it doesn't provide direct integration with the Visual Studio IDE like the Entity Framework does. For this and other reasons, in this book, we will develop our DAL using Entity Framework CTP 5 as our O/RM. We'll use the CTP because for now it is the only one that allows building a Code First version.

Here are the minimum features a custom DAL and an O/RM should be able to provide to be considered a good and reusable data access module:

- *Database-independence:* an O/RM should be database-independent. This means that a domain model mapped with a specific O/RM should be able to be persisted on different databases without any huge reconfiguration on the O/RM side.

- *Autogenerated scripts:* an O/RM should be able to autogenerate the Data Manipulation Language (DML) used to persist or retrieve the domain from the database. The DML should be specific for each database configured with the O/RM.

- *Queries:* an O/RM should provide a set of APIs that allow you to query the model and translate the API so it's understandable by the database.

- *Transactions*: an O/RM should provide an interface for managing transactions like a database does. A transaction is a set of commands that are executed sequentially; if one or more of these commands fails, the entire set of commands is cancelled (rolled back) and no changes affects the database.

- *Concurrency*: an O/RM should be able to manage concurrency. This means that it should be able to return the correct result when concurrent operations are executed against it.

Active Record Pattern

One of the available patterns that can be used with an O/RM and a domain model is the Active Record (AR) pattern. The principal requisites of this pattern are: the domain entity represents a table of the database with a one to one relationship; the domain entity exposes the properties of the corresponding database table, and the Create, Read, Update, and Delete (CRUD) commands and foreign keys relationship are exposed with object references. Listing 6-1 shows a pseudo-code version of the Active Record implementation.

Listing 6-1. *Sample Active Record Pattern Code*

```
Customer customer = new Customer();
customer.FirstName = "Raffaele";
customer.LastName = "Garofalo";
customer.Save();
```

The code creates a new object AR of type `Customer`, then assigns some values to the properties exposed by this object, `FirstName` and `LastName`. Finally, the `Customer` object saves itself to the database by calling the AR method `Save` exposed by the object.

The AR pattern was described by Fowler in the book mentioned earlier as a pattern more for a data source than for a domain model because it explains the behavior and property an object should expose if it is to act as a data source. In fact, an object exposed by a domain that implements the AR pattern can act as a data source and expose methods to perform CRUD operations.

An object that implements the AR pattern is usually specific to the row of the table that the object represents, and it should usually be as close as possible to the real structure of the data row represented.

Usually, an object that implements the AR pattern has three particular characteristics:

- It exposes all the fields of the corresponding table in the form of properties.

- It exposes a set of methods to accomplish the CRUD operations.

- It exposes a set of static methods to execute global CRUD operations with all the records of the table.

Figure 6-1 shows a class diagram of a hypothetical AR entity.

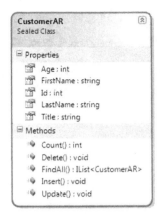

Figure 6-1. Class diagram of an AR object

The AR pattern is a pretty simple and compact implementation of a persistence object pattern and, like any other design pattern, has pros and cons; some basic O/RMs, like LINQ to SQL and LINQ to DataSet, are designed to implement this pattern while others, like Entity Framework and NHibernate, are designed to implement a different type of persistence pattern, one that we will explore in a bit.

Pros and Cons of the Active Record Pattern

Pros

- It forces you to keep the domain simple. In fact, the first requirement of the AR implementation is "*Keep it simple.*"

- It doesn't require lengthy experience writing a custom DAL because, usually, the AR is supported by a mature framework like LINQ To SQL, Castle Active Record, and so forth.

- The object is independent; it carries all the required code for CRUD and for table operations (search, count, and more).

Cons

- It pollutes the domain entities with methods related to the persistence layer; this results in a domain model (the business logic layer or BLL) that interacts directly with the O/RM (DAL).

- The constraint between table and entity forces you to keep both up-to-date because it is the fundamental requirement of the pattern.

- It forces you to expose static methods in the domain entity to perform specific DAL operations (search, count, etc.) that can't be tested properly and that are no longer loosely coupled.

Code First Development

Code First development is the direct application of Domain Driven Design where the flow of the application is driven by the domain and not by the database. Usually this type of approach is accomplished when the database hasn't been designed yet or isn't legacy, so that the datastore has some flexibility that allows you to model the domain in a better way.

As noted earlier, the DDD approach requires a graph of objects that is business-centric. Moreover, with DDD, the domain is totally unaware about the persistence techniques. So, in contrast to the previous AR pattern, with the domain first approach you work on the domain without caring about the datastore. At the end of the development process, when the domain is ready, you map the domain to the database, using an O/RM in order to make the job a little bit easier.

As you can see, the first big difference between the AR and the DDD approach is that the AR is database driven and is directly affected by changes that may occur in the database; the DDD, on the other hand, is domain driven and is developed completely independently of the persistence aspect. Theoretically, a DDD application can be persisted over different database types simply by changing the connection string of the DAL.

Implementing the DDD technique can make an application more complex (easily), and it forces you to introduce additional components in the DAL in order to orchestrate the persistence of one or more domain entities; these components are the *Repository* and the *Unit of Work*. Let's take a look at them now.

The Repository Pattern

When you work with a domain model, you generally try to include in the domain entities only the business logic associated with the relationships and behaviors of the entities. You try to avoid any logic related to the persistence layer because the domain must stay agnostic against the datastore; it's not its role to know how to persist the data or how to retrieve it.

So with the DDD, you need to separate this logic into two layers. The business logic layer will contain the domain-specific logic, while the data access layer will contain the logic specific to the persistence process.

In his book about design patterns, Fowler explains how this logic should be included in a component called Repository. This component mediates between the domain entity and the mapping object, acting like an in-memory collection of entities. Furthermore, the repository is the component that contains the code related to the database transactions, the O/RM calls, and all the other data-layer-specific operations so that there is an additional abstraction between the DAL and the rest of the application. Figure 6-2 diagrams this structure.

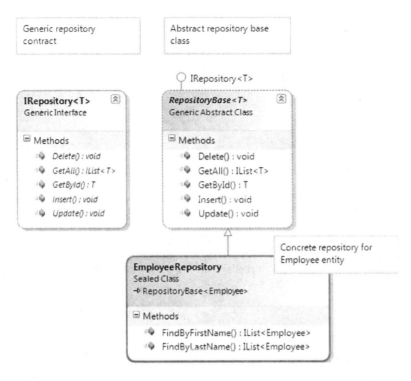

Figure 6-2. *Sample Repository pattern class diagram*

Listing 6-2 shows sample code in which the repository is in charge of retrieving a set of entities of type Person. When a change occurs to one of these objects, the same repository then saves the changes to the database.

Listing 6-2. *Sample Code for the Repository Pattern*

```
CustomerRepository repository = new CustomerRepository();
IList<Customer> customers = repository.GetAllCustomers();
Customer firstCustomer = customers.First();
firstCustomer.LastName = "New LastName";
repository.Update(firstCustomer);
```

The point of this code is to retrieve a list of objects of type Customer. To do so, it first creates a new instance of the CustomerRepository object, which is a repository specifically for the Person entity. It then calls the method GetAllCustomers, which tells the repository to get all the available persons from the data layer. Next, a LINQ extension retrieves the first object of the list by using the extension method First. Finally, the code changes the last name of the object and calls the Update method of the repository to update the change into the database.

As you can see, with this approach the loosely coupled domain doesn't know how it has to be persisted or retrieved from the database, and the DAL (the repository) is acting as the persistence layer.

With this approach, the first important and fundamental concept is that *"The business logic has to stay in the domain model while the database logic has to stay in the data access layer."*

You should generally have a repository component for each domain entity of the domain model, and this class should implement, at least, the basic CRUD methods plus methods that allows you to execute the common query operations like search, count, and so on. It's a good practice, but not mandatory, to use the approach provided by the .NET Framework to create a generic `IRepository<T>` contract that exposes these methods, and then implement the specific methods only in the specific repository.

Take a look at Figure 6-2 again and notice at the top right corner an interface (also known as contract in OOP) that exposes some generic methods that can be used by any repository. In fact, a repository should be able to `Insert` a new entity, `Update` an existing entity or `Delete` an existing entity. A repository should also be able to provide `All` the available entities and a specific entity by `Id` (the unique key that identifies the entity in the database, so we have a unique constraint on the database for all the tables to identify a new row).

The shape to the right in Figure 6-2 represents the base repository class, a class that implements the code exposed in the `IRepository` contract. This class is marked as abstract, meaning it can be used as a base class but it can't be used directly. This is the case because we don't want a generic repository for all the entities but rather a specific repository for each entity of the domain. As you can see, the base repository class is still holding the generic signature because it doesn't yet know which entity it will expose.

The shape at the bottom represents the repository class for a specific entity, in this case an entity called `Employee`. This class exposes only the additional methods (usually query methods) specific to the entity that can't be provided by the generic repository, here the `FindByFirstName` and `FindByLastName` methods.

You will see in the next sections how you can provide a generic repository pattern to the Entity Framework in order to add a further abstraction between the O/RM and the other layers of the application.

■ **Note** In the description of the Repository pattern, Fowler says *"A Repository mediates between the domain and data mapping layers, acting like an in-memory domain object collection."* This concept is not really applied to our repository component because the O/RM, in our case the Entity Framework, is already acting as an in-memory container of entities. This container, also known as the DataContext, is in charge of keeping the entities aligned between the in-memory container and the database store.

The Unit of Work

The repository is a good technique for adding an abstraction layer between the O/RM and the other layers, but it doesn't indicate how to handle operations against the database or against a business transaction. Moreover, unlike the AR approach, it lacks transaction and concurrency management. How do you know that a set of operation executed by a repository object is successful and how do you know that an in-memory object of the repository has been updated in the database? To have more control of these types of operations, Fowler presented the concept of a Unit of Work (UoW), which he defined like this: *"The Unit of Work maintains a list of objects affected by a business transaction and coordinates the writing out of changes and the resolution of concurrency problems."*

This pattern is not specifically required by DDD development and, generally, especially when you work with an O/RM, it is already provided in the framework you are working with. In fact, the O/RMs most often used in the .NET world are all based on this pattern.

Figure 6-3 exposes the Unit of Work pattern in the form of an interface; the contract is composed of three standard CRUD methods: MarkNew (insert), MarkDirty (update) and MarkDeleted (delete). These operations will interact with the DataContext of the O/RM to mark the entities using the specified state (new, deleted, dirty). In addition, the UoW must provide the methods to manage the transaction: begin, commit (confirm), and rollback (cancel).

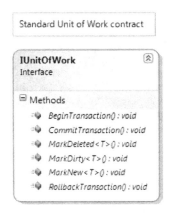

Figure 6-3. *The Unit of Work contract exposed by an interface*

The primary purpose of using a UoW is to provide an abstraction between the database transaction and the business steps that will accomplish the transaction so that the business layer can execute the various steps within a single transaction.

Let's look at the pseudocode in Listing 6-3. The goal is to create a new Customer entity, add an Appointment, and save them both, all within a single transaction.

Listing 6-3. *Multiple Steps of a Business Transaction Using the Unit of Work*

```
// retrieve the three components
IUnitOfWork uow = new UnitOfWork();
uow.BeginTransaction();
CustomerRepository customerRepository = new CustomerRepository(uow);
AppointmentRepository appointmentRepository = new AppointmentRepository(uow);
// create a customer and save it
Customer customer = new Customer();
customerRepository.Insert(customer);
// create an appointment for a customer
Appointment appointment = new Appointment(customer);
appointmentRepository.Insert(appointment);
// commit everything
uow.CommitTransaction();
```

This code takes a different type of approach to using the repository pattern. Here, the two repositories are dependent on the unit of work; in fact, they require an active unit of work in their constructor. After creating a new customer, the code has the repository insert it, then does the same with the appointment. In reality, what the repositories are doing here is calling the method `uow.MarkNew` for each entity, but they are not actually saving the entities. The save (in this case `insert`) method is called only at the end of the script, when it's time for the unit of work to commit the whole transaction.

As you can see, this additional step loosely couples the business logic from the database logic, leaving both active and independent. You could create a new appointment using the appointment business logic (for example you might check that the customer doesn't have already another appointment at the same time) and you could orchestrate this process using a unit of work transaction that is able to roll back all the changes if something goes wrong.

Of course, the more components you add to the project, the more complex and time-consuming the project becomes. Still, the implementation of these two fundamentals patterns (repository and unit of work) in your DAL allows you to keep the domain model intact and totally unaware of the persistence mechanism.

The TimeTracker Domain

Before starting to create the application, you need to consider the domain of the application and you can do this by reading and interpreting the use cases discussed with the customer or with the person who requested the application.

Here are some of the domain entities identified in the TimeTracker application:

- *Employee*: the employee entity represents a unique employee in the domain. It consists of a set of properties that identify an employee, and it also contains a component for the employee login credentials and an address. The entity has a list of roles that grant it rights to the application.

- *Role*: a role represents a specific group an employee entity can be member of that grants access to specific functions of the application.

- *Address*: the address value object is a component that represents the address of an employee entity or a customer entity.

- *Customer*: the customer domain entity represents a unique customer in the domain. It contains a relationship with an address as well as a list of appointments that are themselves entities.

- *Appointment*: the appointment entity represents a unique appointment in the domain and consists of an employee, a customer, and a set of properties that identify the appointment.

The TimeTracker application is brand-new and doesn't have a database yet, and it is going to use DDD. For these reasons, let's build a code-first application where the domain will drive the design of the database. The Entity Framework will be our O/RM and we will use the Entity Framework Designer that comes with Visual Studio 2010 to design the TimeTracker domain model.

Mapping the Domain Model

First, open the TimeTracker solution and in the Solution Explorer pane, locate the solution root. Right-click on the Application solution folder and choose *Add New Project*. From the Project menu under Visual C#, choose *Class Library* and name the library `APRESS.TimeTracker.BusinessLayer` and press OK. You now have a new empty project in your solution that contains just a default file called `Class1.cs`, which you can delete. This is our domain model—the business logic layer.

The Entity Framework

Now create a new Entity Framework Designer file so you can design the domain model entities on the Visual Studio surface; Right-click on the BLL project and choose *Add New Item*. In the left panel, click on the Data group and select ADO.NET Entity Data Model. Then choose the name TimeTrackerModel and press OK; a new window will appear. Now you can choose either *Generate model from Database* (Database First development) or *Empty Model* (Code First development). Choose the latter as this will be a DDD application. You'll see a new file in the Solution Explorer under the `APRESS.TimeTracker.BusinessLayer` project called `TimeTrackerModel.edmx`—an entity data model file. If you double-click this file, it will be opened by Visual Studio with the Entity Framework Designer component, which is nothing more than an advanced class designer with some additional features. An additional file attached to this one is the *designer* file, which is called `[your EF file].Designer.cs` or, in this case, `TimeTrackerModel.Designer.cs`. This file contains the C# code that the EF Designer will generate every time you add or change something in the model using the design surface.

The Role Domain Entity

It is absolutely recommended that you do not manually change this code because it will always be regenerated by Visual Studio; later you'll see how to customize the code generated by EF.

To start, let's create the `Role` entity, which represents a specific security group in the TimeTracker application. To create a new entity in your domain model, drag the shape called `Entity` from the *Visual Studio Toolbox* to the EF design surface. Now you have a new class shape on the design surface that you can customize using the designer and the properties pane.

Here are the steps to follow to get the `Role` entity class ready:

1. With the `Role` shape selected, right-click with the mouse and choose `Properties`.

2. Enter *Role* for the `Name` and *Roles* for the `Entity Set Name` (*see* **Note** *below*).

3. Right-click on the shape and add a new Scalar Property and call it *Name*. With the `Name` property selected, go to the `Properties` pane and change the `Max Length` to **50**.

4. Right-click on the shape and add a new Scalar Property and call it *Description*. With the `Description` property selected, go to the `Properties` panel and change the `Max Length` to **255**.

■ **Note** When you create a new domain entity with the EF Designer, it asks you for two properties. The one called Name represents the name of the object; the one called Entity Set Name represents the name of the collection of this type of entity, stored by the O/RM. Typically, this name is the plural of the name property. When you query the database using EF, it returns a collection of type ObjectSet<your_entity>.

Now you should have the domain entity Role ready to go, like the one displayed in Figure 6-4.

Figure 6-4. The Role domain entity

You probably noticed that there's an additional property on the Role entity called Id of type integer; this property is represented by an icon with a small key on it, indicating that the property is the primary key of the domain entity. In an O/RM, and more in generally in a database, the primary key is a key consisting of one or more fields that represent the uniqueness of the row in table and the uniqueness of the domain entity in the domain model.

In this case, let's generate the unique ID using the integer value. In SQL, this is accomplished by using the int identity(1, 1) data type to add an incremental scalar integer value to every row that's added to the table. You could also do this by setting the data type of the Id property to System.Guid, for example and change the StoreGeneratedPattern to Computed or None. If you set the value to None, you'd have to provide a new, unique value every time you added a new entity to the EF ObjectContext. To avoid extra unnecessary complexity, let's leave our entities' primary keys as the integer identity.

Autogenerated Code

I noted earlier that the EF Designer is essentially a shortcut for generating C# or VB.NET code that creates classes mapped to a SQL database. In fact, after you've created the Role entity, you can navigate in the Solution Explorer pane to the TimeTrackerModel.Designer.cs file, which is just below the TimeTrackerModel.edmx file, and double-click it.

This file contains the C# generated code that represents an EF ObjectContext with the related Role entity mapped. The ObjectContext is also known as the O/RM session; it provides all the methods and functionality to query and execute CRUD operations against the database for the mapped entities. This section is in the Contexts region of the generated code while the entities' code is in the Entities region. Listing 6-4 shows TimeTracker's ObjectContext.

■ **Note** For space reasons I have removed all the comments and #region code generated by the EF Designer, so if you open your EF Designer code-behind file it may looks a little different from Listing 6-4.

Listing 6-4. *The TimeTracker ObjectContext*

```
// we are skipping the "deprecated code" here

public partial class TimeTrackerModelContainer : ObjectContext
    {
        #region Constructors

        public TimeTrackerModelContainer() : base("name=TimeTrackerModelContainer", ↵
    "TimeTrackerModelContainer")
        {
            this.ContextOptions.LazyLoadingEnabled = true;
            OnContextCreated();
        }

        public TimeTrackerModelContainer(string connectionString) : base(connectionString, ↵
    "TimeTrackerModelContainer")
        {
            this.ContextOptions.LazyLoadingEnabled = true;
            OnContextCreated();
        }

        public TimeTrackerModelContainer(EntityConnection connection) : base(connection, ↵
    "TimeTrackerModelContainer")
        {
            this.ContextOptions.LazyLoadingEnabled = true;
            OnContextCreated();
        }

        #endregion

        partial void OnContextCreated();

        public ObjectSet<Role> Roles
        {
            get
            {
```

```
            if ((_Roles == null))
            {
                _Roles = base.CreateObjectSet<Role>("Roles");
            }
            return _Roles;
        }
    }
    private ObjectSet<Role> _Roles;
}
```

The `TimeTrackerModelContainer` is a class than inherits from the `ObjectContext` class, which provides methods and behaviors for interacting with the database and the entities generated by the EF Designer. So far, you have just one entity generated, so it exposes one property—the `ObjectSet` property of the `Role` object set in the designer when you assigned a name to the `EntitySet` property; this special collection represents a typed entity set that is used to perform create, read, update, and delete operations.

The remaining code provides different constructors so you can pass a custom connection string or provide an existing EF connection object.

Listing 6-5 shows part of the generated code for the `Role` entity. (For reasons of space, we won't show all of the generated code.)

Listing 6-5. *The Role Entity*

```
/// <summary>
/// No Metadata Documentation available.
/// </summary>
[EdmEntityTypeAttribute(NamespaceName="TimeTrackerModel", Name-"Role")]
[Serializable()]
[DataContractAttribute(IsReference=true)]
public partial class Role : EntityObject
{
    #region Factory Method

    /// <summary>
    /// Create a new Role object.
    /// </summary>
    /// <param name="id">Initial value of the Id property.</param>
    /// <param name="name">Initial value of the Name property.</param>
    /// <param name="description">Initial value of the Description property.</param>
    public static Role CreateRole(global::System.Int32 id, global::System.String name,↵
global::System.String description)
    {
        Role role = new Role();
        role.Id = id;
        role.Name = name;
        role.Description = description;
        return role;
    }
```

```
#endregion
#region Primitive Properties

/// <summary>
/// No Metadata Documentation available.
/// </summary>
[EdmScalarPropertyAttribute(EntityKeyProperty=true, IsNullable=false)]
[DataMemberAttribute()]
public global::System.Int32 Id
{
    get
    {
        return _Id;
    }
    set
    {
        if (_Id != value)
        {
            OnIdChanging(value);
            ReportPropertyChanging("Id");
            _Id = StructuralObject.SetValidValue(value);
            ReportPropertyChanged("Id");
            OnIdChanged();
        }
    }
}
private global::System.Int32 _Id;
partial void OnIdChanging(global::System.Int32 value);
partial void OnIdChanged();

/// <summary>
/// No Metadata Documentation available.
/// </summary>
[EdmScalarPropertyAttribute(EntityKeyProperty=false, IsNullable=false)]
[DataMemberAttribute()]
public global::System.String Name
{
    get
    {
        return _Name;
    }
    set
    {
        OnNameChanging(value);
        ReportPropertyChanging("Name");
        _Name = StructuralObject.SetValidValue(value, false);
        ReportPropertyChanged("Name");
        OnNameChanged();
    }
}
```

```
    private global::System.String _Name;
    partial void OnNameChanging(global::System.String value);
    partial void OnNameChanged();

    #endregion

}
```

An entity generated for the EF has to inherit from the `EntityObject` class, which informs the EF that this class is an entity generated using the EF tool. Also, with the `partial` keyword added to the class, you can split the declaration of a class or interface in two or more files, as the MSDN definition at `msdn.microsoft.com/en-us/library/wa80x488.aspx` says: "*It is possible to split the definition of a class or a struct, an interface or a method over two or more source files. Each source file contains a section of the type or method definition, and all parts are combined when the application is compiled.*" In this way you can customize your domain entity with methods and other properties not related to the O/RM, so you won't have to worry that they would be blown away by the EF Designer tool every time the code is regenerated.

Let's have a look now at one of the properties available to the `Role` entity—the ID property, which represents the unique identity of the entity in the database. It's an `Int32` property marked with two special attributes:

- `[EdmScalarPropertyAttribute(EntityKeyProperty=true, IsNullable=false)]`, where `EntityKeyProperty` indicates that this property acts as the primary key for the entity and `IsNullable` indicates that null is not an acceptable value.

- `[DataMemberAttribute()]` is a serializable attribute used by EF so that, by default, an EF domain entity can be serialized as an XML structure by a WCF web service.

■ **Note** The analysis of the code generated by the EF Framework ends here as we will accomplish all tasks using only the EF Designer tool. Feel free to open the code-behind file every time you add a new entity to the domain so you can better understand how the EF works behind the scene. Remember, an entire domain of medium complexity can be mapped using only the EF Designer, so you don't have to know how it works behind the scene. In my opinion, however, it is a good practice to at least become familiar with the code.

The Employee Domain Entity

Now let's add an `Employee` domain entity, which will have a strict relationship with the `Role` entity. Drag a new entity shape to the design surface and set the `Entity Set Name` to *Employees* and the `Name` to *Employee*. Add the following properties to the `Employee` entity using the right-click menu command *Add* ➤ *Scalar Property* and the properties panel as with the `Role` entity. Add the properties as shown in Table 6-1.

Table 6-1. *Employee Properties*

Property name	Type	Nullable	Max Length
FirstName	String	False	50
LastName	String	False	50
Title	String	True	10
DateOfBirth	DateTime	False	--
Username	String	False	10
Password	String	False	10

Now you should have an additional shape in the EF Designer called `Employee` with all the properties listed in Table 6-1.

The next step is to make some of these properties into what EF calls a *complex type* and DDD calls a *value object*. A complex type is an object that is consists of two or more properties (like FirstName and LastName) that are represented as a unique property in the domain entity. The purpose of using a complex type is to group some information together into a single component and to recycle this component over other domain entities in the same domain model.

To create a new complex type, hold down the Ctrl key and select the `FirstName` and `LastName` properties of the `Employee` entity, then right-click and choose *Refactor into new Complex type*. Now the entity has a new single property called `ComplexProperty` Instead of the two original properties. With the complex property selected, start typing a new name, like `FullName` and the property name will be changed by the EF. You also have to manually change the `TypeName` value as it will not be updated by the EF Designer.

Now you can edit the property using the following syntax:

```
// how the complex property is exposed in the entity
Employee employee = new Employee();
employee.FullName.FirstName = "John";
employee.FullName.LastName = "Smith";
```

This complex type is available through the Model Browser panel, which Visual Studio opens automatically when you are working with the EF Designer. Here you can edit not only the shapes available on the EF Designer surface but all the objects related to the `.edmx` file. For example, suppose you've created a domain entity and then accidentally deleted it from the Designer. The entity may still be available through the Model Browser panel.

The First Relationship, Role and Employee

A domain model is composed not only of a set of domain entities and value objects but also by behaviors and relationships. For example, to enable an `Employee` entity to be member of one or more `Role` entities, you need to create a many-to-many relationship between the `Role` and the `Employee` entities. The reason to create the relationship as many-to-many is because an employee can be in many roles and a role will have several people in it.

With the EF, you can create different types of *associations* (relationships), depending on how you want to connect two entities together. You can use the `association` object available in the EF Designer, and depending on how you configure it, it will create a different relationship:

- *One-to-one:* this is the simplest relationship and consists of one and only one entity on either side of the relationship.

- *Many-to-Many:* there may be several entities on both sides of the association, and both sides are mapped to a link table that keeps track of the references.

- *One-to-Many:* this is the classic parent/child relationship where the child table has a reference to the parent table primary key.

- *Self-reference:* this is a relationship where an entity has a reference to itself.

This list covers the relationships that can be created on a database using the primary key and foreign key objects, so by using the `association` object you should be able to handle all the possible relationships in your domain.

Now let's create the association between the `Role` and the `Employee` entities.

1. Going back to the EF Designer, locate the `association` shape in the toolbox and select it; now your mouse cursor has the shape of a S.

2. Starting from the `Role` shape, hold down your left mouse button and drag a line from the `Role` entity to the `Employee` entity, this will create a one-to-many relationship that is represented by a straight line that will keep these two entities together.

3. Select the association line, right-click on it and choose `Properties`. Edit the `Properties` panel as shown in Table 6-2.

Table 6-2. Role-Employee Association

Property	Value
AssociationSetName	RoleEmployee
End1 Multiplicity	* (Collection or Role)
End1 Role Name	Roles
End1 Navigation	Employees
End2 Multiplicity	* (Collection of Employee)
End2 Role Name	Employees
End2 Navigation	Roles
Name	RoleEmployee

The result should look like Figure 6-5, which now shows the relationship as many-to-many rather than the one-to-many association created by default by the EF Designer. As you can see, the relationship is now represented using the UML notation *-*.

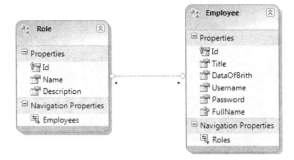

Figure 6-5. *The many-to-many relationship between the Role and Employee entities*

The Address Entity

When you write a new domain model, it may be simple or it may be complex, and you may often debate the nature of some objects, like Address—whether they should be considered an entity, a value object, or something else. In my experience, if you have an Employee, a Customer, or a Person entity, these will always require more than one Address and more than one Contact, and you'll probably need to store the information in a separate table. For this reason, in the TimeTracker application the Address and the Contact entities are going to be two separate and distinct entities and not a simple value object.

Drag a new shape to the EF Designer surface, name it Address, and add the properties shown in Table 6-3 to the new entity.

Table 6-3. *Address Properties*

Property name	Type	Nullable	Max Length
AddressLine1	String	False	150
AddressLine2	String	True	150
Town	String	True	50
City	String	False	20
State	String	False	20
Country	String	False	50
ZipCode	String	False	10

With the `Address` entity on the design surface, locate the association shape on the toolbox and drag a new relationship from the `Employee` shape to the `Address` shape; this will create a new association that has to be, again, of type many-to-many. Table 6-4 show how to specify the relationship.

Table 6-4. *Role-Employee Association*

Property	Value
AssociationSetName	EmployeeAddress
End1 Multiplicity	* (Collection or Employee)
End1 Role Name	Addresses
End1 Navigation	Employees
End2 Multiplicity	* (Collection of Addresses)
End2 Role Name	Employees
End2 Navigation	Addresses
Name	EmployeeAddress

At this point the domain should consist of three shapes, the `Role`, the `Employee`, and the `Address` entities. If you place the `Employee` shape in the middle of the design surface, your result should look like the one shown in Figure 6-6.

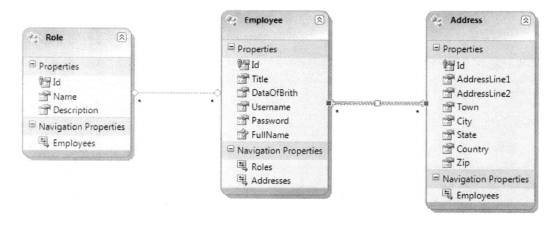

Figure 6-6. *Employee entity with two relationships, roles and addresses*

The Contact Entity

Now let's create the `Contact` entity. This object is very simple; it holds only two properties, the contact number and the contact type, as shown in Table 6-5.

Table 6-5. Contact Properties

Property name	Type	Nullable	Max Length
Number	String	False	20
ContactType	String	False	10

The `ContactType` property is a string but you have to provide an `enum` in order to add some constraint to the user interface; unfortunately right now, EF CTP 5 doesn't yet directly support the `enum` type. It is not a good idea to pollute the domain entities with strange code tricks, so let's leave the property data type as `String` and force the data entry at the `ObjectContext` level.

The `Contact` entity has a relationship of many-to-many with the `Employee` entity, and Table 6-6 shows how this relationship should be handled.

Table 6-6. Employee-Contact Association

Property	Value
AssociationSetName	EmployeeContact
End1 Multiplicity	* (Collection or Employee)
End1 Role Name	Contacts
End1 Navigation	Employees
End2 Multiplicity	* (Collection of Contact)
End2 Role Name	Employee
End2 Navigation	Contacts
Name	EmployeeContact

The `Employee` subdomain is now ready so let's try to generate the database schema that will be used by the application as the mapped schema.

Generating the Database Schema

Before starting to generate the database schema, you need to create a new database using the SQL Server 2008 R2 Express Edition you previously installed on your development machine. If you haven't yet installed SQL Server, now is the time to do so as we'll be using it as a reference datastore for the EF generated model.

To generate a new database, you don't necessarily need to open SQL Server Management Studio (SSMS), but you can do that from the Visual Studio IDE. Locate the Server Explorer; if you don't have it open, just press the shortcut keys Ctrl+W,L and execute the following steps:

1. Locate the Database connection root node, right-click on it, and choose *Create new SQL Server database.*

2. The SQL Connection window pops up. This is where you insert the server name (the default is `.\SQLEXPRESS`) and choose the authentication scheme (the default is Windows Authentication). Then you can click the Test Connection button to be sure that the connection is working.

3. Insert **TimeTrackerDatabase** as the name of the database and press OK; Visual Studio will create a new SQL Server database and store the connection in the Server Explorer tree.

Now right-click on the EF design surface (not on a shape) and select the command *Generate Database from Model.* A Visual Studio window will appear, prompting you to choose a connection string. You should be able to locate the connection you just created in the combo box at the top; choose and tick both options, the option group and the check box. The next window will just ask for a name for the SQL script file that EF generated. Press OK, confirm everything, and at the end of the wizard Visual Studio will open a `.sql` file that contains the T-SQL code necessary to generate the database.

Press Ctrl+Shift+E, or right-click and choose Execute script, and the database schema will be populated in the SQL Server database. You can also add the toolbar at the top of Visual Studio by right-clicking an existing toolbar and choosing the *Transact-SQL Editor toolbar.*

Now refresh the database connection in the Server Explorer pane and look at the Tables folder of the TimeTrackerDatabase connection, and you'll find tables created by the EF-generated T-SQL script. You could also open SSMS and browse the database objects. You'll find some tables you may not have expected; these are the tables used to establish the many-to-many relationships.

The Customer Entity

As you'd expect, the `Customer` entity is the domain entity that represents a `Customer`. It contains all the properties required for a customer, and it is very much like the `Employee` entity—it has a collection of type many-to-many of `Address`es and a collection of type many-to-many of `Contact`s. Create the `Customer` entity using the same process as for the other entities; drag a new entity shape to the design surface of EF and provide the properties listed in Table 6-7.

Table 6-7. *Customer Properties*

Property name	Type	Nullable	Max Length
Title	String	False	10
Company	String	False	100
FullName	ComplexType (FullName)	False	--

Now you need to create associations from the `Employee` shape to the `Address` and `Contact` shapes. To do this, just follow the same procedure as you did earlier, using the properties listed in Tables 6-4 and 6-6 but using the end point names of `Customer` and `Customers` instead of `Employee` and `Employees`.

The Appointment Entity

The last entity to add is `Appointment`, which has a strict relationship between an `Employee` and a `Customer`. The `Appointment` needs to have information like:

- Time of the appointment

- Duration of the appointment

- Place of the appointment

- Activity to be executed during the appointment

- Customer and employee involved in the appointment

Let's drag the last shape of our domain model to the EF design surface and call it `Appointment`. Table 6-8 shows the properties to add to the `Appointment` entity.

Table 6-8. *Appointment Properties*

Property name	Type	Nullable	Max Length
Time	DateTime	False	--
Duration	Int32	False	--
Activity	String	False	MAX
Place	String	False	100

Now you need to create two different relationships that will go from the `Employee` entity to the `Appointment` entity and from the `Customer` entity to the `Appointment` entity. The association this time will be a one-to-many because both `Employee` and `Customer` can have more than one appointment associated with it but an `Appointment` will have only one `Customer` and one `Employee`. To accomplish this, drag the relationship from the `Employee` to the `Appointment` and from the `Customer` to the `Appointment`. The result of this part of the domain model is shown in Figure 6-7.

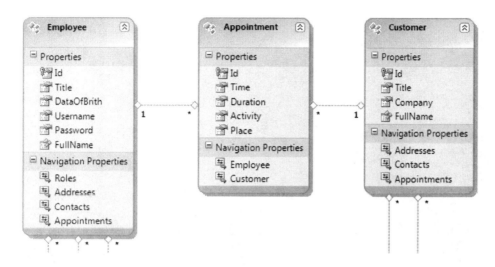

Figure 6-7. *Appointment entity relationships*

Now you can again generate the database schema to obtain the final database schema that will be accessed and used by the Entity Framework and the corresponding Data Access Layer.

The TimeTracker Data Layer

So far we've created, with the aid of the Entity Framework, a simple domain model and the corresponding SQL Server database schema. Now, in order to complete the typical 3-tier application architecture, we need to create an additional abstraction layer that will hide the methods and properties exposed by the Entity Framework to the other layers and that will provide a set of customized query and CRUD methods. To do this, create a new class library project with the name of `APRESS.TimeTracker.DataLayer` if you didn't create it already in the introductory steps.

This new layer will hold the implementation of a simple Unit of Work and four different repository classes: `RoleRepository`, `EmployeeRepository`, `CustomerRepository`, and `AppointmentRepository`. You don't have to create a repository specifically for the `Address` and the `Contact` entities as they are strictly related and managed by the `Customer` and the `Employee` entities.

The Unit of Work

The first object to add to the data layer is the `IUnitOfWork` interface, and the code is shown in Listing 6-6.

Listing 6-6. IUnitOfWork

```
using System;
using System.Data.Objects;

namespace APRESS.TimeTracker.DataLayer
{
    public interface IUnitOfWork : IDisposable
    {
        ObjectContext Session { get; }
        void MarkDirty<T>(T entity);
        void MarkNew<T>(T entity);
        void MarkDeleted<T>(T entity);
        void BeginTransaction();
        void CommitTransaction();
        void RollbackTransaction();
    }
}
```

You saw this object in the "The Unit of Work" section. The only addition to the code here is the IDisposable interface. This interface implements a Dispose method that tells the .NET Framework how to dispose of the resources used by the implementer (Unit of Work), and it also means you can work with the using convention, as we'll see shortly.

Note that the contract exposes a read-only property of type ObjectContext that is exposed by the unit of work; this is the current instance of the EF context.

The next class is a concrete implementation of the IUnitOfWork that's able to work with the Entity Framework CTP 5 and, more precisely, with the TimeTracker ObjectContext component. Add a new class file and name it UnitOfWork. This class will contain the code that I have split into multiple sections to make it easier to grasp. To create the UnitOfWork correctly, you need to add a reference between the data tier and the business tier projects; more precisely, you need to add a reference in the data layer that points out to the business layer project.

First of all, you need to provide the constructors of the UnitOfWork, as shown in Listing 6-7.

Listing 6-7. Constructors of the Unit of Work Class

```
using System;
using System.Data;
using System.Data.EntityClient;
using System.Data.Objects;
using APRESS.TimeTracker.BusinessLayer;

namespace APRESS.TimeTracker.DataLayer
{
    public sealed class UnitOfWork : IUnitOfWork, IDisposable
    {
        private ObjectContext session;
```

```
    public ObjectContext Session
    {
        get { return session; }
    }

    public UnitOfWork()
    {
        session = new TimeTrackerModelContainer();
    }

    public UnitOfWork(EntityConnection connection)
    {
        session = new TimeTrackerModelContainer(connection);
    }

    public UnitOfWork(string connectionString)
    {
        session = new TimeTrackerModelContainer(connectionString);
    }
    }
}
```

As you can see at the beginning of the class, I declared a private field of type `ObjectContext` that I initialize in every constructor with the `TimeTrackerModelContainer` object, which is nothing more the `ObjectContext` created by the EF Designer for our domain model. I left the data type as `ObjectContext` so we can use the `Unit of Work` in a more generic way.

The next step is to make the object *disposable* by implementing the `IDisposable` interface, as shown in Listing 6-8.

Listing 6-8. *The IDisposable Interface*

```
#region Implementation of IDisposable

public void Dispose()
{
    if (session != null)
    {
        if (session.Connection.State != ConnectionState.Closed)
        {
            session.Connection.Close();
        }
        session.Dispose();
    }
    GC.SuppressFinalize(true);
}
```

`#endregion`

The dispose interface is used to free the resources used by a specific component or object. In this case, we are sure that the database resources used by the unit of work, as well as by the EF instance, are properly disposed of so we don't keep references alive for no reason. The garbage collector provided by the .NET Framework is able to recycle and free the resources if they are not in use anymore. Unfortunately, this process is not predictable. Using the Dispose method forces the object to free the resources and to be disposed when you want. The GC.SuppressFinalize call tells the Garbage Collector not to dispose the object because it has been already disposed.

Set Up the First Test Fixture

Now that you've created a component in the data layer, you need to start testing the code to be sure it works correctly. To follow the Test Driven Development approach, you write test cases that satisfy the design requirements of your components, than test the code against the components.

In your solution structure you should have a project of type Test called APRESS.Test; if you don't have it, add a new project of type Test to the APRESS.TimeTracker solution and name it e. When you are done, follow these steps to prepare the test project:

1. Remove the default UnitTest1.cs class created by Visual Studio.

2. Add a new reference that points to the project APRESS.TimeTracker.DataLayer.

3. Add a new reference that point to the project APRESS.TimeTracker.BusinessLayer.

4. Add a reference to the following assemblies:

    • System.Data

    • System.Data.Entity

5. Add a new file of type Configuration file and name it app.config. Now open the app.config file and change its content using the code in Listing 6-9.

Listing 6-9. The app.config *File in the Test Project*

```
<?xml version="1.0" encoding="utf-8"?>
<configuration>
  <connectionStrings>
    <add name="TimeTrackerModelContainer"
        connectionString="metadata=res://*/TimeTrackerModel.csdl|
        res://*/TimeTrackerModel.ssdl|
        res://*/TimeTrackerModel.msl;
        provider=System.Data.SqlClient;
        provider connection string=&quot;Data Source=.\SQLEXPRESS;
        Initial Catalog=TimeTrackerDatabase;
        Integrated Security=True;
        MultipleActiveResultSets=True&quot;"
        providerName="System.Data.EntityClient" />
  </connectionStrings>
</configuration>
```

The contents of this file represents the connection string used by the EF; this app.config file is already available in the BLL project; it was created by the connection wizard when you created the domain model database schema.

Now that the test project is set up, you can start to create the first unit test; the following steps tell how to create the test fixture for the unit of work:

1. Create a new folder in the test project and name it *Fixtures*.

2. Right-click and choose the command *New Test*.

3. Name the test UnitOfWorkFixture.

4. Make the type Basic Unit Test.

Now you have a new class marked with the attribute [TestClass] that represents a set of unit tests. The concept here is that all the test methods exposed in a test class (unit test) are considered a single unit and they should be able to run independently from other components. If the test needs additional dependencies, these dependencies should be resolved using a mockup, a fake concrete dependency.

The first thing to test is the constructor of the unit of work; you want to be sure you can create a new unit of work and that it is not null (see Listing 6-10).

Listing 6-10. *Unit Test for Creating a New Unit of Work*

```
using System;
using APRESS.TimeTracker.DataLayer;
using Microsoft.VisualStudio.TestTools.UnitTesting;

namespace APRESS.Test.Fixtures
{
    [TestClass]
    public class UnitOfWorkFixture
    {
        [TestMethod]
        public void CanCreateAUnitOfWork()
        {
            try
            {
                using (IUnitOfWork uow = new UnitOfWork())
                {
                    Assert.IsNotNull(uow);
                    Assert.IsNotNull(uow.Session);
                    Assert.IsNotNull(uow.Session.Connection);
                }
            }
            catch (Exception exception)
            {
                Assert.Fail(exception.ToString());
            }
        }
    }
}
```

To run the test, you can:

- Right-click on the test file and select Run Tests.
- Open the test panel and run the specific test.

The test should pass and assert that the unit of work has been created successfully, that the `ObjectContext` property is not null, and that it has a connection string.

■ **Note** The static class `Assert` used in Listing 6-10 is provided by the `MSTest` assembly referenced in the Test project. It provides static methods to verify (assert) that the test conditions are satisfied by the code. In the catch section of a test you use the `Assert.Fail` method to force the failure of the test.

Transaction Management

The second part of the unit of work consists of transaction management. A unit of work should be able, at any time, to roll back all the changes included in a transaction or to commit all of them in one shot. With the EF, transaction management is taken care of by the framework, and it happens when you call the `SaveChanges()` method of the `ObjectContext` (session). Unfortunately, what the EF does is to open a transaction, execute all the SQL commands, and commit the transaction in the `SaveChanges` method. We need higher-level management of the changes and the only way to accomplish this is to rebuild the `ObjectContext` every time you want to discard all the changes. For example, if you add a new `Role` entity in the `ObjectContext` and you want to roll back the change, you have to re-create the `ObjectContext` so that the `Role` entity will be detached from the EF session.

The first step is to add is a new read-only property in the `IUnitOfWork` interface that will let you know if it is already in a transaction or not, like this:

```
public interface IUnitOfWork : IDisposable
{
    // ... code omitted
    bool IsInTransaction { get; }
}
```

Now let's start to write the code to implement the transaction management, as shown in Listing 6-11.

Listing 6-11. Unit of Work *Transaction Management*

```
private bool isInTransaction = false;

public bool IsInTransaction
{
    get { return isInTransaction; }
}
```

```
public void StartTransaction()
{
    session = new TimeTrackerModelContainer();
    isInTransaction = true;
}

public void RollbackTransaction()
{
    session = new TimeTrackerModelContainer();
    isInTransaction = false;
}

public void CommitTransaction()
{
    try
    {
        if (isInTransaction == false)
        {
            throw new EntityException("The Unit of Work ");
        }

        session.SaveChanges(SaveOptions.AcceptAllChangesAfterSave);
        isInTransaction = false;
    }
    catch (Exception exception)
    {
        session = new TimeTrackerModelContainer();
        isInTransaction = false;
        throw new EntityException(
            "An error occurred during the Commit of the transaction.",
            exception);
    }
}
```

Every time you start a new transaction, you need to create a new ObjectContext so that any existing session will be dropped by the code, then you mark the Unit of Work as in transaction. In the Commit, you verify that you're in a transaction and if not, you throw an exception and then re-create the object context. If you are in a transaction, you tell EF to accept all the changes and save them into the database, and only if the operation is successful you mark the transaction to false. The rollback simply re-creates a new ObjectContext so that all the changes in the session are discarded.

Let's test the code for the transaction management, as shown in Listing 6-12.

Listing 6-12. *Unit of Work Transaction Test*

```
[TestMethod]
public void CanStartTransaction()
{
    try
    {
        using (IUnitOfWork uow = new UnitOfWork())
        {
```

```
                Assert.IsFalse(uow.IsInTransaction);
                uow.StartTransaction();
                Assert.IsTrue(uow.IsInTransaction);
            }
        }
        catch (Exception exception)
        {
            Assert.Fail(exception.ToString());
        }
    }

    [TestMethod]
    public void CanRollbackTransaction()
    {
        try
        {
            using (IUnitOfWork uow = new UnitOfWork())
            {
                Assert.IsFalse(uow.IsInTransaction);
                uow.StartTransaction();
                Assert.IsTrue(uow.IsInTransaction);
                uow.RollbackTransaction();
                Assert.IsFalse(uow.IsInTransaction);
            }
        }
        catch (Exception exception)
        {
            Assert.Fail(exception.ToString());
        }
    }

    [TestMethod]
    public void CanCommitTransaction()
    {
        try
        {
            using (IUnitOfWork uow = new UnitOfWork())
            {
                uow.StartTransaction();
                Assert.IsTrue(uow.IsInTransaction);
                uow.CommitTransaction();
                Assert.IsFalse(uow.IsInTransaction);
            }
        }
        catch (Exception exception)
        {
            Assert.Fail(exception.ToString());
        }
    }
```

What this does is verify that the transaction property `IsInTransaction` is handled properly, which means that the unit of work is managing the transaction in the correct way. Now let's verify that we can commit changes to the database.

Add, Update, and Remove Objects

The main purpose of the unit of work is to mark one or more entities as new, modified, or deleted; this doesn't mean that the unit of work has to process them by adding, modifying, or deleting the entities from the database. It has just the role of marking the status of the entities. In fact, the EF proxy classes (domain entities created with the EF Designer) are marked using the property `EntityState`, which is an enumeration type with the following values:

- *Added*: the entity is new; it produces an `INSERT` statement in SQL.

- *Deleted*: the entity will be removed, it produces a `DELETE` statement in SQL.

- *Detached*: the entity is not attached to a session (`ObjectContext`); there's no SQL.

- *Modified*: the entity has been modified; it produces an `UPDATE` statement in SQL.

- *Unchanged*: there are no changes.

The transaction suddenly has the role of processing these entities when you commit the changes (which happens in EF when you call `ObjectContext.SaveChanges`). Based on the status of the entity, the EF will execute the specific SQL statement.

The unit of work pattern says that the unit of work has to provide three methods: mark new, mark dirty, and mark deleted.

Add a New Object

Let's start with the mark new method exposed in Listing 6-13.

Listing 6-13. *The* `MarkNew` *Method*

```
public void MarkNew<T>(T entity) where T : class
{
    session.AddObject(typeof(T).Name + "s", entity);
}
```

The code is pretty simple; by default the EF creates for each domain entity an `ObjectSet<T>` property that exposes the in-memory collection of that particular entity, by using the naming convention of `[entity.Name] + s`. This would be translated in `Roles` as an entity of type `Role`. The `ObjectContext` component exposes a generic method `AddObject` that requires the name of the `ObjectSet` collection and the current entity; what it does is add the entity to the collection and mark it with the status `Added`; the first time you call the `SaveChanges` method, the entity will be persisted in the database.

■ **Note** This application declares the ObjectSet<T> names using a final "s" to identify the plural name. In production, you'd probably use a better approach to be sure things will work even if the ObejctSet<T> name doesn't conform to this convention. For example, you might use something like this:

```
If (typeof(T) is EntityObject)
{
    string setName = ((EntityObject)entity).EntityKey.EntitySetName;
    session.AddObject(setName, entity);
}
```

Listing 6-14 shows the corresponding test for this method.

Listing 6-14. TDD for the Unit of Work MarkNew Method

```
[TestMethod]
public void CanAddNewEntity()
{
    try
    {
        using (IUnitOfWork uow = new UnitOfWork())
        {
            uow.StartTransaction();
            int currentCount = uow.Session.CreateObjectSet<Role>().Count();
            // create an entity and verify is still new (id = 0)
            var role = new Role {
                Name = "Administrators",
                Description = "Role for the Administrators."
            };
            Assert.IsTrue(role.EntityState == EntityState.Detached);
            Assert.IsTrue(role.Id == 0);
            // attach the entity as new
            uow.MarkNew(role);
            Assert.IsTrue(role.EntityState == EntityState.Added);
            // save the changes and verified the entity is now saved (id > 0)
            uow.CommitTransaction();
            int expectedCount = uow.Session.CreateObjectSet<Role>().Count();
            Assert.IsTrue(role.EntityState == EntityState.Unchanged);
            Assert.IsTrue(role.Id > 0);
            Assert.AreNotEqual(currentCount, expectedCount);
        }
    }
```

```
    catch (Exception exception)
    {
        Assert.Fail(exception.ToString());
    }
}
```

In the test of the add method, you want to be sure that the entity is marked as new, and after committing the transaction you want to verify that the number of entities of type `Role` is equal of the previous count plus one, as you added a new entity in the database.

The method `CreateObjectSet<T>` is used at runtime to retrieve the collection of type T from the database; you'll see this method in depth in the Repository pattern section of this chapter.

Delete an Existing Object

The second method provided by the unit of work pattern is `MarkDeleted`, which informs the unit of work that a specific object has to be deleted when the next transaction is committed. I previously said that the concept of TDD is that a single test should be totally independent of the rest of the tests, so in order to test the delete method, in the test steps you first need to add a new entity and then assert that the entity has been added to the database. Then you can test that the entity can be deleted by the unit of work, as shown in Listing 6-15.

Listing 6-15. The MarkDeleted Method Test

```
[TestMethod]
public void CanDeleteAnExistingObject()
{
    try
    {
        using (IUnitOfWork uow = new UnitOfWork())
        {
            // add new object
            uow.StartTransaction();
            var role = new Role {
                Name = "Administrators",
                Description = "Role for the Administrators." };
            uow.MarkNew(role);
            uow.CommitTransaction();
            // retreive object
            var expectedRole = uow.Session
                .CreateObjectSet<Role>()
                .Where(r => r.Id == role.Id)
                .FirstOrDefault();
            Assert.IsNotNull(expectedRole);
            // delete the object
            uow.StartTransaction();
            uow.MarkDeleted(expectedRole);
            Assert.IsTrue(expectedRole.EntityState == EntityState.Deleted);
            uow.CommitTransaction();
            //  verify the object doesn't exist
            var finalExpectedRole = uow.Session
```

```
            .CreateObjectSet<Role>()
            .Where(r => r.Id == role.Id)
            .FirstOrDefault();
          Assert.IsNull(finalExpectedRole);
      }
    }
    catch (Exception exception)
    {
        Assert.Fail(exception.ToString());
    }
}
```

The code first creates a new `Role` entity and adds it to the database, then tries to retrieve it using the LINQ syntax by building a `WHERE` SQL statement. (You will see exactly how this works in the Repository section). Finally, after verifying that the entity has been retrieved from the database, the code deletes it and then tries to retrieve it again. Of course, the second time you should get back a null object as the entity has been now deleted from the database.

Note the two new methods in the code:

- *CreateObjectSet<T>*: creates a new `ObjectSet<TEntity>` instance that is used to query, add, modify, and delete objects of the specified type and with the specified entity set name.

- *LINQ to Entities:* provides Language-Integrated Query (LINQ) support that enables developers to write queries against the Entity Framework conceptual model using Visual Basic or Visual C#.

Modify an Existing Object

When you want to modify an existing object using the EF, you must be sure that the object is considered as such by the EF. For example, every time you start a new transaction, the unit of work creates a new `ObjectContext`. When that happens, an existing object may be detached from the EF session and not be considered attached anymore. The EF allows you to verify that the object is already attached. If it is not, you have to attach it and change its state to modified so that the next time you call `SaveChanges`) the object will be updated in the database. Of course, if you stay in the same unit of work while retrieving and updating an object, you don't need to do that.

Another consideration is that every time you change an object property, by default an Entity Framework object raises an `OnPropertyChanged` event that changes the state of the entity to modified.

Listing 6-16 shows the `MarkDirty` method.

Listing 6-16. *The Unit of Work Mark as Dirty*

```
public void MarkDirty<T>(T entity) where T : class
{
    var modifiedEntity = entity as EntityObject;
    if (modifiedEntity == null)
    {
        throw new EntityException("The current entity is not of type EntityObject.");
    }
```

```
    if (!session.IsAttachedTo(entity))
    {
        session.AttachTo(typeof(T).Name + "s", entity);
    }
    if (modifiedEntity.EntityState != EntityState.Modified)
    {
        session.ObjectStateManager.ChangeObjectState(entity, EntityState.Modified);
    }
}
```

Every entity generated by the EF Designer inherits from the class `EntityObject`, so the first step is to be sure in this case that the object passed to the `MarkDirty` method is of type `EntityObject` so that you can cast it back and play with the property `EntityState`. The code first verifies that the object is not null. If it is null, an exception is thrown. Next it verifies that the object is not already attached. If it is not attached, the code attaches it and then changes its state to modified using the helper class `ObjectStateManager` provided by the EF and exposed by the `ObjectContext` (session).

Unfortunately, the EF doesn't provide a method for discovering if an entity has been detached or not from a specific session, so you'll need to *extend* the framework by creating an *extension method*.

■ **Note** Extension methods enable you to "add" methods to existing types without creating a new derived type, recompiling, or otherwise modifying the original type. Extension methods are a special kind of static method, but they are called as if they were instance methods on the extended type. For client code written in C# and Visual Basic, there is no apparent difference between calling an extension method and the methods that are actually defined in a type.

In order to add an extension method, you need a *static* class, so on the DAL project add a new static class and call it `EntityFrameworkExtensions`. In this class you will add the first extension method using the signature shown in Listing 6-17.

Listing 6-17. Entity Framework Extension Method

```
public static class EntityFrameworkExtensions
{
    public static bool IsAttachedTo(this ObjectContext context, object entity)
    {
        ObjectStateEntry entry;
        bool isAttached = false;
        if (context.ObjectStateManager.TryGetObjectStateEntry
                (context.CreateEntityKey(entity.GetType().Name + "s", entity), out entry))
        {
            isAttached = entry.State == EntityState.Detached;
        }
```

```
        else
        {
            isAttached = true;
        }
        return isAttached;
    }
}
```

The signature this in the method tells the compiler that you are extending an object of type
ObjectContext with a method called IsAttachedTo. What the code is doing is calling the method
CreateEntityKey of the ObjectContext to indicate whether the entity is a new entity or an existing one. It
does this by reading the ID property of the entity, whichis equal to 0 only if the object is brand new.

In this case, there will be two tests. One will verify that it can execute an update and the second one
will verify that it can update a detached entity from another unit of work.

The first test, shown in Listing 6-18, verifies that in the same session the object is successfully
updated:

Listing 6-18. A Test That Verifies That an Object Has Been Updated

```
[TestMethod]
public void CanModifyExistingObject()
{
    try
    {
        using (IUnitOfWork uow = new UnitOfWork())
        {
            // add new object
            uow.StartTransaction();
            var role = new Role
                        {
                            Name = "Administrators",
                            Description = "Role for the Administrators."
                        };
            uow.MarkNew(role);
            uow.CommitTransaction();
            // retrieve it
            var expectedRole = uow.Session
                .CreateObjectSet<Role>()
                .Where(r => r.Id == role.Id)
                .FirstOrDefault();
            Assert.IsNotNull(expectedRole);
            // change it
            expectedRole.Name = "PowerUsers";
            uow.StartTransaction();
            uow.MarkDirty(expectedRole);
            Assert.IsTrue(expectedRole.EntityState == EntityState.Modified);
            uow.CommitTransaction();
            // retrieve it again
```

```
            var changedRole = uow.Session
                .CreateObjectSet<Role>()
                .Where(r => r.Id == role.Id)
                .FirstOrDefault();
            Assert.IsNotNull(expectedRole);
            Assert.AreEqual(changedRole.Name, "PowerUsers");
        }
    }
    catch (Exception exception)
    {
        Assert.Fail(exception.ToString());
    }
}
```

The code inserts a new `Role` entity in the database, then retrieves the entity using the `Id` property, which should now not equal 0, thus verifying that the entity exists. Next the code modifies the entity by changing the `Name` property and then verifies that the entity has been successfully updated by executing another query against the EF session. If the property has been changed, the `Name` property should now be equal to `PowerUsers`.

The second test executes the same steps using two different unit of work; in this way you can be sure that the entity is detached when you try to save it. Listing 6-19 shows code that updates a detached entity.

Listing 6-19. *Updating a Detached Entity*

```
[TestMethod]
public void CanModifyADetachedObject()
{
    try
    {
        Role originalRole = null;
        Role updatesRole = null;
        using (IUnitOfWork uow = new UnitOfWork())
        {
            // add new object
            uow.StartTransaction();
            originalRole = new Role
                        {
                            Name = "Administrators",
                            Description = "Role for the Administrators."
                        };
            uow.MarkNew(originalRole);
            uow.CommitTransaction();
            // retrieve it
            updatesRole = uow.Session
                .CreateObjectSet<Role>()
                .Where(r => r.Id == originalRole.Id)
                .FirstOrDefault();
            Assert.IsNotNull(updatesRole);
        }
```

```
            using (IUnitOfWork uow = new UnitOfWork())
            {
                // change it
                updatesRole.Name = "PowerUsers";
                uow.StartTransaction();
                uow.MarkDirty(updatesRole);
                Assert.IsTrue(updatesRole.EntityState == EntityState.Modified);
                uow.CommitTransaction();
                // retrieve it again
                var changedRole = uow.Session
                    .CreateObjectSet<Role>()
                    .Where(r => r.Id == originalRole.Id)
                    .FirstOrDefault();
                Assert.IsNotNull(updatesRole);
                Assert.AreEqual(changedRole.Name, "PowerUsers");
            }
        }
        catch (Exception exception)
        {
            Assert.Fail(exception.ToString());
        }
    }
}
```

Final Consideration for the Unit of Work

You saw how to create a unit of work for the Entity Framework using the TDD approach that consists of constantly testing the code you are writing by verifying the code against the application requirements. We created these tests using the Role entity just because it's the simplest entity in the domain model and because we need a real EntityObject to test the efficiency of the unit of work. Of course, every time we run a test we pollute the database with a mockup Role entity that is probably not necessary. For this reason I suggest you create both an Initialize and a CleanUp method in every test class by marking them with the attributes [TestInitialize] and [TestCleanup] so they will be execute before and after all the tests of that test class are run (see Listing 6-20). In this way you can clear up the pollution from the database caused by the test and leave a new, blank database.

Listing 6-20. CleanUp Test Methods

```
[TestInitialize]
public void TestInitialize()
{
    using (var uow = new TimeTrackerModelContainer())
    {
        // remove all the mockups roles from the database
        foreach (Role role in uow.Roles)
        {
            uow.DeleteObject(role);
        }
        uow.SaveChanges(SaveOptions.AcceptAllChangesAfterSave);
    }
}
```

```
[TestCleanup]
public void TestCleanup()
{
}
```

The Repository

At the beginning of this chapter I mentioned that the repository pattern is used to add an additional
abstraction layer to the DAL so that the other layers won't have direct access to the EF session but will be
forced to use the repository classes exposed by the DAL. A repository class should provide, at least, a set
of methods that allow you to execute the basic CRUD operations plus a basic set of queries, like the
interface in Listing 6-21.

Listing 6-21. The IRepository *Interface*

```
using System.Collections.Generic;

namespace APRESS.TimeTracker.DataLayer
{
    public interface IRepository <T> where T : EntityObject
    {
        void Insert(T entity);
        void Update(T entity);
        void Delete(T entity);
        IList<T> GetAll();
        T GetById(int id);
    }
}
```

In this case you are going to implement the code in an abstract RepositoryBase class that will be
used as a base class for each concrete repository (see Listing 6-22). You want to make the base class
abstract because you don't want it to be used directly. Unfortunately, by doing that you can't test the
implementation of the base repository outside the scope of a concrete repository because an abstract
class can't be tested.

Listing 6-22. Generic Repository Class

```
public abstract class RepositoryBase<T> : IRepository<T> where T : EntityObject
{
    private readonly IUnitOfWork unitOfWork;

    public RepositoryBase(IUnitOfWork unitOfWork)
    {
        this.unitOfWork = unitOfWork;
    }
}
```

This code uses the Dependency Injection pattern to inject a current unit of work into the repository.
Now you need to implement the methods exposed by the IRepository interface and test them.
Because you can't test an abstract class, you will have to create an additional class—RoleRepository—
which of course is a repository for the Role entity (see Listing 6-23).

Listing 6-23. *Role Repository*

```
public sealed class RoleRepository : RepositoryBase<Role>
{
    public RoleRepository(IUnitOfWork unitOfWork)
        : base(unitOfWork)
    {
    }
}
```

The final object is the Test fixture, so in the Test project you have to create a new unit test class and
call it RoleRepositoryTestFixture, then add initialize and cleanup methods as shown in Listing 6-24.

Listing 6-24. RoleRepository *Test Fixture*

```
[TestClass]
public class RoleRepositoryFixture
{
    private IUnitOfWork uow;

    [TestInitialize]
    public void Initialize()
    {
        uow = new UnitOfWork();
    }

    [TestCleanup]
    public void CleanUp()
    {
        // clean up the database ...
        uow.Dispose();
    }
}
```

Add a New Role

When you work with the repository pattern, you have to manage the operation by using a unit of work so
that if something goes wrong, you still have the power to roll back everything outside the scope of the
repository object.

The code in Listing 6-25 is in two pieces; the first is in the RepositoryBase object and it is the
implementation of the Insert<T> method; the second is in the RoleRepositoryFixture test class and is
used to test the method.

Listing 6-25. The `Insert<T>` *Method*

```
// Base repository part
public void Insert(T entity)
{
    unitOfWork.MarkNew(entity);
}

// TDD
[TestMethod]
public void CanCreateANewRole()
{
    try
    {
        uow.StartTransaction();
        var repository = new RoleRepository(uow);
        var role = new Role { Name = "Administrators", Description = "Admin role." };
        repository.Insert(role);
        Assert.IsTrue(role.EntityState == EntityState.Added);
        uow.CommitTransaction();
        Assert.IsTrue(role.Id > 0);
    }
    catch (Exception exception)
    {
        Assert.Fail(exception.ToString());
    }
}
```

As you can see, the test implementation starts a transaction *before* using the repository component and controls the transaction outside the scope of the repository object.

Delete an Existing Role

The delete method is pretty straightforward; you don't have to do anything more than call the unit of work `MarkDeleted<T>` method inside the **RepositoryBase** context, as shown in Listing 6-26.

Listing 6-26. `RepositoryBase` `Delete<T>` *Method and TDD*

```
// RepositoryBase code
public void Delete(T entity)
{
    unitOfWork.MarkDeleted(entity);
}

// TDD
[TestMethod]
public void CanDeleteAnExistingRole()
{
```

```
    try
    {
        // add the entity
        uow.StartTransaction();
        var repository = new RoleRepository(uow);
        var role = new Role {Name = "Administrators", Description = "Administrator Group."};
        repository.Insert(role);
        uow.CommitTransaction();
        Assert.IsTrue(role.Id > 0);
        // delete the entity
        uow.StartTransaction();
        repository.Delete(role);
        Assert.IsTrue(role.EntityState == EntityState.Deleted);
        uow.CommitTransaction();
        // try get it
        var expectedRole = uow.Session
            .CreateObjectSet<Role>()
            .Where(r => r.Id == role.Id)
            .FirstOrDefault();
        Assert.IsNull(expectedRole);
    }
    catch (Exception exception)
    {
        Assert.Fail(exception.ToString());
    }
}
```

Listing 6-26 creates a new Role and saves it in the database. It then deletes the Role using the Repository's method and commits the transaction. Finally, it tries to retrieve the Role to make sure it doesn't exist anymore in the database.

Update an Existing Role

The Update method follows the same pattern as the Insert and the Delete methods. It calls the unit of work methods and waits for a transaction to be committed in order to persist the changes to the database, as shown in Listing 6-27.

Listing 6-27. The Update Entity Method and TDD

```
// RepositoryBase method
public void Update(T entity)
{
    unitOfWork.MarkDirty(entity);
}

// TDD
[TestMethod]
public void CanUpdateAnExistingRole()
{
```

```
    try
    {
        // add the entity
        uow.StartTransaction();
        var repository = new RoleRepository(uow);
        var role = new Role { Name = "Administrators", Description = "Administrator Group."
};
        repository.Insert(role);
        uow.CommitTransaction();
        Assert.IsTrue(role.Id > 0);
        // modify the entity
        uow.StartTransaction();
        role.Name = "PowerUsers";
        repository.Update(role);
        uow.CommitTransaction();
        // try get it
        var expectedRole = uow.Session
            .CreateObjectSet<Role>()
            .Where(r => r.Id == role.Id)
            .FirstOrDefault();
        Assert.AreNotEqual(expectedRole.Name, "Administrators");
        Assert.AreEqual(expectedRole.Name, "PowerUsers");
    }
    catch (Exception exception)
    {
        Assert.Fail(exception.ToString());
    }
}
```

The preceding code creates a new Role and commits it to the database. It then updates the role's Name property and verifies that the corresponding record in the database has the updated value.

GetAll Roles

The GetAll method is a little different from the previous methods. It requires an ObjectSet<T> component in order to create a new LINQ query that will return all the available entities of that type from the database (see Listing 6-28).

Listing 6-28. The GetAll Method

```
// RepositoryBase
public IList<T> GetAll()
{
    return unitOfWork.Session.CreateObjectSet<T>().ToList();
}

// TDD
[TestMethod]
public void CanListAllRoles()
{
```

```
    try
    {
        var count = uow.Session.CreateObjectSet<Role>().Count();
        var repository = new RoleRepository(uow);
        var expectedCount = repository.GetAll().Count();
        Assert.AreEqual(count, expectedCount);
    }
    catch (Exception exception)
    {
        Assert.Fail(exception.ToString());
    }
}
```

What's new here? You already saw the `CreateObjectSet<T>` method and noted that it returns a new instance of an `ObjectSet<T>` object that provides a set of LINQ methods to query the objects in the EF context. LINQ is an integrated query language translated in C#. When used against EF, it is able to translate this SQL-like syntax into a real SQL statement call to the database. The code here uses the `LINQ to Entities` (LINQ for EF) extension method called `Count()` that can be translated to `SELECT COUNT(*) FROM ROLES`.

The task to accomplish here is pretty simple. You want to be sure that the number of entities returned by the repository method `GetAll` is the same as what's provided by the default `ObjectSet<Role>` available through the TimeTracker `ObjectContext` component.

Get a Role by Id

Finally, the `GetById` method returns one and only one entity of the type specified in the generic signature by using the `Id` property that is unique in the database table. The code in Listing 6-29 implements a new way of querying the objects in the EF that uses the `EntityKey` object.

Listing 6-29. The `GetById` *Method*

```
// RepositoryBase
public T GetById(int id)
{
    var fullQualifiedName = string.Format("{0}.{1}s",
        unitOfWork.Session.DefaultContainerName,
        typeof (T).Name);
    var key = new EntityKey(fullQualifiedName, "Id", id);
    return (T) unitOfWork.Session.GetObjectByKey(key);
}

// TDD
[TestMethod]
public void CanGetRoleById()
{
    try
    {
        // add the entity
        uow.StartTransaction();
        var repository = new RoleRepository(uow);
```

```
            var role = new Role {
                Name = "Administrators",
                Description = "Administrator Group." };
            repository.Insert(role);
            uow.CommitTransaction();
            Assert.IsTrue(role.Id > 0);
            // try get it
            var expectedRole = repository.GetById(role.Id);
            Assert.IsNotNull(expectedRole);
            Assert.AreEqual(expectedRole.Id, role.Id);
        }
        catch (Exception exception)
        {
            Assert.Fail(exception.ToString());
        }
    }
}
```

The first part of the code in Listing 6-29 uses a new object called `EntityKey`. The `EntityKey` class represents the key of an entity object. This object needs three pieces of information in its constructor method: the first is the fully qualified name of the `ObjectContext`, which in our case is `TimeTrackerModelContainer.Roles`. The other two parameters are the key name and the key value.

The test simply verifies that the repository is able to return the same `Role` entity that was saved using the `ObjectContext` by querying it using the `Id` property.

Additional Methods

You saw how to create a repository and how to implement the basic CRUD methods, but you haven't yet seen how to implement custom queries. As noted previously, the aim of this pattern is to hide the O/RM methods from the other layers, so it would be good to provide a custom query for each custom method of each repository.

For example, suppose you want to be able to query the roles in the database using a `LIKE` clause to return all the roles that match the string you are passing. To do that, you should create a custom method in the `RoleRepository` like the one in Listing 6-30.

Listing 6-30. The GetByName *Method of* RoleRepository

```
public IList<Role> GetByName(string name)
{
    return unitOfWork.Session
        .CreateObjectSet<Role>()
        .Where(r => r.Name.Contains(name))
        .ToList();
}
```

In order to make the UnitOfWork field visible from a concrete repository, you need to change the field in the `RepositoryBase` class from private to protected. Listing 6-30 uses the `Contains` method of the string class that is translated by LINQ to Entities to `SELECT * FROM ROLES WHERE NAME LIKE %name%`.

LINQ to Entities exposes a lot of methods to query your EF objects and we can't discuss all of them in this book as it would probably take an entire book for just that topic. During the building of the TimeTracker application, we will modify the base repositories classes of the project and you will see

several additional methods. I suggest you visit the MSDN section on LINQ to Entities at
`http://msdn.microsoft.com/en-us/library/bb386964.aspx` to learn how powerful this tool is. I leave to
you the creation of the other repositories, which would be very similar to what you did for the
`RoleRepository` object.

Summary

Domain Driven Design was introduced in the early 2000s in software architect communities to solve
specific business requirements using the most advanced techniques of object-oriented programming.

DDD can be accomplished in different ways, starting from the simplest Active Record pattern,
through the more complex and flexible Domain Driven approach. You can achieve the design by
creating the code before the database exists (Code First) or by creating a domain that will follow the
design of an existing legacy database (Database First).

The TimeTracker application uses the Domain Driven Design technique with the Code First
approach, so the domain model will drive the way we design the application logic and the database
structure.

In order to steer the application flow in the proper way, the domain needs an additional abstraction
layer for controlling how the entities in the database will be persisted. This requirement is accomplished
via a data layer that includes all the components used to persist the data: unit of work, repositories, plus
the O/RM used by the application to generate the T-SQL statements.

You also saw how easy and smooth the creation of such a complex architecture can be if you include
in your code a full set of unit tests.

CHAPTER 7

Data Binding

The primary purpose of WPF is to provide a dynamic, powerful way to build standalone client user interfaces using XAML markup. A user interface consists of different types of controls, such as buttons, textboxes, and datagrids. Each control exposes data and behaviors; the data will be displayed onscreen and edited by the user while the behaviors will make the UI interactive. Typically, the most challenging tasks when developing a UI are binding the data to the View and keeping the data synchronization between the View and the Model up-to-date at all times. For example, if the user modifies the data in the View, you must update the corresponding Model, and if the Model changes, the corresponding View needs to be updated.

WPF exposes a powerful mechanism for keeping the data in the Model and the View up-to-date. This mechanism is known as *data binding* and it provides a way to synchronize the data shared by the View and the Model.

As with any UI technology, you may want to update the data only on one side of the relationship; this is known as *unidirectional* data binding. For example, you may want to update the Model if something changes in the View but you may not want to update the View if the Model changes. If you want to keep the data updated on both sides of the relationship, you use *bidirectional* data binding.

The most powerful feature of this technology is that the data binding to a WPF control can be styled so that the layout of the control is changes completely, depending on the data you are binding to it. With WPF, you can bind the data to just about any XAML element or dependency property so that your View can be totally dynamic.

WPF Data Binding Engine

Data binding in WPF is always comprises two objects, the binding source and the binding target, where the source represents the object that provides the data and the target represents the UI element or property that expose the data value. Figure 7-1 shows a basic representation of this mechanism.

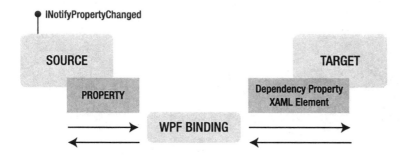

Figure 7-1. WPF data binding mechanism

In Figure 7-1 you can see three major actors involved in the data binding process:

- The source, which can be any CLR object that implements the
INotifyPropertyChanged interface, an interface that uses an event to notify when
the value of a property has been changed.

- The target object and its target property, which must be a dependency property
(we looked at this in Chapter 6).

- The WPF Binding class component, which derives from
System.Windows.Data.Binding and can be created using XAML markup, C#, or
VB.NET in the code-behind file.

The INotifyPropertyChanged Interface

The INotifyPropertyChanged interface implements a contract that notifies the listener when the value of
a property has been modified. This interface doesn't provide the concrete code to notify about the
change, but it does supply a simple event called PropertyChanged that informs the listeners about the
change. Listing 7-1 shows a simple implementation of this interface.

Listing 7-1. INotifyPropertyChanged Implementation

```
// INotifyPropertyChanged implementation

using System.ComponentModel;
namespace APRESS.TimeTracking.DataLayer
{
    public sealed class Person : INotifyPropertyChanged
    {
        public event PropertyChangedEventHandler PropertyChanged;

        public void OnPropertyChanged(string propertyName)
        {
```

```
            PropertyChangedEventHandler handler = PropertyChanged;
            if (handler != null)
            {
                PropertyChanged(this, new PropertyChangedEventArgs(propertyName));
            }
        }
        // there are more properties but they are not
        // shown for semplicity
    }
}

// property inside the Person class

private string firstName;

public string FirstName
{
    get { return firstName; }
    set
    {
        if (value == firstName)
        {
            return;
        }
        firstName = value;
        OnPropertyChanged("FirstName");
    }
}
```

The code first shows a fake **Person** class that implements the **INotifyPropertyChanged** interface. The code provided by the interface consists of a **PropertyChanged** event that requires a **PropertyChangedEventArgs** argument—a string parameter that is the name of the property changed. Next is the method used to raise the **PropertyChanged** event. The only thing to note here is the check that's done before raising the event. If the **PropertyChanged** event is null, it means nobody is listening to the event so it doesn't need to be raised. If it is raised, the .NET Framework throws an ugly **NullReferenceException** error.

The second part of the code shows a property with a private field accessor that implements the notify event when you set the value of the property. If the value has changed from the previous one, you call the method **OnPropertyChanged**.

■ **Note** You may wonder "Why do I have to implement this interface on an object that is bound to a WPF control?" The answer is pretty simple: WPF needs to detect the changes in order to trigger the binding engine and update the target dependency property and/or the source. If you implement this interface in your bind object, WPF has an in-place mechanism to detect the changes and you don't have to worry or to implement any additional mechanism.

Binding Direction

The binding flow in WPF represents the direction of data binding between two objects. In WPF you can use different types of binding as explained in the following list. The list is an enumeration available from `System.Windows.Data.BindingMode`.

- *OneWay*: This is the classic binding, just one direction from the source (Model) to the target (View). The Model updates the View but the View doesn't update the Model. This is also known as read-only binding because a change in the View doesn't affect the underlying Model.

- *OneTime:* As the name indicates, this binding mechanism binds the data just once, the first time, and will not keep either the source or the target updated.

- *TwoWay*: With two-way binding, a change in the Model affects the View and a change in the View affects the Model.

- *OneWayToSource:* In this case, the binding goes in the opposite direction from one-way binding, so it's the View that updates the Model, but not vice versa. This type of binding is hardly used.

As previously noted, when binding the Model to the View, you need to implement the actual change-notification mechanism in order to be able to use the notify mechanism provided by the WPF binding engine.

In order to be notified that something has changed in the source or in the target of the binding expression, you need to specify in WPF the behavior that will set off the change; this behavior is represented in WPF by the property `UpdateSourceTrigger`, which has three different values available from the enumeration `System.Windows.Data.UpdateSourceTrigger`:

- *LostFocus:* this occurs when the affected control loses the focus. This usually happens when another control in the UI gets the focus. This is the default value for the `Text` property of any control.

- *PropertyChanged*: this happens after the property value is changed, and it is fired every time the value changes.

- *Explicit*: this happens only on demand, when the code asks the binding source to update the value.

It's worth noting that some controls, like `TextBox`es, need to bind using the `LostFocus` mechanism due to the high number of changes their `Text` properties can receive, and that may reduce the UI performance overall.

The IValueConverter Interface

When you bind a property of an object to a dependency property of a XAML element, you always use a literal expression, like those shown in Listing 7-2.

Listing 7-2. *Sample Binding Expressions in XAML*

```
<TextBox Text="{Binding Path=Person.FirstName}" />
<TextBox Text="{Binding FirstName, UpdateSourceTrigger = LostFocus}" />
```

By default, the WPF engine is able to convert almost all the primitive values based on the value type of the property you are binding. So, for instance, in Listing 7-2 the `FirstName` property is converted using a string converter with the default `TypeConverter` component, as both the `FirstName` and the `Text` properties are of type `System.String`.

Another example is shown in Listing 7-3. Look at the property values used to customize the `Label` control—there using four properties with three different value types, an integer for the width, a string for the `FontFamily` and a color for the `Foreground` property.

Listing 7-3. *Background Color Value Converter*

```
<Label
   Width="100" Height="25"
   FontFamily="Segoe UI"
   Foreground="SteelBlue">Sample Label</Label>
```

Unfortunately, sometimes you need to format (i.e., convert) the data binding to the UI using a specific approach, a format expression, or some more complicated presentation logic. You may also need to recycle the code used for the conversion all over the WPF application. The .NET Framework provides an interface called **IValueConverter** that forces you to implement a two-way conversion of a specific value type, **Convert** and **ConvertBack**.

Listing 7-4 shows a sample converter that converts a `DateTime` object to a specific value in a string format:

Listing 7-4. *DateTime Converter for WPF*

```
using System;
using System.Globalization;
using System.Windows;
using System.Windows.Data;

namespace ValueConverter
{
    [ValueConversion(typeof (DateTime), typeof (String))]
    public sealed class DateTimeConverter : IValueConverter
    {
        #region Implementation of IValueConverter

        public object Convert(object value, Type targetType, object parameter, CultureInfo↩
culture)
        {
            var date = (DateTime) value;
            return date.ToShortDateString();
        }
```

```
        public object ConvertBack(object value, Type targetType, object parameter,↵
CultureInfo culture)
        {
            var strValue = (string)value;
            DateTime resultDateTime;
            if (DateTime.TryParse(strValue, out resultDateTime))
            {
                return resultDateTime;
            }
            return DependencyProperty.UnsetValue;
        }

        #endregion
    }
}
```

This converter implements the interface IValueConverter, which provides the methods signature to translate the types from the original to the final. The first thing to notice is the attribute ValueConversion on the converter class, which informs the development tools such Visual Studio or Blend about the type of conversion that will occur using this converter. The second thing is the IValueConverter implementation that consists of two methods:

- Convert: this is the method used to convert the original value into the final value displayed in the UI.

- ConvertBack: this method is called when the source tries to get the value modified via the UI so the final value needs to be converted back to the original format.

The first part of the converter simply uses one of the DateTime methods to convert the date value into a short format (mm/dd/yyyy). The second method, because it receives a string as an input, needs first to verify that the value can be converted back to a DateTime. If it can't, the DependencyProperty.UnsetValue object returns a default nullable value.

Now you can add a reference in the XAML View and declare the converter by signing it with an x:key attribute as shown in Listing 7-5.

Listing 7-5. Value Converter XAML Declaration

```
<Window
    x:Class="ValueConverter.MainWindow"
    xmlns="http://schemas.microsoft.com/winfx/2006/xaml/presentation"
    xmlns:x="http://schemas.microsoft.com/winfx/2006/xaml"
    xmlns:ValueConverter="clr-namespace:ValueConverter"
    Title="MainWindow" Height="186" Width="268">
    <Window.Resources>
        <ValueConverter:DateTimeConverter x:Key="DateConv" />
    </Window.Resources>
    <Grid>

    </Grid>
</Window>
```

Once you've attached a new converter instance to the window resources, you can use it in the data bind by using the key `DateConv`, which identifies that specific converter. First of all, you try to bind the `Person` class built previously in the window's `DataContext` by working in the code-behind file, as shown in Listing 7-6.

Listing 7-6. *Attaching an Object of Type **INotifyPropertyChanged** to the **DataContext** of a Window*

```
public partial class MainWindow : Window
{
    public MainWindow()
    {
        InitializeComponent();
        this.DataContext = new Person
            {
                FirstName = "Raffaele",
                LastName = "Garofalo",
                DateOfBirth = new DateTime(2011, 01, 01)
            };
    }
}
```

Finally, you add three controls to the window's `Grid` element, which will expose the three properties of the data-bind object (see Listing 7-7).

Listing 7-7. *Binding the **DataContext** to the XAML Controls*

```
<Grid>
    <Label Content=" First Name :" />
    <Label Content="Last Name :" />
    <Label Content="Full Name :" />
    <TextBox Text="{Binding Path=FirstName}" />
    <TextBox Text="{Binding Path=LastName}" />
    <TextBox Text="{Binding Path=DateOfBirth, Converter={StaticResource DateConv}}" />
</Grid>
```

The result will be a window with three labels and three textboxes. The one bound to the `DateOfBirth` property will expose a datetime value using a short format, as shown in Figure 7-2.

Figure 7-2. *Custom value converter final result*

DataTemplate

One of the most powerful characteristics of WPF is the way it allows you customize the layout of the UI so that a simple `Listbox` control can look like a grid just by customizing the way the control will render the data. By using a data template in WPF, you can customize the layout of a control based on the data you are binding to it.

Figure 7-3 shows the same control (a `Listbox`) bound to a list of `Person` classes but rendered with two different `DataTemplates`. As you can see, the control and the data are the same but the result is totally different.

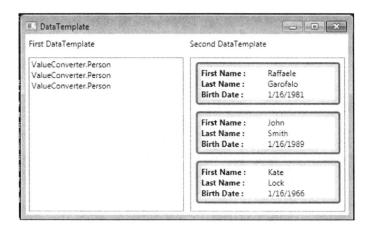

Figure 7-3. A `Listbox` with different `DataTemplates` applied

As Figure 7-3 shows, a collection of type `List<Person>` is bound to these two listboxes. As you can see, the first list uses the default data template provided by the `Listbox` control. In this case, the data template renders the `ListBoxItem` as a `TextBlock` filled by the result of the `.ToString` method of the bind control. Because we didn't implement a custom `.ToString()` method in the `Person` class, the list displays the `FullName` of the object type, `Person` using reflection.

In the second list a custom data template has been defined for an item of the `Listbox`, which is consists of a set of `TextBlock` and other UI elements that are bound to the properties of the `Person` class.

The `Listbox` is a control that is bound to a collection of items so it exposes a dependency property of type `ItemTemplate`, which exposes the data template element for each item in the list. Within this data template you can define the layout of the `Listbox` items, as in Listing 7-8.

Listing 7-8. Defining a Data Template for a `Listbox`

```
<!--in the XAML below we are skipping the UI style code in order to make the XAML more↵
 readable -->
<ListBox ItemsSource="{Binding}">
    <ListBox.ItemTemplate>
        <DataTemplate>
            <StackPanel>
                <TextBlock Text="{Binding Path=FirstName}" />
```

```
            <TextBlock Text="{Binding Path=LastName}" />
            <TextBlock Text="{Binding Path=DateOfBirth}" />
        </StackPanel>
      </DataTemplate>
    </ListBox.ItemTemplate>
</ListBox>
```

The code in Listing 7-8 tells the Listbox that the source of the data is provided by the DataContext of the parent container (you bind a List<Person> to the DataContext of the window). It then specifies that the ItemTemplate will be composed of a StackPanel with three TextBlocks inside, each one bound to a specific property of the Person class.

This example is the first type of approach to bind a specific class to a specific data template. Unfortunately, in this case you can't recycle this code, so every time you need to bind a class of type Person to a control you will need to specify a data template for the control. However, if you put the data template in the window's resources or in a ResourceDictionary, you'll be able to reference the resource in the control without having to rewrite the data template schema every time. See Listing 7-9.

Listing 7-9. *DataTemplate for the Person Class as a Resource*

```
<--Resources of a Window -->
<Window.Resources>
    <ValueConverter:DateTimeConverter x:Key="DateConv" />
    <DataTemplate
        DataType="{x:Type ValueConverter:Person}"
        x:Key="PersonTemplate">
        <StackPanel>
            <Grid>
                <!-- omitted grid implementation -->
                <TextBlock
                    Grid.Row="0" Grid.Column="0"
                    Text="First Name :"
                    FontWeight="Bold"/>
                <TextBlock
                    Grid.Row="0" Grid.Column="1"
                    Text="{Binding Path=FirstName}" />
                <TextBlock
                    Grid.Row="1" Grid.Column="0"
                    Text="Last Name :"
                    FontWeight="Bold"/>
                <TextBlock
                    Grid.Row="1" Grid.Column="1"
                    Text="{Binding Path=LastName}" />
                <TextBlock
                    Grid.Row="2" Grid.Column="0"
                    Text="Birth Date :"
                    FontWeight="Bold"/>
                <TextBlock
                    Grid.Row="2" Grid.Column="1"
                    Text="{Binding Path=DateOfBirth, Converter={StaticResource DateConv}}"
/>
            </Grid>
```

```
        </StackPanel>
    </DataTemplate>
</Window.Resources>

<-- Listbox using the StaticResource -->
<ListBox
    ItemsSource="{Binding}"
    ItemTemplate="{StaticResource PersonTemplate}"
    HorizontalContentAlignment="Stretch">
```

As you can see, the code used to bind a Person class to an ItemTemplate is pretty simple and specific to the Person class, and it can be reused by the whole application, though you may need to add it in a shared application resource file or in a dictionary.

Creating a data template for a specific object is an additional step in the development process but it allows you to:

- Provide a standard layout for a specific object so the object will appear in the same way throughout the application.

- Recycle the XAML markup to style a specific item of a control.

The data template can be used to display the items of an ItemsControl like a Listbox or a ComboBox, but it can also be used to display the content of a ContentControl like a Panel. You can also create personalized behaviors so that the ItemTemplate will choose a specific data template, depending on a specific value in the bind object or on the status of the ItemTemplate (selected or not selected).

You'll find more details about this technology at msdn.microsoft.com/library/ms742521.aspx. Later in this chapter and others you'll see how to create conditional data templates.

UI Validation

WPF introduces a mechanism for validating the data bound to a specific control, and this in combination with the data template and the style mechanisms lets you customize the UI so that it will inform the user about bad input or missing information.

You can use different approaches to validate an object in .NET. You can write a custom validation class that inherits from the ValidationRule class and implements the validation, but the downside of this approach is that you end up with a huge number of custom validation classes. You can also use the System.ComponentModel.DataAnnotations attributes, which provide an in-place mechanism for data validation.

The validation mechanism for WPF is structured as follows:

- Associate one or more validation rules to a binding object; the validation rules implement attributes to check if a specific object or property is valid.

- A validation rule can be overriden by creating a new class that inherits from the ValidationRule class.

- Create a custom ControlTemplate for the attached property Validation.HasError in order to display a specific layout if the bind object has errors.

Listing 7-10 shows a simple validation template for a TextBox.

Listing 7-10. *A Simple Validation Template for a TextBox*

```
<TextBox Name="FirstName">
  <TextBox.Text>
    <Binding Path="FirstName" UpdateSourceTrigger="PropertyChanged">
      <Binding.ValidationRules>
        <ExceptionValidationRule />
      </Binding.ValidationRules>
    </Binding>
  </TextBox.Text>
</TextBox>
```

In this case, the code says that if the property change raises an exception (let's say that if `FirstName` is null, the `Person` class raises an exception), the error will render in the `TextBox`.

■ **Note** In the WPF's validation mechanism, if the source object (ViewModel) bound to the View implements the `IDataErrorInfo` interface, it is able to provide validation feedback for each property bound to the View. The built-in `DataErrorValidationRule` component can be used to check the errors potentially raised by the bound object (ViewModel). An alternative way is to explicitly set `ValidatesOnDataError` to true in the bound property. You'll find more information on this topic in Chapter 12 when we discuss the Model View ViewModel in depth.

By default, WPF renders a validation error using a red border around a control, but with few simple steps you can come up with a cool result, as shown in Figure 7-4.

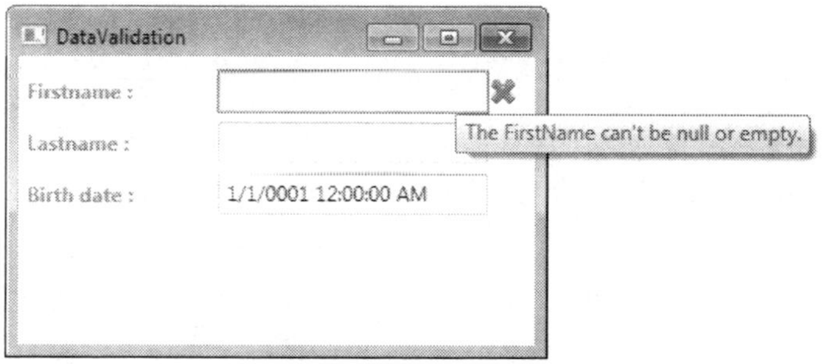

Figure 7-4. *Using a custom error template*

The validation of a bound object's property can happen at different times. For example, you can validate the data entered into a `Textbox` only when the user leaves the control (`LostFocus`) or every time the property value changes (`PropertyChanged`). You may then decide to validate the data using a validation rule or using the exception approach (which I don't suggest).

In the ViewModel section, we'll take a look at an alternative solution—how to create a custom validator class that will validate the data entered in the View using the `DataAnnotations` attributes.

Binding Syntax

The data binding process consists of a syntax that lets you specify the item you are binding, the path to reach the item in the object tree, and the type of binding you are using.

Table 7-1 is a summary of the potential binding path expressions you can use when you bind a property or an object to a XAML element.

Table 7-1. Data Binding Cheat Sheet

Binding Syntax	Description
{Binding}	Bind to current DataContext.
{Binding Name}	Bind to the "Name" property of the current DataContext.
{Binding Name.Length}	Bind to the Length property of the object in the Name property of the current DataContext
{Binding ElementName=SomeTextBox, Path=Text}	Bind to the "Text" property of the element XAML element with name="SomeTextBox" or x:Name="SomeTextBox."

This table shows the classic binding path to use when you create simple binding associations. Table 7-2 shows some less common, more complex binding paths that you may need to use when you have to bind a different element than the classic object property.

Table 7-2. Relative Source Binding Cheat Sheet

Binding Path	Description
{Binding RelativeSource={RelativeSource Self}}	Bind to the target element.
{Binding RelativeSource={RelativeSource Self}, Path=Name}	Bind to the "Name" property of the target element.
{Binding RelativeSource={RelativeSource FindAncestor, AncestorType={x:Type Window}}, Path=Title}	Bind to the title of the parent window using the AncestorType to find the correct type.
{Binding RelativeSource={RelativeSource FindAncestor, AncestorType={x:Type ItemsControl}, AncestorLevel=2}, Path=Name}	Bind the name of the 2nd parent of type ItemsControl. The AncestorLevel talks about how far you back you go on the tree.

Binding Path	Description
{Binding RelativeSource={RelativeSource TemplatedParent}, Path=Name}	Inside a control template, bind to the name property of the element the template is applied to.
{TemplateBinding Name}	Shortcut for the previous example.

Tables 7-1 and 7-2 are adapted from `www.nbdtech.com/Free/WpfBinding.pdf`. Keep them handy for when you will have to write binding expressions.

ViewModels

The ViewModel is an object introduced by the Model View ViewModel (MVVM) pattern, a specific presentation pattern designed for WPF and Silverlight (and right now used also in Windows Phone 7). The core of this pattern is the *Model for View*, i.e., the ViewModel. We will analyze this and other concepts in more detail in the chapter dedicated to UI patterns for WPF, but right now let's just identify this object as the ViewModel and create one for each View of the TimeTracker application.

So, what is the main purpose of a ViewModel object and what should it implement? The ViewModel should implement the `INotifyPropertyChanged` interface so it can be bound dynamically to a View. It should also provide a mechanism for validation, and it should expose the commands and the behaviors executed by the View.

In Chapter 4 you created the base ViewModels for the details and the list views; now let's add validation to the ViewModels and bind them to the entity objects created in Chapter 6. We will also modify how the ViewModels act as now we have an additional component for the application—the domain model that we will bind to the View, the data layer that will retrieve the data from the database, and we know how to use data binding.

The main reason to have a `ViewModel` object instead of binding the business entity directly to the View, like the `Employee` entity for the `EmployeeDetailsView`, is that:

- You want to keep the presentation logic loosely coupled from the business logic.
- You want to keep UI objects like commands, behaviors, and events loosely coupled from the business entity.
- You want to make the presentation logic testable.

A Generic ViewModel Validator

When we created the `BaseDetailsViewModel<T>` in Chapter 4, we didn't include any information about how to validate the data entered by a user because we hadn't yet looked at the WPF validation rule mechanism. Now we've seen that the `System.ComponentModel.DataAnnotations` assembly provides a simple, useful way of validating an object by decorating it with data annotations attributes. What we are going to do is to decorate the ViewModel—and not the business entity—with the validation rules that will be displayed on the corresponding View. Why are we validating the ViewModel and not the domain entity object directly? Typically, with an n-tier application, you recycle the domain objects so the validation rules may be different from application to application. Moreover, the same domain entity should be validated in different ways from one View to another. You may also find a different point of view where the domain model drives the validation rules so you don't need to add them in the presentation logic.

■ **Note** The debate about whether to place the validation on the business entities or on the View models is still open in the software architecture community, not only for WPF technology but for all the technologies that involve a UI layer and one or more business and presentation layers. The validation rules we are using in this application are related more to the data entry done by the end user, and this is another reason for saving the validation in the ViewModel. You can move the validation to the business entity if you believe it is more correct, and validate the Model instead of the ViewModel, but I believe that this approach will end up polluting the domain with presentation validation rules.

Let's open the `BaseViewModel<T>` class and refactor it to provide direct support to the `IDataErrorInfo` interface; we will use reflection to read the `DataAnnotation` attributes and validate the `ViewModel` properties. In order to use it you have to add a new assembly reference to the project, the `System.ComponentModel.DataAnnotations.dll`. See Listing 7-11.

Listing 7-11. Data Validation Using DataAnnotations and IDataErrorInfo

```
using System;
using System.Collections.Generic;
using System.ComponentModel;
using System.ComponentModel.DataAnnotations;
using System.Linq;
using System.Reflection;

namespace APRESS.TimeTracking.ViewModels
{
    public abstract class BaseViewModel<T> : ObservableObject<T>, IDataErrorInfo
    {
        private string viewTitle;

        public string ViewTitle
        {
            get { return viewTitle; }
            set
            {
                if (viewTitle == value)
                {
                    return;
                }
                viewTitle = value;
                OnPropertyChanged(vm => ViewTitle);
            }
        }
    }
```

```
#region Implementation of IDataErrorInfo

public string this[string columnName]
{
    get
    {
        PropertyInfo prop = GetType().GetProperty(columnName);
        IEnumerable<ValidationAttribute> validationMap = prop
            .GetCustomAttributes(typeof (ValidationAttribute), true)
            .Cast<ValidationAttribute>();
        foreach (ValidationAttribute v in validationMap)
        {
            try
            {
                v.Validate(prop.GetValue(this, null), columnName);
            }
            catch (ValidationException ex)
            {
                return ex.Message;
            }
        }

        return null;
    }
}

public string Error
{
    get { throw new NotImplementedException("This method should not be used↩
for validation, it is deprecated."); }
}

#endregion
    }
}
```

The `IDataErrorInfo` interface is implemented by following these steps:

1. Retrieve the `PropertyInfo` object corresponding to the current validated property using the reflection.

2. Retrieve a list of `ValidationAttribute`s of the current property.

3. For each attribute used to decorate the property, validate the property and if there are errors, return them.

Now every property of a `ListViewModel` or a `DetailsViewModel` can validated.

Employee ViewModels

The first entity to tackle is the `Employee` domain entity, which is displayed by the different views. The main View presents a list of the first 10 employees displayed in a `Listbox` control. The `EmployeesListView`

173

displays all the employees using a `DataGrid` control, and a composite View, the EmployeeDetailsView, shows detailed information about a particular employee, as shown in Figure 7-5.

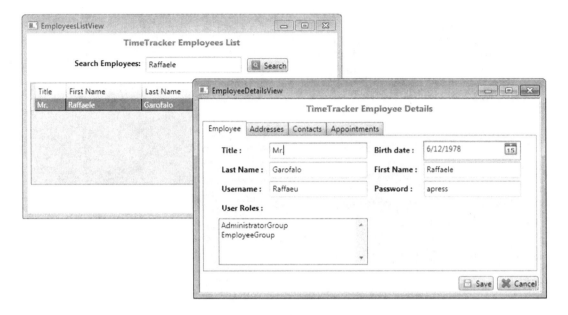

Figure 7-5. *Employee master-details views*

The background screen in Figure 7-5 is a simple `Window` object consisting of a `TextBox` control and a `Button` for searching the employees, as well as a `DataGrid` with a list of results and three `Buttons` for adding, removing, or editing an item. When the user presses the new or edit `Button`, a details View opens that is composed of a set of `TabPages` in a `TabControl`, where each one contains a specific `UserControl` that binds to a specific part of the employee entity.

Each View is bound to a ViewModel that is the model for the View. If you're working with a details View, the ViewModel will be a details ViewModel; if it is a list View, the ViewModel will be a list ViewModel. When the View consists of different parts, like the employee details View, it will be composed of additional ViewModels (details or list), one for each component of the UI.

The ViewModel should expose the properties that are displayed in the corresponding View by hiding the properties exposed directly from the Model; this approach allows you to add an additional abstraction from the View and the Model and it also adds another layer of security to the Model that, otherwise, would be directly exposed in the View.

Employee Details

The first ViewModel you'll create is the EmployeeDetailsViewModel (see Listing 7-12), which will expose the following objects:

- All the properties exposed by the Employee class wrapped around.

- Two ICommand commands, one for the Save command and one for the Cancel command.

Remember, if you didn't yet, to add a reference in the WPF project that points to the BusinessLayer project in order to have the domain model visible in the ViewModel objects.

Listing 7-12. EmployeeDetails ViewModel

```
using System;
using System.Windows.Input;
using System.Collections.Generic;
using System.ComponentModel.DataAnnotations;
using System.Data.Objects.DataClasses;
using System.Linq;
using APRESS.TimeTracking.BusinessLayer;

namespace APRESS.TimeTracking.ViewModels
{
    public sealed class EmployeeDetailsViewModel : BaseDetailsViewModel<Employee>
    {
        public EmployeeDetailsViewModel(Employee currentEntity)
            : base(currentEntity)
        {
        }

        [Required(AllowEmptyStrings = false, ErrorMessage = "The FirstName can't be null
or empty.")]
        [StringLength(50, ErrorMessage = "The FirstName can't be longer than 50.")]
        public string FirstName
        {
            get { return CurrentEntity.FullName.FirstName; }
            set
            {
                CurrentEntity.FullName.FirstName = value;
                OnPropertyChanged(vm => FirstName);
            }
        }

        [Required(AllowEmptyStrings = false, ErrorMessage = "The LastName can't be null
or empty.")]
        [StringLength(50, ErrorMessage = "The LastName can't be longer than 50.")]
        public string LastName
        {
            get { return CurrentEntity.FullName.LastName; }
```

```
            set
            {
                CurrentEntity.FullName.LastName = value;
                OnPropertyChanged(vm => LastName);
            }
        }

        [Required(ErrorMessage = "The Date of Birth can't be null or empty.")]
        public DateTime DateOfBirth
        {
            get { return CurrentEntity.DateOfBirth; }
            set
            {
                CurrentEntity.DateOfBirth = value;
                OnPropertyChanged(vm => DateOfBirth);
            }
        }

        [Required(AllowEmptyStrings = false, ErrorMessage = "The Title can't be null↵
or emtpy.")]
        [StringLength(10, ErrorMessage = "The Title can't be greater than 10.")]
        public string Title
        {
            get { return CurrentEntity.Title; }
            set
            {
                CurrentEntity.Title = value;
                OnPropertyChanged(vm => Title);
            }
        }

        [Required(AllowEmptyStrings = false, ErrorMessage = "The Username can't be null↵
or empty.")]
        public string Username
        {
            get { return CurrentEntity.Username; }
            set
            {
                CurrentEntity.Username = value;
                OnPropertyChanged(vm => Username);
            }
        }

        [Required(AllowEmptyStrings = false, ErrorMessage = "The Password can't be null↵
or empty.")]
        public string Password
        {
            get { return CurrentEntity.Password; }
```

```
        set
        {
            CurrentEntity.Password = value;
            OnPropertyChanged(vm => Password);
        }
    }

    public ICommand SaveCommand { get; set; }

    public ICommand CancelCommand { get; set; }
    }
}
```

Listing 7-12 creates the first part of the details ViewModel that you'll use to display the employee information. Each property of the employee domain entity has been wrapped around a new property, the one that you will bind in the WPF UserControl used to display the data. Each property has also been decorated with the DataAnnotations attributes so that the View will validate the information entered by the user. For more information on the DataAnnotations rules, take a look at msdn.microsoft.com/library/system.componentmodel.dataannotations.aspx.

The ICommand interface exposes methods and properties used to implement the command pattern that's also used by the WPF binding engine; we'll look at this pattern and at other objects like the RoutedCommand in more depth in the next chapter. For now, just create a property in the ViewModel for each command and bind it.

As you've seen, there are three additional tabs in the EmployeeDetailsView but we'll create these properties later as we need the corresponding ViewModels before doing so. The next step now is to edit the EmployeeDetailsUserControl.xaml object that contains only the information exposed by the Employee domain entity and the list of Roles (see Listing 7-13). The tab control in the details View contains only the reference to the specific user control exposed by the View, but the binding will happen in the UserControl directly. In this way, the EmployeeDetailsView will remain clean without any reference to the specific binding object.

Listing 7-13. The EmployeeDetailsView

```
<Window
    xmlns:my="clr-namespace:APRESS.TimeTracking.Views"
    x:Class="APRESS.TimeTracking.Views.EmployeeDetailsView"
    xmlns="http://schemas.microsoft.com/winfx/2006/xaml/presentation"
    xmlns:x="http://schemas.microsoft.com/winfx/2006/xaml"
    xmlns:Controls="clr-namespace:APRESS.TimeTracking.Controls"
    Title="EmployeeDetailsView"
    Height="344" Width="557"
    ResizeMode="CanResizeWithGrip"
    WindowStyle="ThreeDBorderWindow" WindowStartupLocation="CenterScreen">
    <DockPanel LastChildFill="True">
        <TextBlock DockPanel.Dock="Top" Style="{StaticResource TitleBlock}">TimeTracker↵
Employee Details</TextBlock>
```

```
            <StackPanel
                    DockPanel.Dock="Bottom"
                    MaxHeight="30"
                    Orientation="Horizontal" HorizontalAlignment="Right"
                    Grid.Column="1" Grid.Row="3" Grid.ColumnSpan="3">
                <Controls:ImageButton
                        Padding="3"
                        Text="Save"
                        Image="{DynamicResource SaveSmall}"/>
                <Controls:ImageButton
                        Padding="3"
                        Text="Cancel"
                        Image="{DynamicResource CloseSmall}" />
            </StackPanel>
            <TabControl DockPanel.Dock="Bottom" Margin="5">
                <TabItem Header="Employee">
                    <my:EmployeeDetailsUserControl Padding="5" />
                </TabItem>
                <TabItem Header="Addresses">
                    <my:AddressListUserControl Padding="5" />
                </TabItem>
                <TabItem Header="Contacts">
                    <my:ContactListUserControl Padding="5" />
                </TabItem>
                <TabItem Header="Appointments">
                    <my:AppointmentsListUserControl Padding="5" />
                </TabItem>
            </TabControl>
        </DockPanel>
</Window>
```

Now let's bind the Employee entity information to the details user control, as shown in Listing 7-14.

Listing 7-14. Binding the EmployeeDetailsUserControl

```
<UserControl x:Class="APRESS.TimeTracking.Views.EmployeeDetailsUserControl"
            xmlns="http://schemas.microsoft.com/winfx/2006/xaml/presentation"
            xmlns:x="http://schemas.microsoft.com/winfx/2006/xaml"
            xmlns:mc="http://schemas.openxmlformats.org/markup-compatibility/2006"
            xmlns:d="http://schemas.microsoft.com/expression/blend/2008"
            mc:Ignorable="d"
            d:DesignHeight="352" d:DesignWidth="502">
    <Grid>
        <Grid.RowDefinitions>
            <RowDefinition Height="30" />
            <RowDefinition Height="30" />
            <RowDefinition Height="30" />
            <RowDefinition Height="30" />
            <RowDefinition Height="*" />
        </Grid.RowDefinitions>
        <Grid.ColumnDefinitions>
```

```
            <ColumnDefinition Width="15" />
            <ColumnDefinition Width="auto" />
            <ColumnDefinition Width="5" />
            <ColumnDefinition Width="*" />
            <ColumnDefinition Width="5" />
            <ColumnDefinition Width="auto" />
            <ColumnDefinition Width="5" />
            <ColumnDefinition Width="*" />
            <ColumnDefinition Width="15" />
        </Grid.ColumnDefinitions>
        <Label Style="{StaticResource ControlLabel}" Content="Title :" Grid.Column="1"/>
        <TextBox
            Text="{Binding Path=Title,
            Mode=TwoWay, UpdateSourceTrigger=LostFocus,
            ValidatesOnDataErrors=True, ValidatesOnExceptions=True}"
            Grid.Column="3" />
        <Label Style="{StaticResource ControlLabel}" Content="Birth date :"
Grid.Column="5"/>
        <DatePicker
            Text="{Binding Path=DateOfBirth,
            Mode=TwoWay, UpdateSourceTrigger=LostFocus,
            ValidatesOnDataErrors=True, ValidatesOnExceptions=True}"
            Grid.Column="7" />
        <Label
            Style="{StaticResource ControlLabel}" Content="Last Name :" Grid.Row="1"↩
  Grid.Column="1"/>
        <TextBox
            Text="{Binding Path=LastName,
            Mode=TwoWay, UpdateSourceTrigger=LostFocus,
            ValidatesOnDataErrors=True, ValidatesOnExceptions=True}" Grid.Row="1"↩
  Grid.Column="3" />
        <Label
            Style="{StaticResource ControlLabel}" Content="First Name :" Grid.Column="5"↩
  Grid.Row="1" />
        <TextBox
            Text="{Binding Path=FirstName,
            Mode=TwoWay, UpdateSourceTrigger=LostFocus,
            ValidatesOnDataErrors=True, ValidatesOnExceptions=True}" Grid.Column="7"↩
  Grid.Row="1" />
        <Label
            Style="{StaticResource ControlLabel}" Content="Username :" Grid.Column="1"↩
  Grid.Row="2" />
        <TextBox
            Text="{Binding Path=Username,
            Mode=TwoWay, UpdateSourceTrigger=LostFocus,
            ValidatesOnDataErrors=True, ValidatesOnExceptions=True}" Grid.Column="3"↩
  Grid.Row="2" />
        <Label
            Style="{StaticResource ControlLabel}" Content="Password :" Grid.Column="5"↩
  Grid.Row="2" />
        <TextBox
```

```
               Text="{Binding Path=Password,
               Mode=TwoWay, UpdateSourceTrigger=LostFocus,
               ValidatesOnDataErrors=True, ValidatesOnExceptions=True}" Grid.Column="7"↵
  Grid.Row="2" />
          <Label
               Style="{StaticResource ControlLabel}" Content="User Roles :"
Grid.ColumnSpan="3"↵
  Grid.Column="1" Grid.Row="3" />
          <ListBox
               ItemsSource="{Binding Path=CurrentEntity.Roles}"
               DisplayMemberPath="Name"
               ScrollViewer.VerticalScrollBarVisibility="Visible"
               Grid.Row="4" Grid.Column="1" Grid.ColumnSpan="3">

          </ListBox>
     </Grid>
</UserControl>
```

The code doesn't show anything new; it binds a specific property of the corresponding ViewModel to each TextBox of the UserControl, and binds the collection of Role entities associated with the Employee entity exposed by the CurrentEntity property of the ViewModel class to the Listbox. The Role collection has not been wrapped around the ViewModel because it is read-only, so you don't need to add any further abstraction. Now let's modify the NavigationService class and, of course, the corresponding interface so we can pass to the details View a selected ViewModel or a new one when creating a new Employee (see Listing 7-15).

Listing 7-15. NavigationService Method to Open a Details View

```
public Window ShowEmployeeDetailsWindow(object ViewModel)
{
    var window = Container.Resolve<EmployeeDetailsView>();
    window.DataContext = ViewModel;
    window.ShowDialog();
    return window;
}
```

Employee List

The next ViewModel to create is the EmployeeListViewModel (see Listing 7-16), which will expose the following objects:

- A search string that will contain the search text entered by the user.

- Four ICommand objects that will expose the four commands available in this View.

- An IUnityContainer interface that will be used to resolve the dependencies of the ViewModel.

Listing 7-16. *EmployeeListViewModel (First Part)*

```
using System.Collections.Generic;
using System.Linq;
using System.Windows.Input;
using APRESS.TimeTracking.BusinessLayer;
using APRESS.TimeTracking.DataLayer;
using APRESS.TimeTracking.Services;
using Microsoft.Practices.Unity;

namespace APRESS.TimeTracking.ViewModels
{
    public class EmployeeListViewModel : BaseListViewModel<Employee>
    {
        // dependencies resolved with the IoC container
        private readonly IUnityContainer container;
        private readonly IDialogService dialogService;
        private INavigationService navigationService;
        private EmployeeRepository repository;
        private string searchCriteria = string.Empty;

        public EmployeeListViewModel(IUnityContainer container) :
            base(new List<BaseDetailsViewModel<Employee>>())
        {
            this.container = container;
            ResolveDependencies();
            InitializeCommands();
        }

        public string SearchCriteria
        {
            get { return searchCriteria; }
            set
            {
                searchCriteria = value;
                OnPropertyChanged(vm => SearchCriteria);
            }
        }

        public ICommand SearchCommand { get; private set; }

        public ICommand NewCommand { get; private set; }

        public ICommand EditCommand { get; private set; }

        public ICommand DeleteCommand { get; private set; }
```

```
        private void ResolveDependencies()
        {
            repository = container.Resolve<EmployeeRepository>();
            navigationService = container.Resolve<INavigationService>();
        }

        private void InitializeCommands()
        {
            // in the next chapter we will implement the
            // code to create the commands here
        }
    }
}
```

The EmployeeListViewModel has three dependencies, the INavigationService service, the
IDialogService service, and the EmployeeRepository class; they can be all resolved using the unity
container that's already set up in the application's app.xaml.cs file. Because the ViewModel is created by
the IOC container too, you can simply inject in its constructor an instance of the interface
IunityContainer, which will be automatically injected and resolved at runtime.

When the constructor receives the IOC container instance, it tries to resolve the dependencies and
assign a value to the private fields that expose the services and the repository.

The other five properties are a string that represents the search criteria, which will be bound to the
TextBox exposed in the View, and four ICommand objects, which we will explore in the next chapter. For
now, you just need to know that they represent the commands executed in the UI.

The final step is to move back to the app.xaml.cs file and modify the code from Listing 7-13. The
reason for doing this is to test the changes—we want to make the EmployeeListView the startup View and
to change the way the ViewModel is injected in the View (see Listing 7-17).

Listing 7-17. App.xaml.cs Changes to Bootstrap the EmployeeListView.xaml

```
// App.xaml.cs
private void ConfigureContainer()
{
    ...
    // new registrations
    container.RegisterType<IUnitOfWork, UnitOfWork>();
    container.RegisterType<EmployeeRepository>();
    container.RegisterType<EmployeesListView>();
    navigation = container.Resolve<INavigationService>();
}

protected override void OnStartup(StartupEventArgs e)
{
    base.OnStartup(e);
    // init the NavigationService class
    Window employeesView = navigation.ShowEmployeesListView();
}
```

```
// NavigationService.cs
public Window ShowEmployeesListView()
{
    var window = Container.Resolve<EmployeesListView>();
    var ViewModel = Container.Resolve<EmployeeListViewModel>();
    window.DataContext = ViewModel;
    window.Show();
    return window;
}
```

Now if you press F5 the application will start up showing you the `EmployeeListView` window with an empty `Datagrid` and a search `TextBox`. But first, let's bind the ViewModel properties to the View (see Listing 7-18).

Listing 7-18. *Binding the* `EmployeeListView`

```xml
<Window x:Class="APRESS.TimeTracking.Views.EmployeesListView"
        xmlns="http://schemas.microsoft.com/winfx/2006/xaml/presentation"
        xmlns:x="http://schemas.microsoft.com/winfx/2006/xaml" xmlns:Controls="clr-
namespace:APRESS.TimeTracking.Controls" Title="EmployeesListView" Height="320" Width="505">
    <DockPanel>
        <TextBlock DockPanel.Dock="Top" Style="{StaticResource TitleBlock}">TimeTracker
 Employees List</TextBlock>
        <StackPanel Margin="5" MinHeight="30" HorizontalAlignment="Center"
Orientation="Horizontal" DockPanel.Dock="Top">
            <Label Style="{StaticResource ControlLabel}">Search Employees: </Label>
            <TextBox Margin="3"></TextBox>
            <Controls:ImageButton
                    HorizontalAlignment="Right"
                    Padding="3"
                    Margin="3"
                    Text="Search"
                    ClickCommand="{Binding Path=SearchCommand}"
                    Image="{DynamicResource SearchSmall}" />
        </StackPanel>
        <StackPanel Margin="5" MinHeight="30" HorizontalAlignment="Right"
Orientation="Horizontal" DockPanel.Dock="Bottom">
            <Controls:ImageButton
                    Padding="3"
                    Text="New"
                    Image="{DynamicResource NewSmall}"/>
            <Controls:ImageButton
                    Padding="3"
                    ClickCommand="Open"
                    Text="Edit"
                    Image="{DynamicResource EditSmall}" />
            <Controls:ImageButton
                    Padding="3"
                    Text="Delete"
                    Image="{DynamicResource CloseSmall}" />
        </StackPanel>
```

```
        <DataGrid Margin="5" DockPanel.Dock="Bottom"
                ItemsSource="{Binding Path=Collection}"
                SelectedItem="{Binding Path=Selected}"
                AutoGenerateColumns="False">
            <DataGrid.Columns>
                <DataGridTextColumn
                    Binding="{Binding Path=Title}"
                    Header="Title" Width="50" />
                <DataGridTextColumn
                    Binding="{Binding Path=FirstName}"
                    Header="First Name" Width="120" />
                <DataGridTextColumn
                    Binding="{Binding Path=LastName}"
                    Header="Last Name" Width="120" />
                <DataGridTextColumn
                    Binding="{Binding Path=DateOfBirth, StringFormat={}{0:MMM/dd/yyyy}}"
                    Header="Date of Birth" Width="120" />
            </DataGrid.Columns>
        </DataGrid>
    </DockPanel>
</Window>
```

A `BaseListViewModel` exposes only two properties, the collection of `DetailsViewModel<T>` that's represented by the property `Collection`, and the current item that's exposed by the property `Selected`; you bind both properties to the `DataGrid` and every time you select a new row in the grid, the `EmployeeListViewModel` receives a notification from the View and updates the current selected item.

Additional ViewModels and Properties

The `EmployeeDetailsView` requires, of course, additional `ViewModels`. For example, you need a `ListViewModel` for the list of contacts and one for the list of addresses, and you also need to show a list of appointments. Each `BaseListViewModel<T>` also requires a corresponding detail `BaseDetailsViewModel`.

You've seen how to create details and list ViewModel classes. Unfortunately, for reasons of space, we can't show the code for creating each ViewModel object in this book, However, if you understand the process used to create the combination details/list ViewModel, you should be able to create the remaining ViewModels by yourself.

Here are the additional ViewModels you'll need to create:

- Contact entity:

    - ContactDetailsViewModel

    - ContactListViewModel

- Address entity:

    - AddressDetailsViewModel

    - AddressListViewModel

- Appointment entity:
    - AppointmentDetailsViewModel
    - AppointmentListViewModel
- Customer entity:
    - CustomerDetailsViewModel
    - CustomerListViewModel
- MainViewModel (MainView)

Figure 7-6 shows the final resulting graph that contains all the required ViewModels.

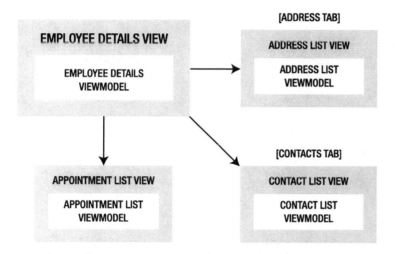

Figure 7-6. *The complete ViewModels graph*

Collection of Child ViewModels

Figure 7-7 shows, for an `Employee` details ViewModel and for a `Customer` details ViewModel, three child collections, each composed of a `ListViewModel`, So, for instance, for a collection of `Contact` entities, the `EmployeeDetailsViewModel` will expose a property of type `ContactListViewModel` that will then be bound to a list container like a `ListBox` control. The code in Listing 7-19 is a trick used with the LINQ extension methods to transform the `EntitySet<T>` collection exposed by the Entity Framework to a list of details ViewModel.

Listing 7-19. *Aggregate Function Used to Transform a Collection of Objects*

```
public AddressListViewModel Addresses
{
    get
    {
        return new AddressListViewModel(
            CurrentEntity.Addresses.Aggregate(
                new List<BaseDetailsViewModel<Address>>(),
                (list, item) =>
                    {
                        list.Add(new AddressDetailsViewModel(item));
                        return list;
                    }));
    }
    set
    {
        CurrentEntity.Addresses =
            value.Collection.Aggregate(
                new EntityCollection<Address>(),
                (list, item) =>
                    {
                        list.Add(item.CurrentEntity);
                        return list;
                    });
        OnPropertyChanged(vm => Addresses);
    }
}
```

This code uses the `Aggregate` extension method to transform a list of `EntityCollection<Address>` to an `AddressListViewModel`; the `Aggregate` function works by using a delegate that iterates over each item of the collection and returns a new type of collection, which must be specified in the `Aggregate` method.

In the set part of the property you do the inverse operation. In this case, you simply associate the list of `ViewModels` back to the `Address` collection using the `Aggregate` function with a different signature. A sample result is shown in Figure 7-7.

Now you can create a `UserControl` for each of these collection properties in the `EmployeeDetailsView`, bind the collection to a `Listbox`, for example, and create a custom `DataTemplate`. Remember also that in Listing 7-19, for example, you are associating a `ListViewModel` of child objects to the `ViewModel` so you can bind not only the collection of child objects but also the currently selected child item.

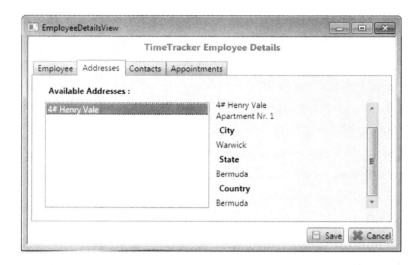

Figure 7-7. *Data Bind Result for the* **Address** *Collection*

Summary

WPF (and Silverlight) exposes a new way of displaying the data and behaviors of objects to the UI by using a technology known as data binding. With this technology you can bind complex objects to the UI and specify templates and behaviors in the UI using rules and styles.

In order to make an object bindable to a WPF UI, you need to implement the `INotifyPropertyChanged` interface, which exposes an event `PropertyChanged` that is able to inform and update the WPF View when something happen between the View and the object bound to it.

The WPF engine is able to translate a value using different data types based on the value converter applied to the bound object; you can also specify a custom value converter in the binding expression and create a custom one by implementing the interface `IValueConverter`.

To use all the power of the data binding exposed by WPF, you have to implement `DataTemplate` objects; with these objects you can radically change the way a specific UI item will appear and behave in the application, depending on the object and the values bound to it.

In the second part of this chapter, you saw how to create a specific `ViewModel` hierarchy and how to make `ViewModel`s interactive with other related `ViewModel`s. You saw how to do that specifically for the `Employee` views; you can try to do the same with the `Customer` views and test the results by tweaking the code in the `App.xaml.cs` file.

CHAPTER 8

■ ■ ■

Command Handling and Event Routing

If you've ever worked with a client technology like Windows Forms or Java Forms, you may already know how the mechanism of reacting to a user request is achieved: you create a control in the UI, the control exposes several **Events** and you listen these events by creating an event handler, which is nothing more than a method with some code inside to handle input to the program.

The downside of using this approach is that you can't recycle and test the code executed in an event handler, and you can't make the relationship between the UI element and the corresponding event handler method dynamic.

WPF exposes a number of predefined events, so for every UI element you can use a set of events available through the Events tab of the Properties panel in Visual Studio, as shown in Figure 8-1.

Figure 8-1. Events tab on Visual Studio 2010

In this case, you can associate an event handler to a `Button` control for when the user presses the button. In the method, you then execute some specific code. Of course the separation of concerns in this case is not satisfied because the code that includes the execution logic of the event is stored in the code-behind file of the WPF XAML file, and the object that invokes the method through an event can't be separated from the event itself. This example, for instance, forces WPF to associate the `Click` event of the `Button` control to a `Click_Button` method.

Introduction to Commands

The Command pattern was not introduced with WPF or Silverlight. Instead, the command-handling technique is a behavioral pattern first presented in the "Gang of Four" book *Design Patterns: Elements of Reusable Object-Oriented Software* by Erich Gamma, Richard Helm, Ralph Johnson, and John Vlissides (Addison-Wesley, 1994). It describes how the logic of a request should be encapsulated in a separate object.

The goal is to separate the semantics and object that invoke a command from the logic that executes the command, so that the same command can be used over different UI elements without having to rewrite the execution logic. For example, the classic commands you may find in a word processing application are `Copy`, `Cut`, and `Paste`. In Microsoft Office Word, you can call these commands in three different ways:

- From the `Edit` menu.

- From the `Context` menu.

- Using keyboard combinations such Ctrl+X, Ctrl+V and so on.

What it is important here is that you would not want to have to write the logic of executing a Cut command more than once, so all of these methods actually execute the same code.

An object of type `Command` can tell you when it can be executed and when it can't. For instance, in Microsoft Office Word, the command `Cut` is disabled until you select some text, but as soon as you select some text, the application triggers the command, saying something like: "*Hey Cut command, look ! Now there's some text selected so you can be executed. Also, you UI element, you can be enabled.*" Of course, this is a funny interpretation of how Word works behind the scene, but in the end, this is what is happening.

The Command Pattern

The Command pattern is a behavioral design pattern; this means its purpose is to describe how to solve a specific behavioral problem associated with an object—in this case, how to separate a request by creating a specific object that represents the request and the information needed by the request. The command pattern is typically used when the request can be invoked by a different client and received by a different receiver. Figure 8-2 shows the class diagram of a command design pattern implemented using Visual Studio and C#.

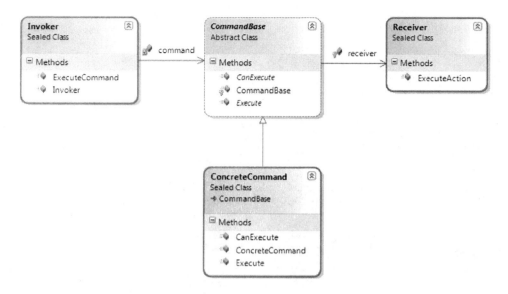

Figure 8-2. *Class diagram of a Command pattern implementation*

The Command is invoked by an Invoker through a standardized method, ExecuteCommand. Inside the method, the Invoker verifies that the command can be executed by calling the CanExecute method of the command object. If the method returns true, the Invoker then call the Execute method of the Command. The Command, inside the Execute method implementation, calls the Receiver.ExecuteAction method so that the receiver method is not standardized as a global command, loosely coupled from the receiver object.

In the original implementation of the Command pattern, the CanExecute method was not introduced and the execution logic was inside the Command object itself. In WPF, the Command pattern has been reinterpreted to satisfy the technology requirements of having a command object that is able to notify about its ability to be executed in a specific context.

Command in WPF

If you are not using any specific design patterns applied to WPF, such as Model View ViewModel (MVVM) or Model View Presenter (MVP), you can still use the core structure of WPF to implement a WPF command, also known as a RoutedCommand. The RoutedCommand is a custom command class available in the System.Windows.Input namespace, and it defines a command object that implements the ICommand interface and that is routed through the entire WPF element tree.

ICommand is a .NET interface that emulates the command pattern by exposing methods such as Execute and CanExecute, and by providing a CanExecuteChanged event that is triggered to re-evaluate the execution of the command. Listing 8-1 shows the decompiled C# code for the ICommand interface.

Listing 8-1. ICommand and RoutedCommand Objects

```
public interface ICommand
{
    // Events
    event EventHandler CanExecuteChanged;

    // Methods
    bool CanExecute(object parameter);
    void Execute(object parameter);
}
```

You can, for example, create a custom Command by implementing the ICommand interface and binding it to a WPF view. Figure 8-3 shows the flow used by WPF to route a command through the UI structure.

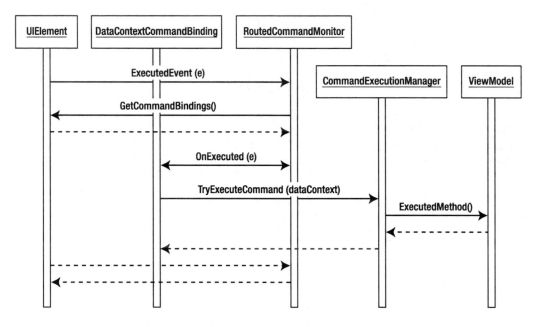

Figure 8-3. Routed Command UI flow

The RoutedCommand Class

WPF can help you use the commands because it provides a set of predefined commands exposed by the ApplicationCommands class. Each of these commands is a RoutedCommand type and can be used in any UI element that supports the ICommand interface.

A RoutedCommand object exposes the Execute and CanExecute methods, which don't contain the application logic for the command. As you would do with an ICommand object implementation, these methods raise events able to traverse the element tree looking for an object with a CommandBinding in order to find the corresponding binding. In the binding, you define the implementations for Execute and

CanExecute. The Execute method raises the PreviewExecuted and Executed events. The CanExecute method raises the PreviewCanExecute and CanExecute events.

You can define a RoutedCommand for a WPF element in two different ways. In the first way you have to explicitly declare and bind the Execute and CanExecute implementations of the command in the XAML and in the code-behind, as in Listing 8-2.

Listing 8-2. Explicit Implementation of Execute and CanExecute

```
// MainWindow.xaml.cs
using System.Windows;
using System.Windows.Input;

namespace CommandHandling
{
    public partial class MainWindow : Window
    {
        public static RoutedCommand CustomCommand = new RoutedCommand();

        public MainWindow()
        {
            InitializeComponent();
        }

        private void CustomExecuted(object sender, ExecutedRoutedEventArgs e)
        {

        }

        private void CustomCanExecute(object sender, CanExecuteRoutedEventArgs e)
        {
            e.CanExecute = true;
        }
    }
}

<-- MainWindow.xaml -->
<Window x:Class="CommandHandling.MainWindow"
        xmlns="http://schemas.microsoft.com/winfx/2006/xaml/presentation"
        xmlns:x="http://schemas.microsoft.com/winfx/2006/xaml"
        xmlns:my="clr-namespace:CommandHandling"
        Title="MainWindow" Height="350" Width="525">
    <Grid>
        <StackPanel.CommandBindings>
            <CommandBinding
                Command="{x:Static my:MainWindow.CustomCommand}"
                Executed="CustomExecuted"
                CanExecute="CustomCanExecute" />
        </StackPanel.CommandBindings>
```

```
        <Button
            Command="{x:Static my:MainWindow.CustomCommand}">
            Classic Routed
        </Button>
    </StackPanel>
  </Grid>
</Window>
```

Listing 8-2 declares a `static` `RoutedCommand` in the code-behind file so that you can access a static resource in the XAML file. The code then declares two methods that respectively implement the `ExecutedRoutedEventArgs` and the `CanExecuteRoutedEventArgs`.

In the XAML file, in the `StackPanel` `CommandBinding` collection, the code created a new command binding associated with the custom `RoutedCommand` created previously, and then bound the `RoutedCommand` to a `Button`. If you now change the code inside the `CanExecute` method and assign a value of false to the event arguments, which means that the command can't be executed, the corresponding UI element will be disabled.

A second and faster way of associating a new `RoutedCommand` to a UI element is to create the `CommandBinding` association in the code-behind file and declare *on the fly* a new `RoutedCommand`, including the `Execute` and `CanExecute` methods, by using the anonymous delegate and lambda expression techniques.

■ **Note** With the anonymous delegate technique introduced in NET 2, you can pass a piece of code to an object as a delegate parameter. With this technique, you can create on the fly a delegate method without needing to declare the delegate method itself.

The following code shows two different ways of creating a delegate method, with and without the anonymous delegate technique:

```
// without the anonymous delegate
button.Click += Click_Delegate;
public void Click_Delegate(object sender, EventArgs args)
{ // custom code }

// with the anonymous delegate
button.Click += (sender, args) => { // custom code };
```

In this case, let's use one of the available `ApplicationCommands`, `RoutedCommand`, so you don't need to declare a `RoutedCommand` object in the code-behind file (see Listing 8-3). This doesn't mean that the custom implementation of the `ICommand` interface is useless. On the contrary, the custom implementation of this interface lets you have more loosely coupled control over the command implementation rather than being forced to use the `RoutedCommand` class.

Listing 8-3. Button Using ApplicationCommands

```
<Button Command="ApplicationCommands.Copy" Content="Copy text" />
```

Then you create a new `CommandBinding` in the code-behind file by using the anonymous delegate in the constructor of the window object as shown in Listing 8-4.

Listing 8-4. CommandBinding with Anonymous Delegate

```
public MainWindow()
{
    InitializeComponent();
    this.CommandBindings.Add(
        new CommandBinding(ApplicationCommands.Copy,
            (sender, args) =>
                {
                    MessageBox.Show("Copy command");
                },
            (sender, args) =>
                {
                    args.CanExecute = true;
                }));
}
```

With this technique you don't need to implement a custom `ICommand` object for each command in the UI, and you don't need to declare the `RoutedCommand` binding association in the XAML file so that the view and the code-behind file are more separated.

Of course, this is not the only technique available, and it actually isn't feasible with the Model View ViewModel pattern we want to apply to the TimeTracker application. In fact, in the previous chapter we exposed in the ViewModel some properties of type `ICommand`.

Implement the ICommand Interface

While a good approach to using a command in a WPF application is to recycle the existing `RoutedCommands` objects exposed by the `ApplicationCommands` class or to create a new instance of a `RoutedCommand`, sometimes you may need to create a more generic and flexible command object that can execute and include business logic code not available from a common `RoutedCommand` object.

Figure 8-4 shows how the `ICommand` custom object will be integrated in the WPF command mechanism.

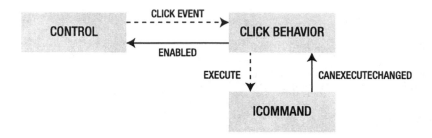

Figure 8-4. ICommand interface implementation schema

The code in Listing 8-5 introduces what in the MVVM community is called a `RelayCommand`, a generic implementation of the `ICommand` design pattern that, like `RoutedCommand`, can be used throughout a WPF application. The main difference is that a `RelayCommand` (which we will call `MvvmCommand`) can be extended to compensate for some lacks in the classic WPF command object.

Listing 8-5. MvvmCommand Interface Implementation

```csharp
using System;
using System.Windows.Input;

namespace CommandHandling
{
    public sealed class MvvmCommand : ICommand
    {
        #region Implementation of ICommand

        public void Execute(object parameter)
        {
            throw new NotImplementedException();
        }

        public bool CanExecute(object parameter)
        {
            throw new NotImplementedException();
        }

        public event EventHandler CanExecuteChanged;

        #endregion
    }
}
```

Listing 8-5 shows the classic implementation of the `ICommand` interface; you need to provide a method for the `Execute` implementation, one for the `CanExecute`, and an event that is raised when the `CanExecute` evaluation happens.

First you need to implement the custom logic to evaluate and execute a command. In the
MvvmCommand you need to provide the method to handle the CanExecuteChanged event and the
implementation of Execute and CanExecute, by using generic and lambda expressions so that the
MvvmCommand implementation can remain generic. See Listing 8-6.

Listing 8-6. MvvmCommand Concrete Implementation

```
private Action<object> execute = null;

private Func<object, bool> canExecute = null;

public MvvmCommand(Action<object> execute, Func<object, bool> canExecute)
{
    this.execute = execute;
    this.canExecute = canExecute;
}

public void OnCanExecuteChanged()
{
    EventHandler handler = CanExecuteChanged;
    if (handler != null)
    {
        CanExecuteChanged(this, EventArgs.Empty);
    }
}
```

The Action<T> represents a generic delegate that will contains the code to execute, the Func<T,
bool> represents a Boolean function that contains the code to enable/disable the command and the
associated UI element. OnCanExecuteChanged is the method used to raise the CanExecuteChanged event.
The last step is to associate the Action<T> and the Func<T, bool> to the corresponding ICommand
methods, as shown in Listing 8-7.

Listing 8-7. Associating Action<T> and Func<T, bool> to ICommand

```
public void Execute(object parameter)
{
    if (this.execute != null)
    {
        this.execute(parameter);
    }
}

public bool CanExecute(object parameter)
{
    if (this.canExecute == null)
    {
        return true;
    }
    return this.canExecute(parameter);
}
```

The first part of Listing 8-7 simply calls Action<T> by passing the parameter (if available) of the command and executing the method. The second part of the code verifies whether Func<T, bool> is null and, if it is null, simply enables the command or verifies that the expression is satisfied.

Listing 8-8 shows how you can create the MvvmCommand command in a XAML window.

Listing 8-8. MvvmCommand Code-behind Implementation

```
// code-behind file
public partial class MainWindow : Window
    {
        public static ICommand MvvmCommand = new MvvmCommand(
                (parameter) => MessageBox.Show("Mvvm Command"),
                (parameter) => true);

        public MainWindow()
        {
            InitializeComponent();
        }
    }

// XAML file
<Button
    Command="{x:Static my:MainWindow.MvvmCommand}">
    Mvvm Command
</Button>
```

Interactive Command, Listen for Changes

What you've done so far is pretty cool, flexible, and testable—you created a generic MvvmCommand, exposed it as an ICommand interface object, and declared the code to execute and to evaluate the execution using the anonymous delegate, which is also fancy and pretty readable.

At this point, you can probably try to create a basic ViewModel object that exposes a couple of properties and an ICommand property, like the one in Listing 8-9, and bind these properties to a View. What you want to do is to enable the FormatCommand property only if the text in the TextBox is not null.

Listing 8-9 shows the ViewModel created for this example. You know already what an ObservableObject<T> is and what an MvvmCommand is.

Listing 8-9. FormatViewModel Object

```
public sealed class FormatViewModel : ObservableObject<FormatViewModel>
{
    private string formattedText;
    private string originalText;
```

```csharp
public FormatViewModel()
{
    FormatCommand = new MvvmCommand(
        (parameter) => { FormatText(); },
        (parameter) => { return !string.IsNullOrEmpty(OriginalText); });
}

public ICommand FormatCommand { get; private set; }

public string OriginalText
{
    get { return originalText; }
    set
    {
        originalText = value;
        OnPropertyChanged(vm => vm.OriginalText);
    }
}

public string FormattedText
{
    get { return formattedText; }
    set
    {
        formattedText = value;
        OnPropertyChanged(vm => vm.FormattedText);
    }
}

private void FormatText()
{
    FormattedText = string.Format("Formatted: {0}", OriginalText);
}
}
```

This `ViewModel` object is pretty simple. It provides two string properties—original text and result text, formatted. The `ICommand` is enabled only if the `OriginalText` property is not null or empty.

Listing 8-10 is the corresponding XAML markup that binds the UI elements to the `ViewModel` properties.

Listing 8-10. FormatView.xaml and FormatView.xaml.cs

```xml
<!-- FormatText.xaml -->
<Window x:Class="CommandHandling.FormatText"
        xmlns="http://schemas.microsoft.com/winfx/2006/xaml/presentation"
        xmlns:x="http://schemas.microsoft.com/winfx/2006/xaml"
        Title="FormatText" Height="226" Width="272">
    <StackPanel>
        <Label
            Margin="5"
            Content="Original Text :" />
```

```
        <TextBox
            Margin="5" Width="200"
            Text="{Binding OriginalText, UpdateSourceTrigger=PropertyChanged}" />
        <Label
            Margin="5"
            Content="Formatted Text :" />
        <TextBox
            Margin="5" Width="200"
            Text="{Binding FormattedText, UpdateSourceTrigger=PropertyChanged}" />
        <Button
            Margin="5" Width="100"
            Command="{Binding FormatCommand}"
            Content="Format the Text" />
    </StackPanel>
</Window>

// FormatText.xaml.cs
using System.Windows;
using CommandHandling.Mvvm;

namespace CommandHandling
{
    /// <summary>
    /// Interaction logic for FormatText.xaml
    /// </summary>
    public partial class FormatText : Window
    {
        public FormatText()
        {
            InitializeComponent();
            DataContext = new FormatViewModel();
        }
    }
}
```

If you press F5, the application starts and the format command is disabled as expected. After you insert some text in the first TextBox, you discover that MvvmCommand has a bug—it stays disabled, as it does as well if there's text in the OriginalText property. Why does this happen?

The CanExecute method of an ICommand object is executed only when the data-binding engine creates the binding between the UI element and the command; then, the command execution is re-evaluated only if something changes and the CommandManager is listening for that change. This means that when you change the text in the TextBox, the CommandManager is unaware of the change and it doesn't update the command so the Button stays disabled.

If the code was not in a ViewModel but in the code-behind of a specific Window or UserControl, you could call the static method CommandManager.InvalidateRequerySuggested method, which raises the RequerySuggested event that re-evaluates all the commands inside the CommandManager. Unfortunately, if you call this method inside the ViewModel object, it doesn't work because you don't have access directly to the View CommandManager object.

Another big disadvantage of using CommandManager is that it doesn't re-evaluate just the execution of one command; instead it re-evaluates all the commands attached to the CommandBinding collection.

One alternative is to manually re-evaluate the command every time the OriginalText property changes, as shown in Listing 8-11.

Listing 8-11. *Manual Re-evaluation of the ICommand Property*

```
public string OriginalText
{
    get { return originalText; }
    set
    {
        originalText = value;
        OnPropertyChanged(vm => vm.OriginalText);
        (FormatCommand as MvvmCommand).OnCanExecuteChanged();
    }
}
```

Now if you run the application, the Button is enabled and then disabled, depending on the content of the OriginalText property. Of course, here we've solved the problem of re-evaluating the command, but can you imagine what would happen if instead of having one command you had ten and you had to re-evaluate all of them for each property of the ViewModel? In the next section you will see how to dynamically re-evaluate the execution of a command.

Attach Listeners to an ICommand

Each ViewModel and, more generally, each object that is bound to a WPF DataContext, should implement the INotifyPropertyChanged interface and raise a PropertyChanged event every time the value of one of its properties changes. Now you know that the command should be triggered when a PropertyChanged event is raised.

Figure 8-5 shows how the ICommand and the INotifyPropertyChanged interfaces flow together.

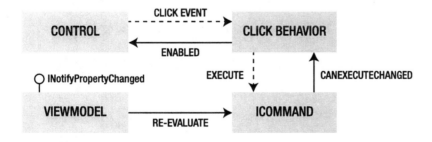

Figure 8-5. *ICommand with INotifyPropertyChanged interaction*

First let's look at how the event model works in C# and, more generally, in .NET. When using a normal event, registering an event handler creates a strong reference from the event source to the listening object, and this strong reference can cause a memory leak—especially when the source object has a longer lifetime than the listener. The only way to avoid this behavior is to manually unsubscribe the listener from the source object so that the resources are free. In C# you can do this by using the -= syntax. But there's another interesting solution, one that uses the WeakEvent, a special type of event manager that is able to automatically free unused resources.

The code in Listing 8-12 uses a WeakEventManager object, introduced in WPF, to manage an event automatically. The WeakEventManager is event-specific, and you have to create an instance of it for each event type you want to listen for. The WeakEventManager provides a base class for managing weak events according to the weak event pattern. This type of manager lets you control the way you add and remove listeners from the manager.

Listing 8-12. Generic WeakEventListener for WPF

```
using System;
using System.Windows;

namespace CommandHandling
{
    public sealed class GenericWeakEventManager<TEventArgs>
        : IWeakEventListener where TEventArgs : EventArgs
    {
        EventHandler<TEventArgs> realHander;

        public GenericWeakEventManager(EventHandler<TEventArgs> handler)
        {
            if (handler == null)
            {
                throw new ArgumentNullException("handler");
            }

            this.realHander = handler;
        }

        bool IWeakEventListener.ReceiveWeakEvent(Type managerType, Object sender, EventArgs
e)
        {
            TEventArgs realArgs = (TEventArgs)e;

            this.realHander(sender, realArgs);

            return true;
        }
    }
}
```

Listing 8-12 creates a new generic WeakEventListener that can listen for any event that inherits from the System.EventArgs class, which is the base class for any event handler's argument object in NET. It then manually implements the IWeakEventListener interface, which exposes a single method— ReceiveWeakEvent. This method simply intercepts the event and fires the corresponding handler (method) associated with the event. The interface has to be manually implemented in order to be used properly in WPF with the WeakEventManager component.

The IWeakEventListener.ReceiveWeakEvent is not required and not used in this code, but it is required by the IWeakEventManager interface, so it has to be included it in our sample code.

The constructor attaches the handler to listen to the private generic field EventHandler<TEventArgs>. Now let's modify the MvvmCommand enable it to listen for specific properties of a ViewModel (see Listing 8-13).

Listing 8-13. *Inside the MvvmCommand*

```
// reference a specific WeakEvent manager
private GenericWeakEventManager<PropertyChangedEventArgs> weakEventListener =
   new GenericWeakEventManager<PropertyChangedEventArgs>(this.RequeryCanExecute);;

//create an handler for the INotifyPropertyChanged
private void RequeryCanExecute(object sender, PropertyChangedEventArgs
 propertyChangedEventArgs)
{
    OnCanExecuteChanged();
}

//create a new constructor that will add a listener
public MvvmCommand(
    Action<object> execute,
    Func<object, bool> canExecute,
    INotifyPropertyChanged source, string propertyName)
    : base(execute, canExecute)
{
    PropertyChangedEventManager.AddListener(source, this.weakEventListener, propertyName);
}
```

Two pieces of information are passed in the constructor of the MvvmCommand; one is the object that implements the INotifyPropertyChanged interface that will listen for changes and the other is the specific property you want to listen for changes. Then you associate the WeakEventListener to the static PropertyChangedEventManager, which is the static WeakEvent manager object provided by WPF for the PropertyChangedEventHandler class. Finally, you inform the weakEventListener that every time the specific property is changed it has to trigger the method RequeryCanExecute.

Now, by refactoring the MvvmCommand a little, you end up with the final result shown in Listing 8-14.

Listing 8-14. *Refactored MvvmCommand*

```
// usage
FormatCommand = new MvvmCommand(
    (parameter) => { FormatText(); },
    (parameter) => { return !string.IsNullOrEmpty(OriginalText); })
    .AddListener<FormatViewModel>(this, x => x.OriginalText)
    .AddListener<FormatViewModel>(this, x => x.FormattedText);
```

```
// inside the MvvmCommand we return the current command object
// by doing this we can chain multiple calls to AddListener together
public MvvmCommand AddListener<TEntity>(INotifyPropertyChanged source,↵
 Expression<Func<TEntity, object>> property)
{
    string propertyName = GetPropertyName(property);
    PropertyChangedEventManager.AddListener(source, weakEventListener, propertyName);
    return this;
}

// Lambda expression translator method
private string GetPropertyName<TEntity>(Expression<Func<TEntity, object>> expression)
{
    var lambda = expression as LambdaExpression;
    MemberExpression memberExpression;
    if (lambda.Body is UnaryExpression)
    {
        var unaryExpression = lambda.Body as UnaryExpression;
        memberExpression = unaryExpression.Operand as MemberExpression;
    }
    else
    {
        memberExpression = lambda.Body as MemberExpression;
    }
    var constantExpression = memberExpression.Expression as ConstantExpression;
    var propertyInfo = memberExpression.Member as PropertyInfo;
    return propertyInfo.Name;
}
```

TimeTracker Commands

In this chapter you've seen how the RoutedCommand works in WPF and what WPF provides out of the box without any need to implement a custom class. Unfortunately, the RoutedCommand is not flexible enough to be used in an MVVM application like TimeTracker where the presentation logic is driven around the ViewModel object.

In the previous chapter you started to create the ViewModels for each view, and added an ICommand property for each command available in the View. With that foundation, you should now be able to complete the EmployeeList/EmployeeDetails combination and make this first part of the application fully functional. It will be then up to you to continue the application by implementing the same logic for the Customer List/Details combination, or you can simply take a look at the source code to view the fully functional project.

In Chapter 12 we will look at the ViewModel class in more depth, at how it works and how it should be implemented. For now, let's just focus on the ICommand object that will be exposed by a ViewModel.

The EmployeeListView

First of all you need to replicate the ICommand implementation from the first part of this chapter in the TimeTracker application. If you created a custom application following the first part of the chapter and you don't want to rewrite the two classes involved (MvvmCommand and the generic

GenericWeakEventManager), you can add them to the TimeTracker WPF project by right-clicking the project and choosing Add existing item. Then select those two files from the project.

After this step you should have the objects shown in Figure 8-6 in the TimeTracker application.

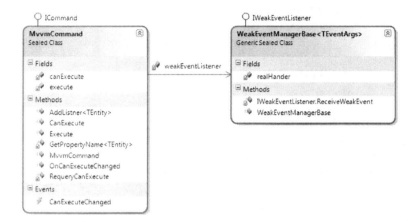

Figure 8-6. *MvvmCommand implementation with GenericWeakEventManager*

Search for an Employee

The EmployeeListViewModel object has a method called InitializeCommands where you will initialize the four commands. The first one is the SearchCommand that should be enabled only if there is some text in the search TextBox, so that the user will not accidentally fire a full search on the entire database. See Listing 8-15.

Listing 8-15. *SearchCommand and SearchMethod*

```
// SearchCommand initialization inside the InitializeCommands method
SearchCommand = new MvvmCommand(
    (parameter) =>
        {
            this.SearchEmployees();
        },
    (parameter) =>
        {
            return !string.IsNullOrEmpty(this.SearchCriteria);
        }
    )
    .AddListener<EmployeeListViewModel>(this, x => x.SearchCriteria);

//SearchEmployees method
private void SearchEmployees()
{
    List<Employee> result = repository.SearchEmployees(SearchCriteria);
```

```
        if (result == null || result.Count == 0)
        {
            dialogService.ShowAlert("No Employees found.", "There are no Employees using
    the following criteria.");
            return;
        }
        Collection.Clear();
        foreach (var employee in result)
        {
            Collection.Add(new EmployeeDetailsViewModel(employee));
        }
}
```

The implementation of the search method is pretty simple; you attach a WeakEvent to the SearchCommand so that if the TextBox is not empty the SearchButton will be enabled. The search method is calling the EmployeeRepository object to search for any employee that matches the search criteria. If there are no such employees, you advise the user by popping up a MessageBox using the IDialogService service.

Select and Edit an Employee

The next step is to select an employee from the grid and edit the entry using the EmployeeDetailsView. In this case, the EditCommand should be enabled only when a row in the grid is selected. If the grid doesn't have any row, the EditCommand should be disabled, as in Listing 8-16.

Listing 8-16. EditEmployee Command Implementation

```
// InitializeCommands
EditCommand = new MvvmCommand(
    (parameter) =>
        {
            this.EditCurrentEmployee();
        },
    (parameter) =>
        {
            return this.Selected != null;
        }
    )
    .AddListener<EmployeeListViewModel>(this, x => x.Selected != null);

// EditCurrentEmployee method
private void EditCurrentEmployee()
{
    navigationService.ShowEmployeeDetailsWindow(Selected);
}
```

In this case, you are checking that no employee is selected in the grid. If that's the case, you should disable the editing process as the EmployeeDetailsView will receive a null ViewModel. The trigger for the command is the Selected property that is bound to the SelectedItem property of the Datagrid.

Delete an Employee

The last step is to delete an employee in the grid if one is selected and if the user also presses yes in the confirmation message he receives (see Listing 8-17).

Listing 8-17. Delete a Selected Employee

```
// InitializeCommands
DeleteCommand = new MvvmCommand(
    (parameter) => { DeleteCurrentEmployee(); },
    (parameter) => { return Selected != null; }
    ).AddListener<EmployeeListViewModel>(this, x => x.Selected);

// Delete with Confirmation
private void DeleteCurrentEmployee()
{
    if (Selected == null)
    {
        dialogService.ShowAlert("No Employee selected.", "There are no employees
selected.");
        return;
    }
    bool canDelete = dialogService.AskConfirmation("Delete Employee",
                                        "Do you want to delete the current
employee?");
    if (canDelete)
    {
        try
        {
            unitOfWork.StartTransaction();
            repository.Delete(Selected.CurrentEntity);
            unitOfWork.CommitTransaction();
            SearchEmployees();
        }
        catch (Exception exception)
        {
            unitOfWork.RollbackTransaction();
            dialogService.ShowError("Delete error", "An error occured during the Delete
command.");
        }
    }
}
```

Here the code is a little bit more complex. First you need to verify that an employee has been selected, then you need to ask the user to confirm the deletion as you want to be sure he wants to drop the current employee record.

If you get a confirmation message from the user, you need to start a transaction with the unit of work and delete the record with the EmployeeRepository object that is created using the current unit of work. If the operation is successful, you can commit the transaction but if something goes wrong, you need to roll back the operation and advise the user.

Suggested Steps

You should now be pretty confident about creating a `ViewModel` and an `ICommand` object that has one or more triggers. Here's what you need to accomplish to complete the CRUD steps of the Employee List/Details Views.

- Create two commands for the `DetailsView`, one for confirmation and one for cancellation. Based on the command selected by the user, you persist the changes or cancel them.

- When the user selects the `NewCommand` in the `ListView`, you need to create a new `Employee` entity, attach it to the repository, and pass it to the `DetailsView`.

- Following the same logic, you need to provide the Views for creating or modifying existing: `Contact`, `Address`, and `Appointment`, and, of course, do the same for the `Customer`.

Summary

In this chapter you saw how the event handling approach has been changed in WPF with the introduction of `RoutedCommands` and `WeakEventManagers`. You can implement a WPF command in three different ways. The first approach is to recycle one of the existing `RoutedCommands` provided by WPF in the `ApplicationCommands` class and provide the implementation of the `Execute` and the `CanExecute` methods in the code-behind file of a `Window` or `UserControl`.

The second way is to create a custom `RoutedCommand` and attach it to the `CommandBinding` collection of the corresponding View. The third approach, more complex but also more flexible, is to create a custom command class that implements the `ICommand` interface and that is also able to trigger its execution based on events external to the command.

In the second part of the chapter you created a flexible `MvvmCommand` using the `ICommand` interface and the `WeakEvent` pattern in order to avoid overtaxing the resources used by the event listening technique. You also created a fancy syntax that makes the creation of an `MvvmCommand` more readable and understandable.

It is up to you now to complete the remaining commands of the application and make the Views interactive.

CHAPTER 9

■ ■ ■

Testing with TDD

One of the main reasons for writing a loosely coupled application that uses the latest design patterns and layering technique is are to increase, as much possible, the testability surface of the application, to make the various components of the application separate and independent and so more testable.

Visual Studio 2010 provides, out of the box, a set of tools and assemblies that allow you to write testable applications, which means writing applications that can be tested even outside the scope of the UI that the user will interact with. To get started, you need to look at Test Driven Development (TDD), part of the Agile approach, which supports the "test first" principle of Extreme Programming (XP). However, TDD can be used independently of the other Agile XP approaches. In the company where I work, for example, we apply TDD to every project but we don't use other Agile XP techniques.

Visual Studio and MSTest aren't the only unit test frameworks for .NET. On the Web you'll find many others, most of them open source, that are also suitable for writing unit tests, like the following:

- nUnit: www.nunit.org/

- xUnit.NET: http://xunit.codeplex.com/

- mbUnit: www.mbunit.com/

Before using the TDD approach, the only way of testing a specific set of code commands was to build and execute the application and debug inside the application code. By *debug* I mean that process used to find and fix the number of bugs in a specific application. With this approach, you have to first identify the bug that is the cause of the problem, and after it is identified you step through the code that is causing the bug and you try to fix it. Then you re-execute that piece of code in order to be sure that the bug is fixed and that the change you made did not affect other parts of the application.

Of course the two approaches are drastically different, but they can easily coexist in the same application. It is very good to write your application following TDD principles, but it is still necessary, sometimes, to step into the code and identify the root cause of the problem.

In this chapter we will explore how to write the TimeTracker application following the principles of TDD, and how Visual Studio 2010 can help apply these principles to every layer of the application. We will then look at the basic code coverage principles that come from TDD, and finally we will see how to test the various layers of the TimeTracker application.

Test Driven Development

If you look as a purist at the TDD principles, you'd say that TDD is a technique for developing software based on a set of small development cycles, where each cycle consists of a test case that defines the code requirements and the code that will satisfy these requirements. TDD is also known as *red-green-refactor* because the lifecycle of a test includes three simple steps:

- Write the test and the assertions and fail them (red).

- Implement the code to pass the assertions (green).

- Refactor the code and test it again.

This type of approach may look strange to you at the beginning, but you will realize that if you write the code that identifies an application requirement before the requirement has been written in code, the test shouldn't pass; at that point, the code implementation should just satisfy the requirement, nothing more. The final refactoring step is accomplished to clean up the code written to pass the assertions.

TDD is not a pattern but a development methodology, so you may find some people positive about this approach and others that don't like to develop using TDD. Here are some pros of using the TDD technique as we will for the TimeTracker application:

- It forces you develop according to the requirement and to refine the code to respect and honor the application requirements.

- It forces you to write code that is loosely coupled, as the code must be quick and easy to test.

- It allows you to test the code you write in an incremental process without having a graphical layer to execute the core code.

- It forces you to write a lot of single tests in order to cover at least 80-85% of the code with tests, and this approach helps make you and other developers confident about the quality of the code and the number of defects covered by tests.

TDD can't be used everywhere, especially if the requirements arise from code that can't easily be tested with automation, like a WPF View. In the case of a GUI object, you should introduce in your testing environment a more complex mechanism of UI automation, and a UI macro that will guarantee the correctness of the test execution.

TDD may also not fit properly when the requirements have some dependencies that are can't be emulated in the test environment, for example, testing a data layer against a backup copy of a production database.

One good way to measure the amount of code covered by the test is the Code Coverage approach. Let's take a look at that now.

Code Coverage

One of the metrics used in TDD is called *Code Coverage* because it represents the amount of code covered by a specific test or set of tests, i.e., the amount of code executed by the tests while the tests are running. Listing 9-1 shows a simple class that exposes a method to execute a calculation between two integers. The code uses some Visual Studio features that we will analyze in the next section; for now let's just focus on the code coverage concept.

Listing 9-1. *Code Coverage Example*

```
using System;

namespace Calculator
{
    public sealed class Engine
    {
        public int Sum(int a, int b)
        {
            if (a == 0 || b == 0)
            {
                throw new ArgumentNullException(
                    "The arguments a and b must be greater than 0.");
            }

            return a + b;
        }
    }
}
```

Now let's write a test for this class so that we can test that a sum of two integers, both greater than 0, will cover the class `Engine` (see Listing 9-2).

Listing 9-2. *Unit Test for the Sum Method*

```
using Microsoft.VisualStudio.TestTools.UnitTesting;

namespace Calculator.Test
{
    [TestClass]
    public class EngineTest
    {
        [TestMethod]
        public void SumTest()
        {
            var target = new Engine();
            int a = 5;
            int b = 4;
            int expected = 9;
            int actual;
            actual = target.Sum(a, b);
            Assert.AreEqual(expected, actual);
        }
    }
}
```

If you execute this test in Visual Studio, the code coverage window will tell you that you are partially covering `Sum`, as Figure 9-1 shows.

◢ Calculator.dll	3	37.50 %	5	62.50 %	
◢ {} Calculator	3	37.50 %	5	62.50 %	
◢ Engine	3	37.50 %	5	62.50 %	
Sum(int32,int32)	3	37.50 %	5	62.50 %	

Figure 9-1. Code coverage window in Visual Studio 2010

Because Listing 9-2 didn't cover the occurrence where one of the parameter can be equal or less than 0, MSTest (the TDD framework integrated into Visual Studio) tells you that you didn't cover all the code. The next test, shown in Listing 9-3, will cover that part of the Sum method

Listing 9-3. Covering an Exception

```
[TestMethod]
[ExpectedException(typeof(ArgumentNullException))]
public void ThrowExceptionWhenSum()
{
    var target = new Engine();
    int a = 0;
    int b = 0;
    int expected = 0;
    int actual = target.Sum(0, 0);
    Assert.AreNotEqual(expected, actual);
}
```

with a final result of 100% coverage, as shown in Figure 9-2.

◢ Calculator.dll	0	0.00 %	8	100.00 %
◢ {} Calculator	0	0.00 %	8	100.00 %
◢ Engine	0	0.00 %	8	100.00 %
Sum(int32,int32)	0	0.00 %	8	100.00 %

Figure 9-2. Code coverage 100% for the Sum method

In this case, for a single method, we wrote two test methods so that the amount of code used to test the requirement was more than the amount of code used to satisfy the requirement. Code coverage doesn't always indicate quality of the TDD process, especially when the code and the tests are written by the same developer. In any case, setting your minimum code coverage requirement to 95+ % is a good starting point and should guarantee a certain code quality level. The more coverage, the better.

TDD with MSTest

When you develop an application using the TDD approach, you need an environment that lets you run the tests in a context different from the one represented by the application. In Visual Studio you can do this by creating, in the same solution you are testing, a new project of type "Test" that will contain the methods and tests for your testing.

■ **Note** Unfortunately the Express editions of Visual C# or Visual VB.NET don't allow you to install or run plug-ins, and since the MSTest engine available in Visual Studio (any version except Express) is a sort of plug-in, in order to follow the examples provided in this chapter, you need a demo version of Visual Studio 2010 Professional, Premium, or Ultimate, available for download at `www.microsoft.com/visualstudio/en-us/download`.

Let's explore the MSTest engine by creating a simple project, the project you saw in the "Code Coverage" section, which is composed of a class library that contains a simple Calculator engine that can execute sums only of integers greater than 0.

Calculator Example

Open a new instance of Visual Studio and create a new Project under Visual C# ➤ Windows ➤ Class Library. Give the Solution the name `Calculator` and press OK. Now you should have a blank class library project that contains only a file called `Class1.cs`. Delete this file and create a new class with the name of `Engine`, This class will contain the same code used in Listing 9-1.

Now that you've created the class to test, let's write the two requirements for the test:

- Assert that `Engine` can calculate the sum of two integer greater than 0.

- Assert that `Engine` will throw an exception if one of the numbers is equal to 0.

To create a new test, you can either create a test project in Visual Studio and reference the Calculator project, or you can right-click in the `Engine.cs` class file content (any place in the code editor) and choose the command Create Unit tests....This command pops up a new dialog like the one in Figure 9-3.

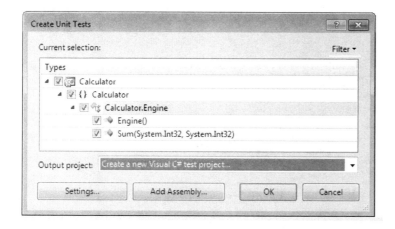

Figure 9-3. *Create unit test dialog*

213

The dialog lets you select the methods and properties you want to test, so select the constructor and the Sum method of the class Engine. The next window asks for a name for the new C# project. Call it Calculator.Test so you know that it represents the test Test for the Calculator assembly. At this point Visual Studio will create two different methods as shown in Listing 9-4.

Listing 9-4. *Constructor Test*

```
[TestMethod()]
public void EngineConstructorTest()
{
    Engine target = new Engine();
    Assert.Inconclusive("TODO: Implement code to verify target");
}
```

It will also create the method represented in Listing 9-2. Notice that at the end of the test method in Listing 9-4, Visual Studio added an Assert call to the Inconclusive method. This method is added to let you know that a test skeleton has been created but now you have to write the correct test assertions. You can do this using the Assert class, which exposes a list of methods to verify a lot of different types of assertions. You can find a detailed list of assertions verifiable with the Assert class at msdn.microsoft.com/library/microsoft.visualstudio.testtoolsunittesting.assert.aspx.

Now, what you want to verify in this method is that the object is not null. Because you are testing the constructor of the engine class, the correct implementation of Listing 9-4 would be something like what's shown in Listing 9-5.

Listing 9-5. *TDD Class Constructor*

```
[TestMethod()]
public void EngineConstructorTest()
{
    Engine target = new Engine();
    Assert.IsNotNull(target);
    Assert.IsInstanceOfType(target, typeof(Engine));
}
```

You want to verify that the object is not null and that it is of type Engine. Right-click the [TestMethod] attribute and select the command Run Tests. A Visual Studio window will pop up showing the running tests and the execution results, as in Figure 9-4.

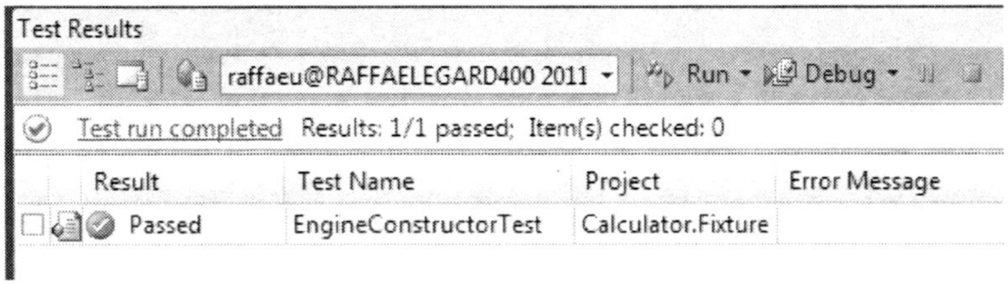

Figure 9-4. *Test results window in Visual Studio 2010*

The window in the Figure 9-4 shows that you can access all the features of the MSTest engine using the Test Results panel. You can look at the test results, the test execution statistics, and more. You can also select any test and rerun it, or run them with the debug option.

The other two tests were shown already in Listing 9-2 and Listing 9-3. Listing 9-2 verifies that `Engine` can execute a normal operation with two integer numbers greater than 0, while Listing 9-3 is used for verifying the exception. Of course, the two tests have been changed from the original ones that Visual Studio provides.

The method in Listing 9-3 uses the attribute `[ExpectedException()]` available from the `Microsoft.VisualStudio.TestTools` namespace. The attribute is used to test whether an expected exception is thrown. The test method will pass if the expected exception is thrown; of course, for it to pass the test you can't include in your test method a try/catch block that will catch the exception.

Another option for creating a new Test in Visual Studio is to right-click, in Solution Explorer, on a test project and select Add New Test. This brings up in a dialog all the tests that VS provides; you'll see the same list in the context menu when you right-click on a Test project (see Figure 9-5).

The next section gives is a short overview of what each of these test objects is used for.

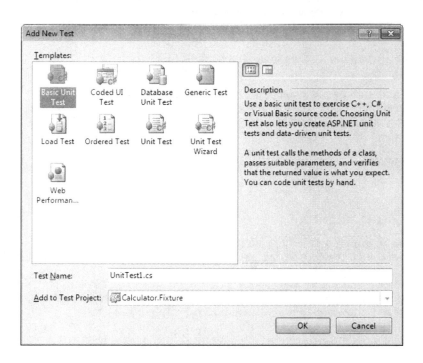

Figure 9-5. Add New Test dialog

Available Tests

- *Basic Unit Test:* A class marked with the attribute [Test], which can include various test methods.

- *Coded UI Test:* A special test that can record user actions in a UI to test a graphical component, such as a Window, Page, or UserControl.

- *Database Unit Test:* A special test used to verify objects in a database, such as stored procedures, tables, and more.

- *Generic Test:* A generic program or .dll wrapped to work and act as a test.

- *Load Test:* An aggregation of tests that can run together.

- *Ordered Test:* A way to execute a set of tests in a specified order.

- *Unit Test:* The classic unit test like the one created in this section.

- *Unit Test Wizard:* A way to bring up the AddNew Test wizard shown in Figure 9-5.

- *Web Performances:* A way to test the performance of Web applications such ASP.NET.

In this book you'll learn how to create a unit test and then see how much code was covered with the test. If you plan to cover your application by testing all the layers and components, and to develop using the TDD approach, you will probably also use the Load and the Ordered tests so you can test an entire component or an entire layer by sequentially running a set of unit tests that will cover all your application requirements.

The only test that you will never use for a WPF application is the Performances test for a Web application.

Code Coverage with Visual Studio

In the previous section you saw that an important measure of the correctness of your tests is the Code Coverage metric that is a core part of the TDD methodology, but you haven't seen yet how to use this technique in Visual Studio.

In Visual Studio 2008, the code coverage feature was preconfigured so that after you ran a unit test you could immediately verify the test's coverage. In the 2010 version , the code coverage is not enabled by default and to enable it you need to understand how Visual Studio 2010 configures the test environment.

Figure 9-6 shows the default layout of the Calculator project after the first set of unit tests was created.

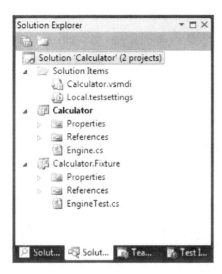

Figure 9-6. *Solution Explorer view of the Calculator project*

Visual Studio created two additional files and one folder in the root of the application. The folder is called `Solution Items` and the files are `Calculator.vsmdi` and `Local.testsettings`.

The file with the extension `.vsmdi` is used by Visual Studio. If you double click it, you'll see a panel showing all the available tests in the solution.

The file with the `.testsettings` extension includes all the information the tests require to run. You can have more than one `testsettings`, so you can specify different requirements for your tests. Let's say that in your tests you reference an assembly located in `C:\MyAssembly`, and that a colleague's PC doesn't have the same location for that dependency. You can create an additional `testsetting` for your colleague that will resolve the specified dependency in a different way.

If you double-click the `.testsettings` file, Visual Studio will show a dialog like the one in Figure 9-7.

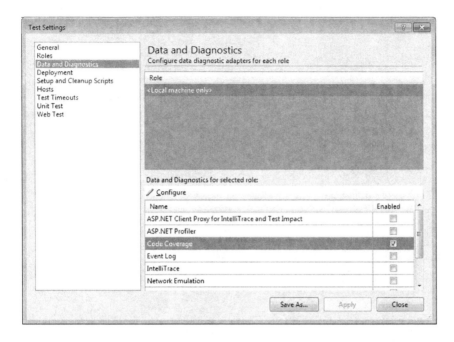

Figure 9-7. Visual Studio test settings

You can access each section in the dialog using the list on the left; the option you need to modify is the one labeled Data and Diagnostics, which contains information about the tools you want to add to your test. Note, though, that this section is available only in the Ultimate and Premium versions of Visual Studio, so if you have a lower version, like Professional, you won't be able to access this section of the test configuration.

Select the Code Coverage tool and then click the Configure button at the top of the Data and Diagnostics list. You'll then see another window with a list of assemblies you can instrument. In this window you select the Assembly you want to test, so choose `Calculator.dll`.

What did you do in this step? Visual Studio needs to know what code you are executing and covering in your tests so it can modify the corresponding assembly code in order to *instrument* it, so that when you run the code MSTest will be able to monitor it and give you back a code coverage result.

Now if you run your tests again, the Visual Studio test engine should also create code coverage statistics that you can explore after all the tests are executed. The code coverage is calculated only after a specific test is executed and its asserts are all successful. If the tests fail, VS will not calculate the code coverage.

You can view the code coverage window in different ways:

- From the menu select Test ➤Windows ➤ Code Coverage Results.

- Right-click a test result in the Test Results windows and select View Code Coverage.

Look back at Figure 9-2, which shows the Code Coverage panel in action; for each method or property exposed by the instrumented assembly, code coverage shows you the number of blocks of code that can be covered by tests, the number already covered, and a percentage.

From this window you can double-click one of the tested methods or properties and verify the amount of code covered. But before doing that you should enable the code-coloring feature. Code coloring can be switched on and off by clicking on the fourth icon in the toolbar of the Code Coverage panel. After you enable code coloring and you click, for example, on the Sum method of the Engine class, it will appear as shown in Figure 9-8.

```
public int Sum(int a, int b)
{
    try
    {
        if (a == 0 || b == 0)
        {
            throw new ArgumentNullException(
                "The arguments a and b must be greater than 0.");
        }

        return a + b;
    }
    catch (Exception exception)
    {
        throw new Exception("An error occured during the Sum calculation", exception);
    }
}
```

Figure 9-8. *Code coloring*

You can configure the colors in Visual Studio by opening the color preferences available through the menu Tools ➤ Options ➤ Fonts and Colors. I assigned red to the noncovered regions, green to the covered regions, and orange to the partially covered regions.

Figure 9-8 shows the Sum method modified from its original implementation just to show you how the code coverage coloring works in Visual Studio 2010.

TDD: the TimeTracker Application

Now that you've seen how the TDD methodology can be applied to a project and the tools that Visual Studio provides to implement TDD, let's take a look at the TimeTracker application and see how to test the various layers of the application.

You may already understand, from reading this chapter, that even though the TDD technique is very helpful, it is also verbose and time-consuming; in fact, the common rule of TDD is that you will end up writing 45% code more in the tests than in the production code. So, for instance, if your production code consists of 100 lines, you will probably end up with 245 lines—100 lines of production code + 145 lines of testing code. Of course, this example is purely theoretical.

In any case, let's take a look at how to test each of the existing layers (DAL, BLL, UI) of the application, and how to do this using the common TDD best practices. It is not the goal of this section to show you the full testing code of the entire application.

When you write a layered application, like the TimeTracker WPF application, you usually create an additional test project for each layer so you can keep the tests of one layer separate and loosely coupled to the tests of another layer.

The order in which you test your layers is usually development driven, so you should expect to create a test project for the domain layer, then create the domain requirements in the test, and one by one create the corresponding code in the domain assembly. When the domain is ready, you should create the data layer part and then the presentation layer (ViewModels, Views).

Test the Business (Domain) Layer

Because we created all the TimeTracker code before writing the tests, in the following example we are not really writing TDD but simply writing tests for the existing code. Since the purpose of this book is to create a layered WPF application and not to learn TDD, the idea is just to show you how to implement TDD. In the real world, of course, the approach should be opposite to the one used in this book—you should create the tests first and then the corresponding code.

In Solution Explorer, right-click the TimeTracker solution node and add a new solution folder called Tests. This folder will keep the test projects separate from the rest of the application. You may have already created this in the previous chapters when you created the unit tests for the data layer. I'm repeating it here just to be sure you have everything in place.

In the TDD syntax, a test is called Fixture but Visual Studio calls them Test. In this book I use the Test naming convention just to stay in line with the Visual Studio syntax, but it may happen that you see a project where the tests are called using the prefix/suffix Fixture instead of the Test one.

Now, right-click on the Tests folder and create a new project of type Test Document ➤ Test Project. Name it `APRESS.TimeTracking.BusinessLayer.Test` and press OK. Visual Studio will create a new test project with a default unit test called `UnitTest1.cs` that you have to delete.

Now choose to add a new test to the project and select the Unit Test file type. Visual Studio opens a dialog showing all the available projects in the application; navigate through the Business Layer project and select the `Role` domain entity with all its properties and methods and press OK.

Visual Studio will now add all the required references and it will also create a new file called `RoleTest.cs` containing all the required test Tests for the `Role` object. You can simply right-click on the `RoleTest [TestClass()]` attribute and select the Run test command and execute all the related tests.

You will receive a failure for some tests and a question mark for others; this is due to the fact that VS adds at the end of each test the `Assert.Inconclusive` method, which informs VS that your tests are inconclusive and that you have to verify the final result.

What you can do now is to remove all the `Assert.Inconclusive` methods and rerun all the tests. Then read the Code Coverage to understand how much amount of code the Visual Studio wizard has already covered for you. You should get 0 coverage as the code implemented by Visual Studio in your tests is just the starting point.

For a domain entity created by Entity Framework, you should test the following components and methods:

- Test the constructor and verify that the properties are initialized correctly.

- Write a test for each property by adding a mockup value to the property and verify that the value is properly injected.

- Write a test for each method exposed by the entity and a corresponding test to also verify the well-known exceptions it may throw.

For the domain model, you should cover almost 100% as it doesn't have any dependencies and it represents the core of the application.

Testing the Data Layer

Testing the DAL of an application can be a more challenging task because it has a direct dependency on the database. When you work with an O/RM, the testing you do using the data layer is to be sure that the data can be persisted and retrieved as expected using the O/RM and the data layer that is wrapping it around.

So, how can you test a data layer properly?

First create a new test project but this time name the project APRESS.TimeTracking.DataLayer.Test as it will include tests for the DAL of the TimeTracker application.

The first component to test is the UnitOfWork—not the IUnitOfWork—as in the TDD methodology, you test the implementation and not the contract. So as you did for the Role entity in the previous section, using the Test creation wizard create a new test project, this time for the UnitOfWork component of the DAL. But don't select any method this time so that the test will be created with all the corresponding references but without any method inside.

The second step is to add a new file of type "Configuration file (app.config)" in the test project and provide a connection string like you did in the WPF application so that the Entity Framework will be able to read the configuration section and run against a database. See Listing 9-6.

We've actually done this already in Chapter 6, but now we're also taking a closer look the TDD technique.

Listing 9-6. *Configuration File for the DAL Test Project*

```
<?xml version="1.0" encoding="utf-8"?>
<configuration>
  <connectionStrings>
    <add name="TimeTrackerModelContainer"
    connectionString="metadata=res://*/TimeTrackerModel.csdl|
    res://*/TimeTrackerModel.ssdl|
    res://*/TimeTrackerModel.msl;
    provider=System.Data.SqlClient;
    provider connection string=&quot;
    Data Source=.\SQLEXPRESS;
    Initial Catalog=TimeTrackerDatabase;
    Integrated Security=True;
    MultipleActiveResultSets=True&quot;"
    providerName="System.Data.EntityClient" />
  </connectionStrings>
</configuration>
```

By doing this you are using the local SQL database as your test environment, so you should be careful that the connection string does not point to a database that will be used in production for your DAL!

For the UoW, you want to verify that it can be created; that when it's created the connection is not null; and that the connection string inside the app.config is configured properly, as shown in Listing 9-7.

221

Listing 9-7. Unit Test for the Creation of a Unit Of Work

```
[TestMethod]
public void CanCreateAUnitOfWOrk()
{
    using (IUnitOfWork uow = new UnitOfWork())
    {
        Assert.IsNotNull(uow);
        Assert.IsNotNull(uow.Session);
        Assert.IsNotNull(uow.Session.Connection);
    }
}
```

Then you should test the properties, such as to verify that the transaction can be started and can be committed and rolled back. You should also test that if you try to start a transaction twice in a row without committing the first one, the UoW will throw an exception.

In order to test the `MarkNew<T>`, `MarkDelete<T>` and `MarkDirty<T>` methods, you need to provide a domain entity and save, delete, or update it using the EF session. However, because this step has already been accomplished in every repository test, you can skip this in the UoW test as the code will be covered in the repository test.

For each repository you should do the same, adding a new test class and covering all the methods exposed by the base plus the concrete repository, because for each repository the corresponding domain entity is different. Listing 9-8 shows an example test for the `RoleRespository` delete method.

Listing 9-8. Test the `RoleRespository` delete method.

```
[TestMethod]
public void CanDeleteAnExistingObject()
{
    using (IUnitOfWork uow = new UnitOfWork())
    {
        // add new object
        uow.StartTransaction();
        var repository = new RoleRepository(uow);
        var role = new Role
                    {
                        Name = "MockupRole",
                        Description = "Role for the Test."
                    };
        uow.MarkNew(role);
        uow.CommitTransaction();
        // retreive object using the UoW
        Role expectedRole = uow
            .Session
            .CreateObjectSet<Role>()
            .Where(r => r.Id == role.Id)
            .FirstOrDefault();
        Assert.IsNotNull(expectedRole);
        // delete the object
        uow.StartTransaction();
```

```
        repository.Delete(role);
        Assert.IsTrue(expectedRole.EntityState == EntityState.Deleted);
        uow.CommitTransaction();
        // verify the object doesn't exist
        Role finalExpectedRole =
            uow
            .Session
            .CreateObjectSet<Role>()
            .Where(r => r.Id == role.Id)
            .FirstOrDefault();
        Assert.IsNull(finalExpectedRole);
    }
}
```

The purpose of this code is to verify that the UoW is able to delete an existing object. Because the TDD requires that the testing environment be rolled back to its initial state when the test is done, you should always leave the test database empty and prepare it based on the test you are running.

In this case you need an entity in the database before you can delete one, so the first thing to do is to create a new entity and verify that is has been created properly in the database. Then you delete it using the repository, and finally retrieve it again using the UoW. The creation of a new entity should be a test on its own as well, but to keep things simple in this book, we just assembled the two tests together.

If you are wondering why we are not using the repository to insert and retrieve the entity, the answer is very simple. It's because this test class is used to test the repository itself and this method is used specifically to test the delete method. At this point you still don't know if the insert method is working so you shouldn't add additional dependencies to test.

The same process should be done for the remaining repositories of the data layer.

Testing the UI

The process of testing the UI can be accomplished with two different steps. For example, the APRESS.TimeTracker WPF project consists of a set of services and ViewModel objects that can be tested using the normal approach of creating a new unit test and asserting the corresponding requirements. In contrast, something like the EmployeeListView.xaml object can be tested only by having a user that interacts with the view.

Let's create a new test project and call it APRESS.TimeTracker.Test. It will include tests for the services, tests for the ViewModels, and tests for the UI.

You can use the Wizard test to test all the ViewModels, the Services, and the command objects in the same way as with the domain entity. So, for instance, if a ViewModel object has some properties and methods, you need to verify that they are all created and instantiated as expected. In this case, with a ViewModel, you want to verify that the value exposed by the ViewModel is the same as that of the corresponding property in the corresponding model, as in Listing 9-9.

Listing 9-9. Testing the AddressDetailsViewModel Object

```
[TestMethod()]
public void AddressLine1Test()
{
    Address currentEntity = new Address();
    string expected = "MockupAddress";
    currentEntity.AddressLine1 = expected;
    AddressDetailsViewModel target = new AddressDetailsViewModel(currentEntity);
    Assert.AreEqual(expected, target.AddressLine1);
}
```

To test a View, you need to have the UI layer running properly as you will track your mouse movements and then verify the result in the code.

Right-click on your test project and select a new Coded UI test that will present a dialog asking if you plan to test a UI by recording an action or by using an existing one. Choose the first option and press OK. Note that this can be executed only if you have VS Premium or VS Ultimate.

From that point, Visual Studio will allow you to track every action you accomplish on your development machine by recording it as a macro. For instance, if you record the execution of the APRESS.TimeTracker application, you should get an icon over the application window like the one in Figure 9-9.

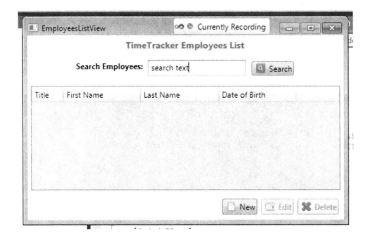

Figure 9-9. Recording actions in Visual Studio UI testing

In this case, we insert a "search text" string in a TextBox so the corresponding test should verify that the ViewModel property has that same value.

Writing tests for the UI is not as easy as writing tests for non-UI objects as you need to consider additional factors, like all the possible options offered by the UI elements, the user interactions, and more. Finally, with the UI testing you can't get real code coverage as you aren't testing the code coverage of the application but the UI behavior requirements.

Summary

Test Driven Development is an agile methodology used to invert the order in which you develop and test an application. Instead of writing the code and then debugging it, with TDD you write the test to verify the application requirements and then you write the code to satisfy these tests and consequently also the application requirements.

Writing a TDD application may require time, and when it is your first TDD application, it may require double the time you normally need to write an application. The advantage of using TDD is really discovered in the future, when you move from the development phase of the application to the maintenance phase. In this phase you typically spend a lot of time testing, debugging, and trying to fix and sort out bugs discovered by your QA department. If you've adopted TDD methodology, this phase will be much easier because you will already have a set of tests that can verify whether the application is still stable and covered and if a new feature might compromise the existing structure of the software.

When you test a layered application like TimeTracker, you need to provide a test project for each layer and use a different approach based on the type of code you are testing. For instance, the testing code you write for a domain entity is totally different from the code you write to test a user interface like a WPF View.

TDD can be measured using code coverage—the amount of code covered by a specific set of unit tests. Code coverage is one metric for TDD but it should not be considered the only metric because sometimes it doesn't really provide an absolute measure of code quality.

Visual Studio 2010 provides a set of panes, tools, and assemblies that can make the creation of a TDD application fast and easy. Within the Visual Studio IDE you can access all the aspects of the TDD and control code quality and code coverage. Unfortunately, all these nice features are not available in the Express edition of Visual Studio.

CHAPTER 10

■ ■ ■

Reports with Microsoft Reporting Services

Giving the user a way to print out the data he's working with is a very common application requirement, especially when this data is used for business purposes. In the TimeTracker application, one of the tasks the user can accomplish is to organize appointments between an employee and a customer, and this requires a set of reports that should be displayed and printed within the UI using a report viewer component.

A report is a digital document that displays information, retrieved from a database in the form of ordered data, typically as a grid or matrix, or graphically as in a chart. The report becomes more useful to the user when it can be printed and when it can be exported from the application and used with different software, for example if it can be exported as a Portable Digital Format (PDF) and saved to the local file system or sent with an e-mail.

Visual Studio 2010 offers two different types of reporting you can use in your applications. One is the Microsoft SQL Server Reporting Services software, a subset of the reporting technology in Microsoft SQL Server 2008 R2; the second is a third-party technology that is now provided for free within the Visual Studio environment—the famous Crystal Reports (CR).

The Microsoft reporting technology can be hosted using your SQL Server 2008 R2 Windows SharePoint Services if you have that, or directly within your WPF application using the Windows Forms control ReportViewer that VS provides. It produces a file with extension `.rdlc`, which can be edited in the Visual Studio IDE. It lets you have a preview of the final result by simply querying the data available in the database and by showing you a preview of the final result.

SAP Crystal Reports for Visual Studio 2010 is a subset of the SAP Crystal Reports engine available from SAP, which bought the Crystal Reports company a few years ago. Though CR was integrated in Visual Studio, it was not free; you had to purchase a development license. Moreover, the integration with Windows Forms was not easy at all. Now, however, SAP Crystal Reports has released a version for Visual Studio 2010 that is completely free and easy to redistribute. You just need to register your version and download the runtimes from this web site in order to have a full working version `www.sap.com/solutions/sap-crystal-solutions/query-reporting-analysis/sapcrystalreports-visualstudio/index.epx`.

In this chapter we will configure the Microsoft reporting technology and build some reports so you'll get a nice overview of the product. We will host the reports in our WPF application or on a SQL Server Reporting Service web site.

■ **Note** In order to follow the next tutorials, your database should be populated with some dummy data so that you will be able to view the data displayed in the reports and verify that it's correct. In case you haven't completed the UI of the TimeTracker application, you can edit the data in the TimeTracker database by opening Microsoft SQL Server Management Studio, right-clicking on a table, and selecting the command "Edit all rows." This opens the table in edit mode and you will be able to add, remove, or modify the data.

SQL Server Reporting Services

Visual Studio 2010 provides a tool for creating `.rdlc` reports, which can be hosted in a Windows Forms or WPF application (the second option uses a simple, approved way of embedding the Windows Forms ReportViewer control in WPF) or by deploying them to a SharePoint SQL Report Server to be displayed using a web browser.

During the writing of this book, I omitted some steps, like creating the `Customer` entity data-entry views, as I believe that as part of the learning process the reader should emulate the steps described in the book to generate new features in the application. For this reason, the book includes the entire code to search for an `Employee` entity and to edit, create, or delete an `Employee` entity. In the same way, we will build reports for the `Employee` entity, and then you can follow the steps to build reports for the `Customer` entity on your own.

We want to produce three different reports for an `Employee` domain entity. The first one is a simple list of all the available employees ordered by first name and last name, with a summary overview of the employee information. The second one is a more detailed report that shows all the information and all the activities of a single employee, and it will be shown from the Details View. The third report is a list of appointments for each employee.

Configure SQL Server Reporting Services

When you install SQL Server 2008 R2 with advanced services and you choose to install the Reporting Services feature, the setup will create and install all the required components and services for running RS from your development machine or from wherever you've installed such service. Unfortunately, the setup doesn't prepare the server so you'll have to configure it manually using the wizard available through Start ➤ All Programs ➤ Microsoft SQL Server 2008 R2 ➤ Configuration Tools ➤ Reporting Services Configuration Manager.

As soon as you open the wizard, it asks you to identify the server name in the first `TextBox` and the SQL Server instance in the second one, which by default should be `SQLEXPRESS`. When you have located the correct server, press OK and the wizard will start (see Figure 10-1).

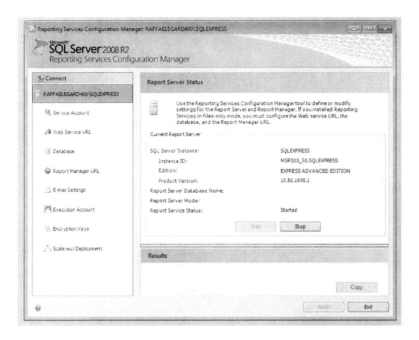

Figure 10-1. *SQL Server Reporting Services Configuration Manager*

The configuration wizard consists of a series of steps that are independent of each other; each step allows you to configure a specific functionality of the SQL Server Reporting Services (SSRS). After you set up the configuration in one step, press the Apply button before moving on to a new one. The first step is simply verifying that SSRS is up and running. Then you follow these steps:

1. **Service Account:** In this step you select a specific Windows account to run the SSRS service; you can just leave it to the default (Network Service) so you don't need to press Apply.

2. **Web Service URL:** This step configures the web application in IIS that will host the SSRS web site. You can leave the settings as proposed by the wizard and click Apply, then click the link in the middle of the dialog that points to the current SSRS URL. If you already have other web sites running on IIS port 80, consider installing SSRS on a different port.

3. **Database:** In this step you need to tell SSRS where to save the reports you'll create. Select Change database and follow the wizard to create a new SSRS database. In the Database server section, be sure to substitute the database name with `.\SQLEXPRESS` if you installed SSRS on your development machine. Then set up credentials and authentication and create the database following the wizard. This step creates two databases, one using the name you inserted and one with the suffix TempDb.

4. **Report Manager URL:** This step creates an additional IIS web application that you will use to administer the reports. Press Apply and verify that the application has been created.

5. **E-mail Settings:** This is used to configure e-mail settings if you plan to deploy reports through an e-mail service like Microsoft Exchange Server. This step is not mandatory.

6. **Execution Account:** In this step you can change the account that is used to process the reports if you need to apply additional security.

7. **Encryption Keys:** This step allows you to create and back up an encrypted key for keep your data safe. If you plan to use this option, remember to back up the encryption key and save it as it will be the only way to restore or change the SSRS configuration in the future.

Once your machine is set up, you need to restart it to allow SSRS to properly reconfigure IIS and user access control so you can navigate the SSRS portal.

■ **Note** If you have a machine that is running Windows 7 or Windows Vista, you'll have to disable UAC in order to allow through the browser to authenticate in the SSRS portal. You can find information about how to disable UAC for Windows Vista and Windows 7 at `http://windows.microsoft.com/en-US/windows-vista/Turn-User-Account-Control-on-or-off`.

Now try to access the report portal, which should be located at `http://[yourserver]//Reports_SQLEXPRESS/e` the browser should display a project portal page like the one in Figure 10-2.

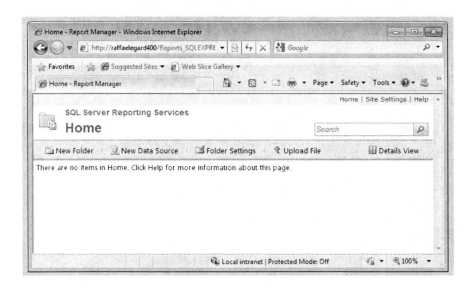

Figure 10-2. SSRS portal page with default settings

Now, on the SSRS home page, add a new folder and call it TimeTracker. This folder is where you'll create the reports for the application.

TimeTracker Reports

As noted earlier, we are going to use Microsoft SQL Server Reporting Services (SSRS) in this chapter. Unfortunately, if you want to create a new report for SSRS right now, you can't use Visual Studio 2010 as Microsoft hasn't yet provided integration between the two products. The only way you can create a new SSRS report is to open the Visual Studio 2008 shell installed with SSRS and create a new report project from there. Then you can publish your reports and display them within your WPF application.

First Report: EmployeeListReport

The first report you'll create is the list of employees that will be used to print a summary list of the employees in the database. Then you'll apply some style and layout to the report.

To start, locate the VS 2008 Business Intelligence shortcut on your computer that the SQL Server 2008 R2 Express Edition setup installed. (If you didn't install it, you can run the setup again and add more features to the current installation.) Or you can go to Start ➤ All Programs ➤ Microsoft SQL Server 2008 R2 ➤ SQL Server Business Intelligence Development Studio.

After you open this, you'll see the VS 2008 IDE but with fewer features and project templates as this version of VS 2008 just uses the VS shell to host the Report Designer and other features provided by SQL Server.

Now go to the File menu and create a new project by selecting Business Intelligence Projects ➤ Report Server Project. Name the new project `TimeTracker.Reports` and click OK. VS creates a new empty solution that will host reports and data sources for SSRS.

Figure 10-3 shows the default structure in Solution Explorer after you create a new Report Server Project. Bby default, VS adds three different folders in your projects:

- **Shared Data Sources:** In this folder you'll create the data sources shared by the report project and hosted in SSRS.

- **Shared Dataset:** This folder will hold the datasets you create that will provide the data for your reports.

- **Reports:** This folder should be used to store your reports.

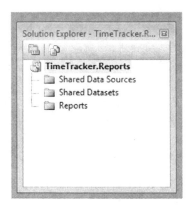

Figure 10-3. Default layout of a Report project in VS2008

You can't change the names and the structure of this layout because it is used by VS to deploy the objects to the SSRS portal and also to provide a context menu for each folder type.

Create a DataSource

Before even starting to create the first report you need to set up the data source for the project and host it on SSRS so that the reports you publish can retrieve the data in the same way as in the VS IDE.

To create a new datasource, right-click on the corresponding folder in the Solution Explorer tree and select Add New Datasource; Visual Studio brings up a dialog that asks for a name and credentials for the connection string, and of course the connection string that points to the TimeTracker database you are using.

Name the datasource `TimeTrackerDatasource`, provide a connection to the database by pressing the Edit button, and verify that the connection is working. Press OK and save the new datasource. Remember to also select a database in the connection window and to press the Test button to verify that the connection is properly configured. If you want, you can also provide different credentials in the datasource that will be used by the report engine, for example to let an ordinary user on the network run the reports.

Now you should see the new datasource in the corresponding folder of VS, ready to be deployed.

The next step is to configure the VS solution to be deployed in the SSRS portal. To do this, select the Solution node (root) in Solution Explorer and then select Properties from the context menu. A properties dialog will be displayed, as shown in Figure 10-4.

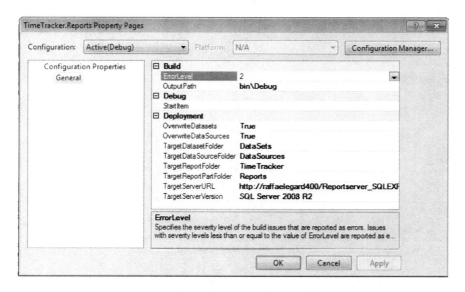

Figure 10-4. SSRS Project configuration

Figure 10-4 shows the dialog used to configure SSRS project properties. You should change the information to match what's in Figure 10-4. Pay attention to the TargetServerURL, which in your case should be http://[yourSSRS]/[reportserverurl]/. Now all the reports, datasources, and datasets will be deployed to the corresponding folders in the TimeTracker root folder of the SSRS web site.

You can try this by applying the changes in the Properties dialog and then right-clicking the report solution and choosing the Deploy command. If you've properly configured the solution, you should be able to see in the SSRS root a new folder called DataSources and in it the shared datasource object.

Create the Dataset

The next step consists of creating your first report using the shared datasource. Right-click on the report folder of the VS Solution and choose Add ➤ New Item…. Select the Report item, call it EmployeeListReport, and press OK. If you select Add New Report from the folder menu instead of Add New Item, VS will bring up the report creation wizard, which we won't use in this project (we want to create a more complex report).

The next step is to provide a dataset for the report, and this can be accomplished in two different ways. You can create a new dataset in the solution folder and share it with other reports in the future, or you can use the Report Data panel on your left and add a new report dataset that is visible only to the current report and, of course, is not recyclable.

I personally create only shared datasets so I can recycle their queries in the future. Unfortunately, the Express version of SQL doesn't allow sharing datasets so let's point to the VS Report Data panel and on the New… menu, click and add a new dataset. VS will show a dialog for creating the new dataset.

Figure 10-5 shows the Shared Dataset Properties dialog where you can create a new dataset. The dialog has a set of panels that you can navigate using the list on the left. In the first panel you can set up the query that will retrieve the data you want to display in the report. You can generate the query by simply writing in the Query text box the T-SQL statement if you have it already, or you can use a dataset created previously in the report or available through the shared datasets (this option isn't available for SQL Server Express edition).

Figure 10-5. Create new dataset dialog

What we are going to do is to generate a new query using the query generator provided with this dialog window. To do that, click the "Use dataset embedded in this report" option and the layout of the dialog will change, allowing you to type in some T-SQL code or to select a specific table or stored procedure. You will be typing in the T-SQL code so select the first option and press the New command on the datasource combobox. This command lets you select a datasource for the dataset or create a new one. Select the second option, "Use shared datasource reference" and choose the datasource you just created, then press OK. Now you can click the Query Designer command and the wizard will bring up a new dialog that you can use to build the query (Figure 10-6).

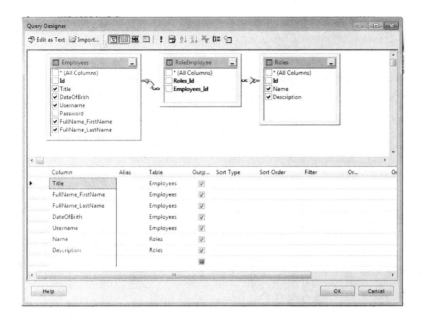

Figure 10-6. *The Query Designer window*

Within the window shown in Figure 10-6, you can create a query to retrieve the data for the report. Using the commands available on the toolbar, you can edit the query using the custom query designer or by typing T-SQL code. You can select tables and views, create joins between the tables, select fields and criteria, and test the result by simply running the query using the "!" command from the toolbar. When you are all set, click OK and the generated T-SQL code will appear in the previous window.

For this report you want to select the **Employee**, the corresponding **Role**, and the **Appointment**s he has scheduled. To be able to do that by pressing the + command, you need to add the four tables shown in Figure 10-6. The query designer will render the joins using the foreign keys created by the Entity Framework when you created this database. Now select the fields for the **Employee** (except the **Id** and the **Password**—you don't want to show a password in a report) and select the Name and Description fields from the Column list.

The final result should also use **SUM** and **COUNT** functions to aggregate the total number of appointments for each employee; due to space limitations, only the T-SQL code is posted in Listing 10-1.

Listing 10-1. *List Employees Plus Count Appointments*

```
SELECT
    Employees.Title, Employees.FullName_FirstName, Employees.FullName_LastName, ↵
Employees.DateOfBirth, Employees.Username, COUNT(Appointments.Id)
                        AS Appointments, Roles.Name, Roles.Description
FROM
    Roles RIGHT OUTER JOIN
    RoleEmployee ON Roles.Id = RoleEmployee.Roles_Id RIGHT OUTER JOIN
    Employees ON RoleEmployee.Employees_Id = Employees.Id LEFT OUTER JOIN
    Appointments ON Employees.Id = Appointments.Employee_Id
```

```
GROUP BY
    Employees.Title, Employees.FullName_FirstName, Employees.FullName_LastName, ↵
    Employees.DateOfBirth, Employees.Username, Roles.Name, Roles.Description
```

If you never worked with the GROUP BY and COUNT functions of T-SQL, you can find a nice, detailed description of how they work at msdn.microsoft.com/library/ms177673.aspx. For now, just press OK in the query designer and you should have the T-SQL code available in the text box. If you don't have the same as the book, you can simply write the T-SQL in the code space of the query designer and click in the design surface to see the final result. Click OK in the first dialog and Visual Studio will create a dataset node in the Report Data panel containing the fields you selected from the database.

Design the Report

Before starting to drag the fields from the dataset to the report design surface, you need to define a header and footer for the report so that every page of the report will look almost the same and the final result will look more professional.

To edit the header and footer of a report, you need to make them visible. Right-click on the report design surface (inside the report area) and from the menu select Insert ➤ Header and Insert ➤ Footer and Visual Studio will add two new horizontal lines to the report area, showing you that there's a header, the content of the report, and a footer.

In the header, right-click and select a TextBox from the context menu and insert the content "Employees List report." Then, from the toolbar, select the font Segoe UI, with a size 20 and a color of SteelBlue. Drag the TextBox to the top left corner of the report and resize it so the entire text is visible and it looks like Figure 10-7.

Now it's time for the footer. Locate on the Report Data panel the Built-in Fields folder and expand it; select the PageNumber field and drag it to the bottom left corner. Do the same for the Execution time field but move it to the opposite corner. For both, select the Segoe UI font and resize them. You should end up with a result like the one in Figure 10-7 (note that in the figure I added few more controls, like the line).

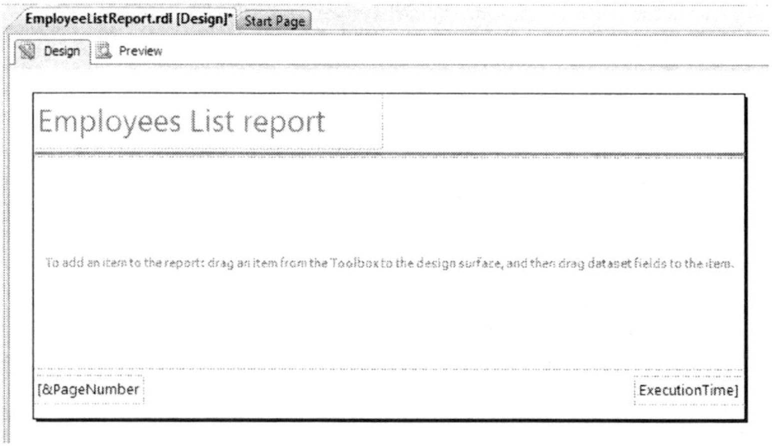

Figure 10-7. Preview of the EmployeeListReport first draft

Now you need to create a `Table` object in the report that will display the data you extracted from the table using the dataset. In this case, let's group the data into different groups, each one for a `Role` existing in the dataset.

Click inside the design area (in the middle of the report) and add a new `Table` object from the Insert menu and resize it so it covers the entire surface in width. Now for each column, select a corresponding field by clicking on the menu available in the details cell. Double-click the header content, then use the toolbar to select the cells and change the font to Segoe UI and the column header to Bold. Right-click on the Date of Birth column (the cell value) and select Textbox Properties, and then select the Number panel, the Date section, and format the date in the short datetime format (dd/mm/yyyy). Rename the column headers using the names shown in Figure 10-8.

Now if you select the Preview tab, you should be able to see the report, with a table populated with the data you've extracted. The last step is to group the data using the table group function. To do that, select the gray square at the beginning of the table row, before the first cell. Right-click on it and select Add group ➤ Parent group, then select the [Name] field from the dialog and then Add group header and press OK. Rename the Name label to Group and switch again to the Preview tab. You should see now the row grouped by the Group name as shown in Figure 10-8.

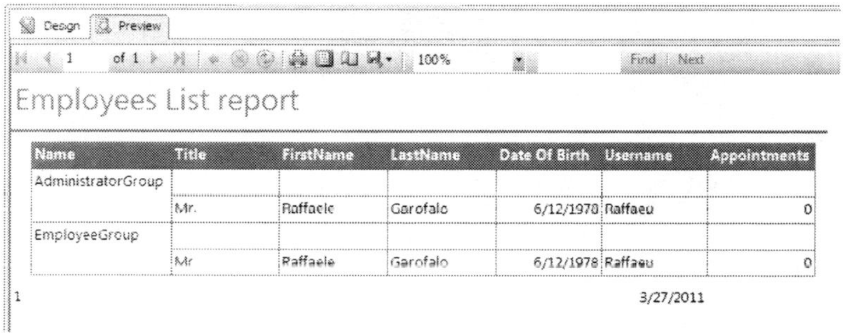

Figure 10-8. *Final report result*

Now let's design the detailed report for a selected employee. We will create a generic detail report with a query that will require a parameter, the Employee Id.

From Solution Explorer, select the Deploy command on the context menu and verify that the menu is uploaded properly into the SSRS folder on the report portal.

EmployeeDetailsReport

The TimeTracker application has two views that allow you to interact with the registered employees. The first one is a list of employees and you just created the corresponding report. The second is the detailed view for the employee so let's create the report for that view.

In Solution Explorer select the Reports folder and click Add ➤ New Item ➤ Report, name it `EmployeeDetailsReport` and press OK.

Create a header and a footer using the same settings as for the `EmployeeListReport`, but change the title of the report to Details instead of List and save it. It should look like the report in the Figure 10-7 except for the title.

Now you need to create a dataset for this report, so in the Report Data panel select New and create a new dataset. Choose the option of creating a new dataset embedded in the report and open the query designer as you did for the previous report.

Create a Query with a Parameter

This time you want to select all the tables that provide information related to the Employee entity and you don't need to run any aggregate function because you just want to display all the information related to a specific employee in a form-style report.

Figure 10-9 shows the information and the tables to select from the database.

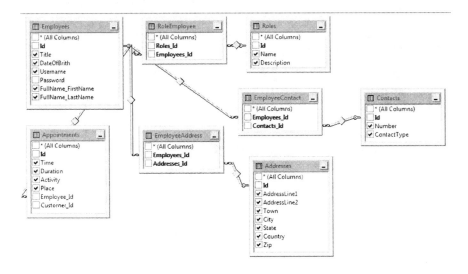

Figure 10-9. Database query for the EmployeeDetailsReport

The last step is to add an additional line of T-SQL at the end of the generated T-SQL code like this:

```
WHERE        (Employees.Id = @Id)
```

Press OK and look at the Parameters section of the Create Dataset dialog. You should see that the report now has a parameter that requires the current Employee Id in order to display the employee information. After you confirm this, the Report data panel will have two new objects, the new dataset and, in the Parameters folder, the new parameter.

Now you need to provide a ComboBox in the report so whether the user wants to run the report from the SSRS web site or from WPF, he will be able to select the employee from a ComboBox and run the report.

Create a new dataset and call it AvailableEmployees. This report will show the list of employees using the following query:

```
SELECT          Id, Title + ' ' + FullName_FirstName + ' ' + FullName_LastName AS FullName
FROM            Employees
ORDER BY FullName
```

Press OK and save the new dataset. It will provide a list of employee names in this form: "Mr. FirstName LastName" and the corresponding Id.

In the Parameters folder of the Report Data panel, locate the @Id parameter and double-click it to open a new dialog that allows you to configure the parameter values.

Select the Available Values section using the Listbox on the left and click the option "Get values from a query." Now select the newly created dataset and specify the Id for the value and the Fullname field for the label. Press OK and save this setting.

Now you can test the report by switching to the Preview tab; you should see a header that will prompt you to select an employee from the list.

Create the Details

In the previous report you used a component called Table that allows you to create a list of rows using features like Group By, Sum, and more. Now let's create a simple details view so you don't need to embed the data into a specific container. You can simply drag the fields from the dataset in the Report data panel directly into the report. Unfortunately, SSRS doesn't have a feature that if you drag a field of a dataset to a report surface it will add a label, so you need to create a label for each property of the Employee entity, like FirstName, LastName and so on.

When you are done with the first part of the report, which is the Employee details section, you need to create three distinct tables, one for the Contacts, one for the Addresses, and one for the Appointments.

Just right-click on the design surface of the report, select Insert ➤ Table, and then specify in the table to use the dataset that provides the data and not the dataset that provides the list of employees.

When you are done your result should look like the one in Figure 10-10.

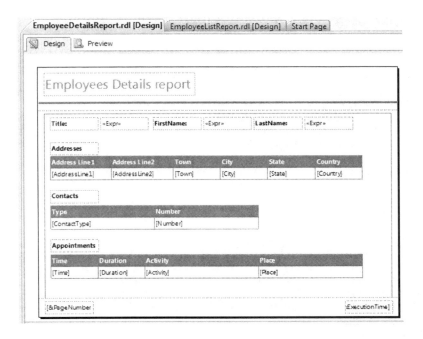

Figure 10-10. *Final Employee details report*

After you add the tables to the report, they will be dynamically filled with all the rows coming from the dataset, filtered by Employee Id. The last step is to Group By every table for the specific Id you're showing. For example, the table that shows all the contacts should be grouped by the Contacts Id field. This process has to be done because the SELECT we are using is returning additional rows because of extra JOINS being executed; this type of SELECT will return duplicate rows for the joined tables (Addresses, Contacts and Appointments).

To group a table without showing the group on the design surface, you have to execute the following steps:

1. Select a table you want to group.

2. In the Row Groups panel positioned below the report design surface area, select the little arrow on the right of the lines called Details.

3. Select the last menu item, Group Properties.

4. In the Group By dialog, select Add and choose the corresponding Id field of the table.

Now the report should be fine and ready to be deployed to the report server folder so that it can be used by the users and by the TimeTracker application.

Additional Reports

In the first part of this chapter you saw how to create two different types of reports, a simple list of information retrieved from the database without any filtering but using a Group By function to aggregate some information, specifically the number of appointments per employee.

The second type of report is one that requires a parameter, which means that the data displayed in the report is filtered by a specific criterion that can be decided on the fly by the user or by the application that is running the report.

In the TimeTracker application, you'll probably need a lot more reports. For example, all the reports we created for the `Employee` entity should be created for the `Customer` entity, and you should create a report for the Appointments, including its details and the invoice that has to be sent to the customer.

For space reasons, we can't create all these reports in this chapter, but you can use the two previous reports as a path to follow to create new reports, filtered or not filtered. If you want to take a more in-depth look at SSRS and learn more about the many different types of reports you can create, here are a few very useful resources:

- *Pro SQL Server Reporting Services* (Apress, 2004)

- *Foundations of SQL Server 2008 R2 Business Intelligence* (Apress, 2011)

- "SQL Server Reporting Services," `msdn.microsoft.com/library/ms159106.aspx`

Keep in mind that the business intelligence part of SQL Server 2008 R2 comprises a very big area, and in this chapter you are seeing how to create only some very simple reports and how to integrate them in your WPF application using the MVVM pattern and the Windows Host control. This is only a small part of what can be achieved with this very powerful tool.

Hosting the Reports in a WPF Control

SSRS provides a component called `ReportViewer` that can be used to host (display) a report inside a Windows Forms control. Unfortunately, the control for WPF hasn't been created yet, so to display a report in WPF using the Windows Forms control you need to run the control in a special container that can provide forward compatibility between Windows Forms and WPF.

In WPF you can use a control of type `WindowsFormsHost`, which is available from the `WindowsFormsIntegration.dll` assembly provided with .NET 4. This control is a full, rich WPF control that provides tons of methods, events, and properties to fully integrate and host a Windows Forms control in a WPF control. The control can be used in your WPF XAML markup to instantiate and create additional controls in it that derive from the `System.Windows.Forms` namespace.

In order to use the control, you need to add the following references to the WPF application that will host the control:

- `System.Windows.Forms`

- `WindowsFormsIntegration`

Then you can integrate the control in your XAML markup, as in the example in Listing 10-2.

Listing 10-2. Sample to Show a Windows Forms Control in a WPF Window

```
<Window x:Class="APRESS.TimeTracking.Views.ReportView"
        xmlns="http://schemas.microsoft.com/winfx/2006/xaml/presentation"
        xmlns:x="http://schemas.microsoft.com/winfx/2006/xaml"
        xmlns:wf="clr-namespace:System.Windows.Forms;assembly=System.Windows.Forms"
        Title="ReportView" Height="300" Width="300">
    <Grid>
        <WindowsFormsHost>
            <wf:Panel>
                <wf:Panel.Controls>
                    <wf:Label Text="MyLabel"></wf:Label>
                    <wf:TextBox Width="100" Height="29"></wf:TextBox>
                </wf:Panel.Controls>
            </wf:Panel>
        </WindowsFormsHost>
    </Grid>
</Window>
```

The only downside of using this control is that you can't control in design time the layout of the control's content because it doesn't render the layout until you execute the application. The suggested approach, if you plan to use this control, is to host a Windows Forms `UserControl` in it, already designed so you get fancy layout results at runtime.

Display the Report in a WPF View

The `ReportViewer` is a Windows Forms control used to display local and remote reports in a Windows Forms application. The control is not available in the default Visual Studio installation so you need to download it separately. You can find the download for the Microsoft Report Viewer 2010 Redistributable Package at `www.microsoft.com/downloads/en/details.aspx?FamilyID=a941c6b2-64dd-4d03-9ca7-4017a0d164fd`.

After you've installed it on your development machine, you'll find some new assemblies in the Visual Studio Add reference window:

- Microsoft.ReportViewer.Common V9 and V10

- Microsoft.ReportViewer.WebForms V9 and V10

- Microsoft.ReportViewer.WinForms V9 and V10

To display a report in the TimeTracker application, you have a few tasks to accomplish, but nothing really complicated:

- Prepare a ViewModel for the report view that will set up the report viewer component.

- Prepare a simple WPF Windows that will host the report ViewModel.

- Modify the `INavigationService` to load the `ReportView`.

- Modify the `EmployeeList` and `EmployeeDetails` Views and ViewModels to load the reports.

The first step is to prepare in the TimeTracker WPF project a new ViewModel object specifically for the report viewer you've installed on your machine (see Listing 10-3).

Listing 10-3. ReportViewModel

```
using System;
using System.Windows.Forms.Integration;
using Microsoft.Reporting.WinForms;

namespace APRESS.TimeTracking.ViewModels
{
    public sealed class ReportViewModel : BaseViewModel<ReportViewModel>
    {
        private WindowsFormsHost viewer;

        public ReportViewModel(string reportPath)
        {
            viewer = new WindowsFormsHost();
            var reportViewer = new ReportViewer();
            reportViewer.ProcessingMode = ProcessingMode.Remote;
            // here you have to point to your machine URL
            reportViewer.ServerReport.ReportServerUrl =
                new Uri("http://raffaelegard400/Reportserver_SQLEXPRESS");
            reportViewer.ServerReport.ReportPath = reportPath;
            reportViewer.RefreshReport();
            viewer.Child = reportViewer;
        }

        public WindowsFormsHost Viewer
        {
            get { return viewer; }
            set
            {
                viewer = value;
                OnPropertyChanged(x => x.Viewer);
            }
        }
    }
}
```

This code exposes a WindowsFormsHost control as a property that you will bind to the XAML view. The report path must be in the constructor; in this case it will be something like /TimeTracker/myreport/. Finally, the code binds the report to the report viewer, refreshes and generates the report, and then binds the report viewer to the WindowsFormsHost control.

Now you have the ViewModel, which will host the report viewer; it has to be created in the Views folder and it is a Windows component.

Listing 10-4 creates the View that will host the report viewer and uses a ContentPresenter WPF control to put a placeholder in the view. This placeholder will be filled using the Viewer property of the DataContext, which in our case is the WindowsFormsHost control exposed by the ViewModel.

Listing 10-4. ReportView WPF Window

```
<Window x:Class="APRESS.TimeTracking.Views.ReportView"
        xmlns="http://schemas.microsoft.com/winfx/2006/xaml/presentation"
        xmlns:x="http://schemas.microsoft.com/winfx/2006/xaml"
        Title="ReportView" Height="300" Width="300">
    <Grid>
        <ContentPresenter
            Content="{Binding Viewer, UpdateSourceTrigger=PropertyChanged}" />
    </Grid>
</Window>
```

Now let's modify the navigation service and the corresponding interface, as shown in Listing 10-5.

Listing 10-5. Modification on the INavigationService Interface and Concrete Class

```
// INavigationService
void ShowReportDialog(string report);

// Navigation Service
public void ShowPrintDialog(string report)
{
    var window = Container.Resolve<Views.ReportView>();
    ReportViewModel vm = new ReportViewModel(report);
    window.DataContext = vm;
    window.ShowDialog();
}
```

The `NavigationService` class creates a new `ReportView` using the Unity IoC container. You don't need to preregister the `ReportView` in the container because the container will resolve it using the default constructor of the view. Next the code creates a new `ViewModel` for the report by injecting the report path received from the `ShowReportDialog` method, and finally it binds the `ViewModel` to the `View` and then displays the `View` as a dialog so that the user can't do anything until the report is closed.

Load a List of Employees Report

The first view to modify is the `EmployeeListView`. You need to add a new `Button` that will display the report, associate a `PrintCommand` to the `Button` and create the delegate that will be used to call the `NavigationService` from the `EmployeeListViewModel`.

To start, open the `EmployeeListViewModel` and create a new command and the corresponding implementation as shown in Listing 10-6.

Listing 10-6. EmployeeListViewModel

```
// add a new property
public ICommand PrintCommand { get; private set; }

// modify the InitializeCommands method by adding this one
PrintCommand = new MvvmCommand(
    (parameter) => { PrintEmployees(); },
    (parameter) => { return true; });

// method to display the report
private void PrintEmployees()
{
    this.navigationService.ShowPrintDialog("/TimeTracker/EmployeeListReport");
}
```

The first part of this listing creates a new command in the ViewModel and modifies the existing InitializeCommands method by adding an additional initialization, the one used for the PrintCommand object. Next it associates a delegate to the PrintCommand that will simply call the INavigationService method to display the report by passing the report path.

The final step is to create the Print button in the EmployeeListView and verify that everything works as expected. See Listing 10-7.

Listing 10-7. Modification of the EmployeeListView

```
// add a new Button in the toolbar
<Controls:ImageButton
        Padding="3"
        Text="Print"
        ClickCommand="{Binding Path=PrintCommand, UpdateSourceTrigger=PropertyChanged}"
        Image="{DynamicResource PrintSmall}" />
```

The final result should look like the one displayed in Figure 10-11.

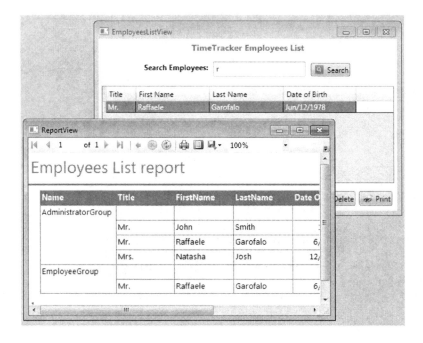

Figure 10-11. *Employee List report, with new print button*

Load a Detailed Report

The code to load a single employee is almost the same; you need to create a new `Button` in the `EmployeeDetailsView` and associate a command in the corresponding `ViewModel`, then modify the `NavigationService` and create a new method that will ask also for the `PrimaryKey` of the record you want to print out, as in Listing 10-8.

Listing 10-8. *The NavigationService Method to Show a Details Report*

```
public void ShowDetailsPrintDialog(string report, int id)v
{
    var window = Container.Resolve<Views.ReportView>();
    ReportViewModel vm = new ReportViewModel(report, id);
    window.DataContext = vm;
    window.ShowDialog();
}
```

Now you need to modify the `ReportViewModel` by creating a new constructor that will require the `Id` as a parameter, which you'll inject into the corresponding report (see Listing 10-9). Remember to adapt the `NavigationService` class for these new methods and the corresponding interface.

Listing 10-9. *New Constructor of the* `ReportViewModel`

```
public ReportViewModel(string reportPath, int id)
{
    viewer = new WindowsFormsHost();
    var reportViewer = new ReportViewer();
    reportViewer.ProcessingMode = ProcessingMode.Remote;
    // remember to change the address to the URL you have
    reportViewer.ServerReport.ReportServerUrl = new↵
 Uri("http://raffaelegard400/Reportserver_SQLEXPRESS");
    reportViewer.ServerReport.ReportPath = reportPath;
    ReportParameter[] parameters = new ReportParameter[1];
    parameters[0] = new ReportParameter("Id", id.ToString());
    reportViewer.ServerReport.SetParameters(parameters);
    reportViewer.RefreshReport();
    viewer.Child = reportViewer;
}
```

The only difference here is the `ReportParameter` array, an array of parameters you can pass to the report server to filter the data of the report without requiring user interaction. So, in this case, the user will not need to select a specific employee from the report combobox.

Finally, you need to define the report command for the details view and, of course, you need to add a new Button also in the Details view as you did for the list view. Listing 10-10 shows the `PrintCommand`.

Listing 10-10. *PrintCommand for the Employee Details ViewModel*

```
public ICommand PrintCommand { get; set; }

private void InitializeCommands()
{
    navigationService = container.Resolve<INavigationService>();
    PrintCommand = new MvvmCommand(
        (parameter) => { PrintEmployee(); },
        (parameter) => { return true; });
}

private void PrintEmployee()
{
    this.navigationService
        .ShowDetailsPrintDialog(
            "/TimeTracker/EmployeeDetailsReport",
            this.CurrentEntity.Id);
}
```

Finally, the code calls the new method on the navigation service and passes the current entity id and the name of the report. The final result looks like the one in Figure 10-12.

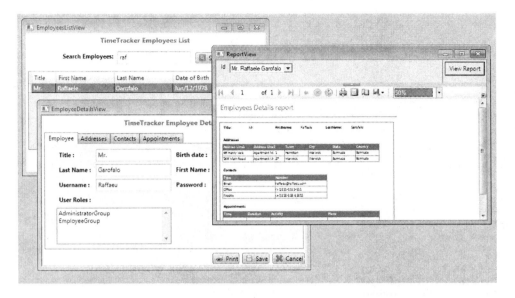

Figure 10-12. Employee Details View and Report

Now you can refactor the code used previously and pass a `Dictionary<string, string>` instead of a simple `int` as the report parameter so that you can use the method to display any report, with or without parameters. Here is a possible application of how you can call it:

```
// Create the parameters
Dictionary<string, string> parameters =
    new Dictionary<string, string>
    {
        "Id", "1"
    }

    this.navigationService
        .ShowDetailsPrintDialog(
            "/TimeTracker/EmployeeDetailsReport",
            parameters);
```

Summary

In this chapter you saw how to configure SQL Server Reporting Services (SSRS), a powerful business intelligence reporting system provided with SQL Server 2008 R2 and also available with the Express edition (of course with some architectural limits).

SSRS works by creating a Windows SharePoint Server portal that you can use to share and run the reports deployed on it.

In order to create a report for SSRS, you need to open the special version of Visual Studio 2008 installed with the SSRS tools, which is called SQL Server Business Intelligence Development Studio. This version of VS lets you create, run, and deploy datasources, datasets, and reports of any type.

You saw how to create a simple list of records and how you can create a more complex report of type master-detail, and how to filter the data by using report parameters. You can provide a set of values for a report parameter so that the user will not be forced to remember, for example, the Id of the employee he wants to show in the report.

Finally, you saw how to host a Windows Forms control in WPF and, more precisely, how to execute the `ReportViewer` component to load and run remote reports, all using the Model View ViewModel pattern so that the View stays loosely coupled and unaware of the `ReportViewer` control.

CHAPTER 11

■ ■ ■

Deploy the Application Using ClickOnce

When the application is complete and ready to be distributed to the final user, whether in your organization or an external customer, you need to prepare a package or a deployment solution that lets this user install and run the application in few easy steps.

In this phase of the deployment process, it's really important that you focus on the simplicity of the end result. Remember that the user will probably be completely unaware of the technology requirements of the application and you have to be able to give him everything he'll need to install and run the application.

For example, if the user's computer doesn't have the .NET Framework 4 runtime files and your application has been developed using .NET 4, you have to provide an easy way to install these mandatory files without too many hassles.

The .NET Framework provides different ways to install and distribute an application to the end user. You can distribute a setup package (.msi) that the user can download and install, but with this solution, the application will have to provide a mechanism to be "upgradable." A good alternative is ClickOnce, a technology available in the .NET Framework for distributing packages across the Internet that are safe and auto-upgradable.

ClickOnce Deployment

When you deploy an application, you have to satisfy three major requirements:

- Make the setup process safe especially if it is distributed through the Internet.

- Make the installation process easy; the user should be aware of the application .requirements and prerequisites and should be able to run a setup and get the application running.

- Make the application auto-upgradable or easily upgraded, and there should be a way to notify the user of new updates.

The ClickOnce technology is designed to be distributed using the Internet, a file share, or media such as a CD-ROM or USB drive. You simply set up the distribution configuration and then deploy the application and Click Once will do the rest.

With ClickOnce you can make the application self-upgradable using different options that we will discuss in this chapter. You can also sign and certify the application and you can include prerequisites like the .NET Framework 4 or other redistributable packages.

The web distribution of ClickOnce, right now, works with any version of Internet Explorer and Mozilla Firefox; it also works with Chrome, but this browser is not yet included in the official list on MSDN.

In the next sections we will take a look at distribution, security, certificates, and updates; then we will apply the knowledge's to the TimeTracker application.

ClickOnce Security

ClickOnce provides a complete mechanism for securing your distributable package using technologies like certificates, code access security policies (CAS), and authentication. If you plan to distribute your application using ClickOnce, the first step is to use the Windows Authenticode certificate to sign your package and make it safe. When the user downloads the package, he will see the certificate and be able to identify you as the author of the package.

Certificates and Authenticode

There are different types of certificates you can use in Windows. You can use certificates to sign the contents of an e-mail; certificates to sign access to a web site; and certificates to sign an application's code. The latter are classified as code-signing certificates and can be obtained in the following ways:

- Purchase a certificate online from one of the well-known companies that sell certificates, like www.verisign.com/code-signing/.

- Get a certificate from you company or your company's network administrator.

- Create a certificate of your own using the Makecert.exe .NET tool.

The type of certificate you need depends on the type of application you're publishing. For example, if you are publishing the TimeTracker application as a software vendor and you want to distribute it using a public web site, your authority should be certified using a trusted publisher like VeriSign. On the other hand, if you are publishing the application to your company intranet, using the Makecert.exe utility is more than enough.

In any case, remember that a certificate is not "forever" and usually will expire in a year or two. Also, consider that a VeriSign certificate may cost you $895 per year (at the time of this writing). You should be able to recoup this cost out of the application income; otherwise, you might want to use a self-signed certificate. Remember, though, that it won't provide the correct user experience and that it shouldn't be used for an external application.

To run Makecert.exe, select Start ➤ All programs ➤ Visual Studio 2010 ➤ Visual Studio tools ➤ Visual Studio command prompt. Inside this (DOS) window, type Makecert and press OK. The dialog will show you a list of commands and options available for this tool. A detailed guide to creating certificates with Makecert is available at msdn.microsoft.com/en-us/library/bfsktky3(v=VS.100).aspx.

To generate a certificate with this tool, to run it using options like the following:

```
// simple certificate
makecert testCert.cer

// create a certificate with a key
makecert -sk XYZ -n "CN=XYZ Company" testXYZ.cer
```

■ **Note** The ClickOnce deployment panel in Visual Studio 2010 (in the project properties under the Signing panel) lets you create a temporary certificate that can be used to deploy your ClickOnce application within your intranet. If you are working for a company that has an internal IT infrastructure, ask your network administrator about certificates. He should be able to create one using the Certificate Authority server on your network.

Code Access Security

Code Access Security is a ClickOnce option used for limiting the access of the ClickOnce application to specific resources and components of the client running the application. For example, you may want to disable access to the local file system or you may need to increase the application's rights to access a local file system folder on the client in order to be able to write, for example, a custom log file.

By default, ClickOnce installs the application with full trust rights, and this type of configuration can be harmful for the client. Moreover, if the client computer has some restricted configuration, the full trust provided by ClickOnce may not work and the user may be forced to grant additional permissions to the application.

The only way to configure the security access is to use the security page available in Visual Studio. Figure 11-1 shows an example of the security page options.

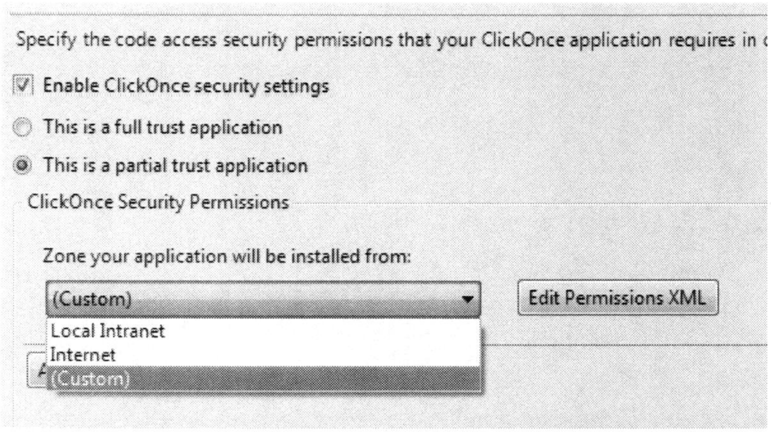

Figure 11-1. Security options for ClickOnce

When you set up the security, you need to also consider the distribution technique you'll use for the application. For instance, if you plan to grant full trust and distribute the application using an Internet URL, ClickOnce will ask the user to grant additional permissions because an Internet setup doesn't have full-trust permission by default.

Publishing Options

When you set up the ClickOnce options for the application, you can specify any prerequisites for the application, how to update the application or one of its components, where to publish the application, and what components will included in the deployment package.

You can specify all this information using the Publish option panel available in Visual Studio in the properties window of the WPF project you are configuring.

Updates

One of the most interesting features that make ClickOnce a handy way of distributing applications is the ability to provide a self-checking mechanism for updates. You can configure ClickOnce so that the application can make decisions about updates and force the user to install the latest version or take different actions.

The options related to the update strategy used by your ClickOnce deployment are available in the Publish panel of the Project properties window.

In the first TextBox of the Publish panel you can set up where you want to deploy the application files, which can be a UNC path (i.e., \\mymachine\mysharedfolder), a URL, or an FTP address. If you press the browse button next to the TextBox, you'll see a dialog that will help you choose the destination folder. You can use the dialog to locate a local IIS web site, a remote FTP folder, or a file system location.

In the second TextBox, you can choose a different path for the installation. It could, for example, be a web site address like http://mywebsite.com/install.html.

After you've decided where to deploy the application files, you need to configure the update strategy you plan to use, and you can do this by choosing the appropriate options in the Application Updates dialog shown in Figure 11-2.

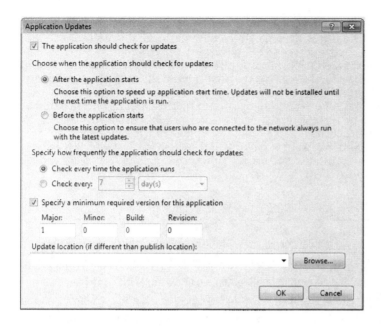

Figure 11-2. *The Application Updates dialog*

For example, if the updates you will release aren't critical, you can allow the user to run the application without the latest update and check for updates when the application is shut down. Or you can force the application to look for updates at startup, and you can also force the user to run a specific version number so that any previous version will be invalid. Every update of the application can override these settings.

These settings can also be changed using the corresponding deployment manifest file, which can be edited using a text editor or the `MageUI.exe` utility, an alternative UI tool that allows you to create different application manifest files for ClickOnce deployment.

With `MageUI` you can create two different files:

- `APRESS.TimeTracker.Application`, the application manifest file used to specify how the application will be deployed.

- `APRESS.TimeTracker.exe.manifest`, the manifest file that describes the application settings and requirements.

These files can replace the one published by the ClickOnce wizard, so you can control the deployment process with more granular settings.

Application Files and Prerequisites

Another section in the Publish tab is related to the application's file dependencies. For example, the TimeTracker application uses some external components and some .NET assemblies that must be deployed with the application; otherwise, the client who runs the installation package won't be able to execute the software because the dependencies aren't available.

If you press the Application Files button, you'll get a dialog showing you all the dependencies Visual Studio identifies for the application. This window is divided in four columns, the first one shows you the name of the file (.dll) needed by the application; the second one shows you the current status in the deployment process, which can be include, prerequisite (already installed), or exclude. The third column shows you the group to which the item will be published, and the final column shows the hash result of the assembly and asks you if you want to publish this as well.

In the prerequisites window, also on the Publish tab, you can use the corresponding button to force the ClickOnce deployment to check for some specific prerequisites that the client must have installed in order to run your application. You can then specify that the setup will update the missing components or it will fail the installation. For example, you may want to check that the client has installed SQL Server 2008 R2, the NET Framework 4, and the Visual Studio 2010 Report Viewer components. If they are not installed, you can force the client to download them from a location or you can include them in the deployment package.

■ **Note** ClickOnce technology has been introduced to help developers distribute and update their applications with less effort and pain. If you plan to deploy your application on a network folder or web site and to distribute it using only this technique, you should be careful about the application requirements. For example, the .NET Framework plus the Visual Studio Report Viewer packages can easily amount to 50MB of data that the client will have to install the first time. On a slow network link, a download of 50MB can take quite a while, so you should keep such application requirements in mind when you design the ClickOnce part.

Additional Options

The final section of the Publish tab contains some additional information that you can provide to the installation package to better describe your company and the application. The options dialog window consists of four different sections:

- **Description:** This section allows you to insert more information about the application, the publisher, and the language. You can also provide a URL for support and another URL in case the application setup encounters an error.

- **Deployment:** In this section you can specify the deployment web page or leave it blank so that VS will create a default one for you. You can open the deployment page when the build and publish process is complete, and you can also configure the settings for the CD-ROM version of ClickOnce.

- **Manifests:** In this section you can add more granular control of the setup process.

- **File Associations:** This section can be used to associate a file extension of a particular type to the application. You can also specify a unique Id and an icon file that will be used by Windows to identify the file extension. The unique Id is a ProgID used by Windows.

ClickOnce technology provides additional settings and setup configurations for more advanced use that we won't analyze here. If you plan to take advantage of ClickOnce for more advanced use, I suggest you look at the exhaustive guide to ClickOnce at msdn.microsoft.com/library/t71a733d.aspx.

Deploy the TimeTracker Application

In the first part of this chapter you saw how to sign a ClickOnce application using an Authenticode certificate, how to set up the code access security (CAS) for the application, and how to prepare IIS to distribute the application. Now let's apply all these concepts to the TimeTracker application so you will have a full working example of a redistributable application that can be hosted in IIS.

First, you need to open the TimeTracker application. Right-click on the TimeTracker WPF project in Solution Explorer and select **Properties**; this opens the WPF project properties window, showing a set of tabs that identify all the information related to the application.

The Application tab provides information related to the application. In the Icon and Manifest sections, you need to provide an icon (the size depends on your operating system; usually a 32px is pretty good) for the application that will be used by ClickOnce to create a custom shortcut on the desktop and on the application folder. Leave the settings as is for the manifest.

Next you need to get all the information needed to sign and identify the WPF application. You can accomplish this by clicking on the Assembly information button, which will bring up a dialog that requires the information used to sign and identify the assembly. Figure 11-3 shows the information for the TimeTracker application.

Figure 11-3. Assembly properties window

Now you can press OK, save the file in Visual Studio, and move to the Signing tab, which will be used to create a certificate for the application.

Create a Temporary Certificate

In this book we can't use a Code Signing certificate for the TimeTracker application because we didn't purchase one from an authorized company, nor have we a network administrator who can provide a Code Signing certificate. This may be the same situation you have on your development machine, but you need to be able to test and deploy the ClickOnce application anyway, so what can you do?

If you go to the Visual Studio project properties Signing panel, you will see a set of information that's grayed out by default. To enable this information, select Sign the ClickOnce manifests. Now you have three options to provide a ClickOnce certificate: you can select one available on a certificate store; you can select one from a file system; or you can create a test certificate. Let's use the third option.

The only information required by the dialog used to create a temporary certificate is a password for the certificate, which will be used by Authenticode to sign a temporary key file. Because this is a temporary test certificate, you can leave the password blank and press OK.

The result is a custom certificate that ClickOnce will use to identify you as the creator of the application, as Figure 11-4 shows. You can also click the More Details button to view the standard certificate dialog showing that the certificate is untrusted.

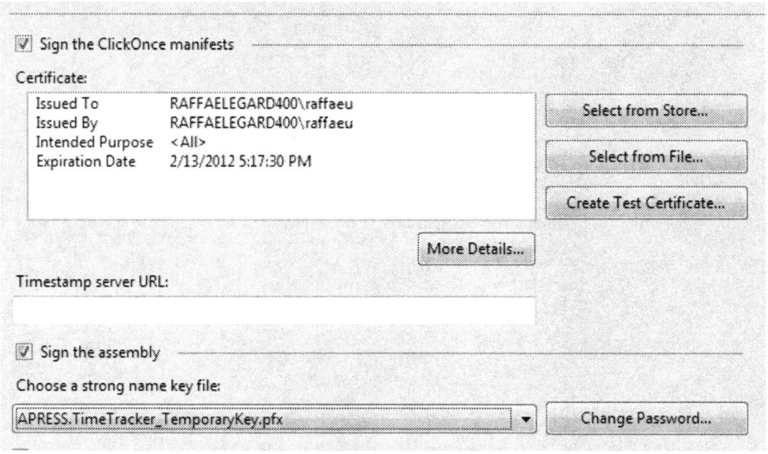

Figure 11-4. Test certificate created using Visual Studio 2010

The certificate has been created as a file with the extension .pfx and you can now choose to sign the assembly and certify it using your custom certificate. Note that as soon as you mark the assembly with the certificate, the application will not build anymore because the BusinessLayer and the DataLayer assemblies are not signed with the same certificate. To fix this problem you need to open the properties panel of each TimeTracker application project and sign the assembly using the same certificate, which is available from the Sign the Assembly combobox option.

Security

The security settings for the TimeTracker application are pretty simple as you'll be running the application from the development machine. If you plan to distribute the application over your company network, you can easily change these settings later.

Go to the Security tab of the TimeTracker properties page and select the option "This is a Full trust application" and then save the settings.

This configuration will not cause any security issue while you are testing your deployment package.

Publish TimeTracker

Now it's time to publish the TimeTracker application and verify the installation process, so click on the Publish tab.

First you need to decide where to publish the application. Let's use the local Internet Information Service (IIS) already created by the SSRS setup in the previous chapter.

On your C :drive, create a new folder and call it TimeTrackerDeployment. This folder is where you'll save the deployment package.

If you have Windows 7 or Windows Vista, simply type IIS in the search **TextBox** of the Start menu and select Internet Information Services. If you have Windows XP (or Windows Vista or Windows 7), you should be able to locate IIS in Control Panel ➤ Administrative Tools ➤ Internet Information Services.

In the IIS panel, locate the Sites folder and expand it. You should have a Default Web Site node; expand it, right-click on it, and select Add Application. Use the settings shown in the dialog in Figure 11-5.

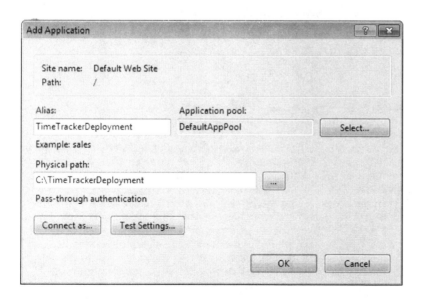

Figure 11-5. IIS web application settings

In the previous step you created a new web application called TimeTrackerDeployment, which will be reachable from your development machine at `http://localhost/TimeTrackerDeployment`, where you'll put the deployment files.

Now go back to the Publish tab and set the Publish folder location to: `C:\TimeTrackerDeployment\` and the Installation folder URL to `http://localhost/TimeTrackerDeployment/` and save the settings.

You can try to publish the application as is now by right-clicking on the WPF application project in the solution folder and choosing Publish, or by pressing the Publish button on the Publish tab. Visual Studio will build the application and publish it to the destination folder. It will then open your default browser by pointing to the URL `http://localhost/TimeTrackerDeployment/publish.htm`.

The `publish.htm` page is a static page created by the Visual Studio publishing template, which includes a brief description of the application package that can be enriched by using the Options page. That page includes an Install button for installing the application on your machine. It will also create a shortcut icon and a Program menu item.

Now, based on the Update settings you have configured, every time you run the TimeTracker application, it will or will not check for updates and additional versions of the application.

■ **Note** The ClickOnce technology in Visual Studio 2010 has a well-known bug that sometime happens when you press the Publish button on the Publish tab. It displays a generic error saying that the application can't be deployed because one of the projects can't be built. If this happens, you can fix the problem by calling the Publish command from the context menu of the WPF project. This solution has been exhaustively described in the following Microsoft Connect thread: `https://connect.microsoft.com/VisualStudio/feedback/details/551674/` `vs-2010-rtm-returns-error-cannot-publish-because-a-project-failed-to-build-even-though-` `solution-builds-fine`.

Summary

With ClickOnce you can distribute the application you are producing without the hassles of creating complicated distribution packages and worrying about application updates and dependencies.

ClickOnce is a proven technology introduced with Visual Studio 2003 and now tested and extended to satisfy all the major requirements an application setup package may have. You can create a shortcut on the client desktop, an application menu item in Windows, and take advantage of many other features like providing a help URL or an error URL.

ClickOnce also lets you certify your packages by signing the code with the Authenticode technology using a custom-generated certificate or a third-party certificate like the ones provided by VeriSign, for example.

With ClickOnce, you can carry with your application deployment package all the dependencies required by the application, and if you believe the dependencies are too heavy, you can just force the client computer to check if the prerequisites are satisfied or provide an alternative way of obtaining them, for example by using a download URL.

ClickOnce is flexible and easy to use, and with the help of IIS, it lets you create and deploy an application setup file in few minutes and make it available to your entire company network just by sharing a static IIS web site.

CHAPTER 12

■ ■ ■

Design Patterns in WPF

The main purpose of creating a layered application and loosely coupling presentation logic to business logic is to have a larger testable surface area and to remove, as far as possible, code dependencies so that each layer of the application can be testable and independent.

Probably this concept can be applied, from a purist point of view, only in a perfect world where the model is completely independent of anything else and the UI doesn't know anything of the data model that is rendering on the screen.

Throughout the entire book we've applied design patterns to every component of the TimeTracker application. We created a domain model using the domain driven design techniques; we created a data layer using the UnitOfWork and the Repository patterns; and we applied some Test Driven Development concepts to these components.

The advantage of using these techniques is amazing. You can change something in the domain model and, by testing, understand right away if the change will or will not affect the remaining components of the application. You can also verify the impact of such change and understand if the application can be deployed with the new changes or not. Of course, this process is covered by a complex set of tests; as soon as you tackle one layer, say the data layer, you should execute all the unit and integration tests for all the layers to make sure that the changes will not affect, indirectly, a different layer that has not been tested again.

Unfortunately, though we added all this flexibility to the TimeTracker application, we didn't (completely) isolate and loosely coupled the UI logic from the rest of the application logic. In short, we didn't apply a design pattern specifically for the presentation logic to make the presentation part more testable.

To be honest, although you've already seen a whole lot about the MVVM pattern, we haven't really analyzed it in depth or looked at the available alternatives. Let's do that now.

Patterns for the UI

The point of applying a design pattern to the graphical layer of an application is to loosely couple the business logic to the presentation logic so that, for example, you can recycle the same components for a different View.

However, with presentation patterns, the idea is not to apply them in order to loosely couple the Model to the View. In the first place, all the information carried from the model is exposed by the View and there's no reason to hide it. Moreover, the amount of effort you have to put in and the amount of code you have to write to totally loosely couple the view to the model is too much to gain any other advantage.

If you look at all the other presentation patterns (not just for WPF), they all include the word model: Model View Controller (MVC), Model View Presenter (MVP), Presentation Model (PM). and Model View ViewModel (MVVM), so it seems clear that you shouldn't be afraid of exposing the model to the view to display the information you need to display. What you should be more afraid of is sticking business logic in the view and mixing logic code for the view with logic code for the model.

For example, if you have a model that is not valid (there's no data), you shouldn't write this logic in the view just because the view is in charge of notifying the user with a validation error. Instead, you should use a middle component, like a presenter, to orchestrate between the view and the model so that the view requirements don't affect the model requirements.

In this book we use the MVVM pattern, a design pattern designed for WPF and subsequently applied as well to Silverlight and Windows Phone 7. However, MVVM is not the only design pattern applicable to WPF, so let's take a short tour of the design patterns that can be easily applied to WPF.

■ **Note** You may notice that in discussing design patterns for WPF we skip some of the most well-known presentation patterns, like MVC. This is quite deliberate because I believe that the MVC pattern is not practically applicable to WPF—even if it is theoretically possible to build an MVC WPF application. First of all, MVC requires an architecture (framework) behind the scenes that is not easy to build and not feasible with client technologies like WPF or Windows Forms. Second, and more important, with the MVC pattern you can't use a number of WPF's powerful features, like data binding, commands, and delegates, because the MVC pattern is driven by the Controller and not by the View.

Model View Presenter

The Model View Presenter (MVP) pattern has been around developer communities since 1990 when it was first used by Taligent and IBM. It was introduced because the parent Model View Controller (MVC) pattern lacked a middle component to take care of the presentation logic. The MVP pattern has three components: the Model, the View, and the Presenter; the last one is in charge of the presentation logic.

In this pattern, the main role is given to the Presenter, which is in charge of listening for the View's events and reacting appropriately to these events. The Presenter also makes logical decisions based on the View state.

Since its development, this pattern has been examined, especially by Martin Fowler, a software architect who analyzed this and other presentation patterns in depth. (If you are interested in the topic, you may find his book *Patterns of Enterprise Applications Architecture* (Addison-Wesley, 2003) very useful).

Now let's take a look at the MVP pattern, also known as Passive View, and at a variant called Supervising Controller.

■ **Note** The next sections use some sample code that can be easily downloaded from this book's page on the Apress web site. The sample code does not refer directly to the TimeTracker application and is used just to explain the design pattern.

The Passive View MVP

The Passive View MVP pattern is the original version of the MVP, the one introduced by IBM in 1990, which was then changed and adapted by various exponents of the pattern communities.

Figure 12-1 shows the structure of the MVP pattern.

MVP – PASSIVE VIEW

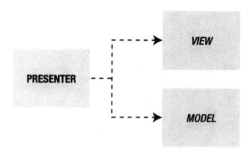

Figure 12-1. *MVP Passive View structure*

In this version of the MVP pattern, the orchestrator is the Presenter, which is in charge of listening to the View's events and reacting to them, as well as updating the model and passing the Model information to the View. The diagram shows that the View is totally passive and does not have a real dependency on the model. In this case, the Presenter is in charge of everything and this is the reason this version of the MVP pattern is called the passive view.

Listing 12-1 shows an interface that represents a `Calculator` View—a simple WPF `Window` that has two `TextBoxes` and a `Button`, and performs integer addition. This simple WPF application was created with Visual Studio 2010 and is downloadable from the APRESS download section related to this chapter. This example creates an interface that represents the View that will be displayed. The View contains two pieces of information, `NumberA` and `NumberB` of type `System.Int32`; it exposes a public method that will be used to perform a calculation with the two numbers.

Listing 12-1. *ICalculatorView Interface*

```
using System;

namespace UIPatterns.PassiveView
{
    public interface ICalculatorView
    {
        int NumberA { get; set; }
```

```
        int NumberB { get; set; }

        void Calculate(object sender, EventArgs args);
    }
}
```

The view has two properties of type integer, NumberA and NumberB, and a method that will be used as a delegate for the Calculate button. Now we need to create a WPF view with two TextBoxes and a Button and implement the interface in the code-behind file, as in Listing 12-2.

Listing 12-2. Implementation of the ICalculateView

```
using System;
using System.Windows;

namespace UIPatterns.PassiveView
{
    /// <summary>
    /// Interaction logic for PassiveView.xaml
    /// </summary>
    public partial class PassiveView : Window, ICalculatorView
    {
        public PassiveView()
        {
            InitializeComponent();
            btnCalculate.Click += Calculate;
        }

        #region Implementation of ICalculatorView

        public int NumberA
        {
            get { return Convert.ToInt32(txtA.Text); }
            set { txtA.Text = value.ToString(); }
        }

        public int NumberB
        {
            get { return Convert.ToInt32(txtB.Text); }
            set { txtB.Text = value.ToString(); }
        }

        public void Calculate(object sender, EventArgs args)
        {
            // the implementation will be analyzed later in this section
        }

        #endregion
    }
}
```

As you can see, the code implements the View by manually binding the properties of the ICalculatorView to the objects of the WPF View and also attaches the Calculate method to the corresponding Click event of the btnCalculate Button.

Now we just need to implement the Presenter and bind it to the View, as shown in Listing 12-3.

Listing 12-3. *The Presenter and Its Reference in the View*

```
// Presenter class
namespace UIPatterns.PassiveView
{
    public sealed class CalculatorPresenter
    {
        private readonly ICalculatorView view;

        public CalculatorPresenter(ICalculatorView view)
        {
            this.view = view;
        }

        public void Calculate()
        {
            CalculationModel model = new CalculationModel(view.NumberA, view.NumberB);
            model.Calculate();
        }
    }
}

// Reference in the WPF View
    public partial class PassiveView : Window, ICalculatorView
    {
        private CalculatorPresenter presenter;

        public PassiveView()
        {
            InitializeComponent();
            this.presenter = new CalculatorPresenter(this);
            btnCalculate.Click += Calculate;
        }

        public void Calculate(object sender, EventArgs args)
        {
            this.presenter.Calculate();
        }
        // omitted code
}
```

In this case, the View notifies the Presenter that the user has requested a calculation; the Presenter will process the numbers entered in the View and execute the calculation.

As you can see, the View is totally agnostic and unaware of the presentation logic, which is left completely to the Presenter.

Of course, this is a very simple example just to show you how the MVP Passive View can be applied to WPF. It's pretty obvious that this kind of presentation pattern doesn't use the binding engine of WPF or the commands at all because everything has to be left to the Presenter. In this example, the `CalculatorModel` is nothing more than a class with two properties of type `Int32` and a method `Calculate` that sums the two properties.

The Supervising Controller

The Supervising Controller uses an alternative representation of the MVP pattern. In this case, the View is not passive and it is able to interact directly with the Model. Figure 12-2 shows the main difference between the MVP Passive View and the MVP Supervising Controller. In the latter, the View has a direct reference to the Model.

MVP – SUPERVISING

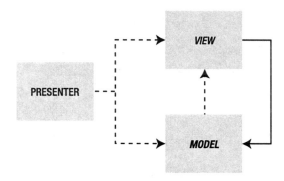

Figure 12-2. MVP Supervising Controller

This version of the MVP pattern can be used only if the technology of the View, in our case WPF, has a binding engine that is able to keep an interaction between the Model and the View alive. In our case, the View is much simpler; it has just a reference to the Model and a method to invoke the Click Button event. See Listing 12-4.

Listing 12-4. View Implementation in the Supervising Controller Version

```
using System;

namespace UIPatterns.SupervisingController
{
    public interface ICalculatorView
    {
        CalculatorModel Model { get; set; }

        void Calculate(object sender, EventArgs args);
    }
}
```

And the implementation in the WPF View will use the binding engine of WPF to keep the Model alive (see Listing 12-5).

Listing 12-5. *WPF Implementation of the View*

```
using System;
using System.Windows;

namespace UIPatterns.SupervisingController
{
    /// <summary>
    /// Interaction logic for SupervisingController.xaml
    /// </summary>
    public partial class SupervisingController : Window, ICalculatorView
    {
        private readonly CalculatorPresenter presenter;

        public SupervisingController()
        {
            InitializeComponent();
            this.presenter = new CalculatorPresenter(this);
        }

        #region ICalculatorView Members

        public CalculatorModel Model
        {
            get { return DataContext as CalculatorModel; }
            set { DataContext = value; }
        }

        public void Calculate(object sender, EventArgs args)
        {
            this.presenter.Calculate();
        }

        #endregion
    }
}
```

In this case, the View will be in charge of keeping the Model up-to-date directly and the call to the Presenter's `Calculate` method will call the `Calculate` method of the Model exposed by the View.

The View has two roles now; it has to provide feedback for the user's input and it has to update the Model with the data provided from the UI. The Presenter still has the job of managing return values or executing business operations or presentation logic.

When to Use the MVP

If you are working with WPF, there shouldn't be any particular reason to use MVP instead of MVVM, but if you're not building a brand-new application and are simply migrating an existing application designed with the MVP pattern to WPF, you may wonder when to use the MVP Passive View and when the Supervising Controller version.

Let's start with the Passive View; in this version of MVP you can test almost the entire surface of the presentation logic because the View is a pure abstract container of information for the UI and nothing more. The testability of the application is very high and all the presentation logic can be tested without the need of mocking the UI part because all the hard work is left to the Presenter.

The downside of using the Passive View is that it requires a lot of additional code, especially on the View side because you probably won't expose the Model directly into the View. This additional code can make a huge difference if the View you are building is complex and rich in information.

On the other hand, there may be some situations where the testability of the presentation logic is not the only concern or requirement, and the complexity of the Model you are exposing to the View is so great that it may turn out to be very difficult to create an abstract View that represents the corresponding Model. In that case, you might consider using the Supervising Controller MVP version. Of course, if you plan to use this version of the MVP, you have to bear in mind that you are forcing the application to lose flexibility because the View is strictly bound to the corresponding Model, and this will probably remove abstraction from the View.

Model View ViewModel

In 2004, when rich UI technologies like WPF and Silverlight were just in beta, Martin Fowler introduced a new presentation pattern called Presentation Model (PM). In this pattern, Fowler presented some of the features that are now in WPF but in simpler way. The PM pattern consists of two components, the PresentationModel and the View that is bound to it. The PM is in charge of providing the information and the presentation logic used by the View, and the View is bound to it using a binding engine, which in our case, is the WPF binding engine.

In 2005, John Gossman, WPF software architect at Microsoft, revised the PM pattern a little bit, introducing a new specialized version more specific to WPF, the Model View ViewModel pattern. The main difference between this presentation pattern and the MVP is that MVVM, like PM, does not need a reference to the View, while in MVP you have to reference the View in the Presenter. This difference can have a big advantage in terms of flexibility, as with the MVVM pattern you recycle the ViewModel over different Views.

The MVVM pattern consists of three major objects: the Model, the View, and the ViewModel; the structure of the MVVM is shown in Figure 12-3.

MVVM

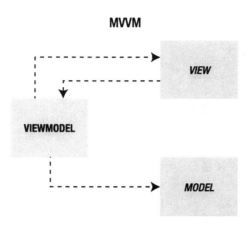

Figure 12-3. *Model View ViewModel (MVVM) pattern*

Let's take a look now at how the MVVM pattern is made up and at the role of each component.

- The Model: The model can be considered the domain entity of the application, the component in charge of carrying the data and the domain logic. It does not have any presentation logic or UI logic. It can be tested in complete isolation from the Presentation and the View.

- The View: The view is the user interface, the UI; it is the only component visible to the user and the only component that can interact with the user. In MVVM, the view is an active component and thanks to its binding engine it interacts directly with the viewmodel.

- The ViewModel: The viewmodel is in charge of synchronizing the data displayed in the view with the data of the model, and with updating the state of the view by exposing commands, behaviors, and other methods.

The ViewModel, in order to be implemented in WPF, needs to satisfy some design requirements to keep the View synchronized and to allow communication between the View and the ViewModel.

The INotifyPropertyChanged Interface

To create a new ViewModel object, you must first provide a notification mechanism between the ViewModel and the View that will be bound to it. This mechanism can be obtained by implementing the `INotifyPropertyChanged` (INPC) interface available with the .NET Framework. This interface exposes an event, `PropertyChanged`, that should be raised by every property of the ViewModel when the underlying data is changed. See Listing 12-6.

Listing 12-6. Implementation of the INPC Interface

```
using System.ComponentModel;

namespace UIPatterns.MVVM
{
    public sealed class CalculatorViewModel : INotifyPropertyChanged
    {
        #region Implementation of INotifyPropertyChanged

        public event PropertyChangedEventHandler PropertyChanged;

        #endregion

        public void OnPropertyChanged(string name)
        {
            PropertyChangedEventHandler handler = PropertyChanged;
            if (handler != null)
            {
                PropertyChanged(this, new PropertyChangedEventArgs(name));
            }
        }
    }
}
```

The WPF binding engine is designed to listen for the **PropertyChanged** event exposed by this interface if the object databound to the **DataContext** of the View is implementing the **INPC** interface. For more information, see Chapter 7, which has an entire section dedicated to this mechanism.

For the **Calculator** model, the second step is to inject the Model into the ViewModel and replicate the Model properties in the ViewModel, then raise a **PropertyChanged** event for each, as shown in Listing 12-7.

Listing 12-7. Implementation of the Model in the ViewModel

```
    public sealed class CalculatorViewModel : INotifyPropertyChanged
    {
        private CalculatorModel model;

        public CalculatorViewModel(CalculatorModel model)
        {
            this.model = model;
        }
```

```
        public int NumberA
        {
            get { return this.model.NumberA; }
            set {
                If (this.model.NumberA != value)
                {
                    this.model.NumberA = value;
                    OnPropertyChanged("NumberA");
                }
            }
        }
    }
    // INPC implementation omitted
}
```

In this listing, the Model is not directly exposed in the View but is wrapped around a ViewModel property so you don't have to pollute the domain entity with the INPC interface.

Now you can easily data bind the ViewModel in the View using only pure XAML markup, as shown in Listing 12-8.

Listing 12-8. *Data Bind the ViewModel to the XAML View*

```xml
<Window
    x:Class="UIPatterns.MVVM.ModelViewViewModel"
    xmlns="http://schemas.microsoft.com/winfx/2006/xaml/presentation"
    xmlns:x="http://schemas.microsoft.com/winfx/2006/xaml"
    xmlns:MVVM="clr-namespace:UIPatterns.MVVM"
    Title="ModelViewViewModel" Height="300" Width="300">
    <Window.DataContext>
        <MVVM:CalculatorViewModel />
    </Window.DataContext>
    <Grid>
        <TextBlock>Calculator MVVM</TextBlock>
        <TextBlock >Calculate the Sum between A and B</TextBlock>
        <Label>Number A:</Label>
        <TextBox Text="{Binding Path=NumberA}"></TextBox>
        <Label>Number B:</Label>
        <TextBox Text="{Binding Path=NumberB}"></TextBox>
        <Button>Calculate</Button>
    </Grid>
</Window>
```

■ **Note** The preceding example shows one possible approach to binding a Model to a ViewModel. You can also consider exposing the Model directly in the ViewModel or creating a ViewModel that reflects the Model properties and data bind the Model to the ViewModel backwards and forward. You'll find much debate about which technique is the best and which is the worst. I personally believe that it always depends on what you are doing and on the complexity of the Model/ViewModel structure.

Exposing the Commands

In Chapter 8, you looked at how commands work in WPF and how this is handled by the data binding engine. WPF itself exposes the RoutedCommand object, which is nothing more than a custom implementation of the ICommand interface, designed for the WPF engine.

In MVVM, you expose the commands available for the UI as simple read-only properties of type ICommand that are implemented inside the ViewModel object as in Listing 12-9. (Please refer to Chapter 8 to see how to create an MvvmCommand object).

Listing 12-9. Exposing an ICommand *in a ViewModel*

```
public sealed class CalculatorViewModel : INotifyPropertyChanged
{
    public ICommand CalculateCommand { get; private set; }

    private CalculatorModel model;

    public CalculatorViewModel()
    {
        this.model = new CalculatorModel();
        this.CalculateCommand = new MvvmCommand(
            param => model.Calculate(),
            param => NumberA != 0 && NumberB != 0)
            .AddListener<CalculatorViewModel>(this, x => x.NumberA);
    }
}
```

This listing creates a new ICommand that is re-evaluated every time the property NumberA of the ViewModel is changed, and this executes the Calculate method of the ViewModel model property. The reason for re-evaluating the command execution is that WPF binds it to the Command dependency property of the Button and this re-evaluation process will enable/disable the button depending on the Boolean result returned by the CanExecute method of the ICommand implementation.

The main concept here is how to use the ICommand interface in WPF (discussed extensively in Chapter 8), then in the ViewModel you just have to expose the ICommand interface and data bind it to the corresponding XAML element of the View, like a button, as shown in Listings 12-10 and 12-11.

Listing 12-10. Binding to a Button

```
// sample ViewModel
public class SampleViewModel : INotifyPropertyChanged
{
    // INotifyPropertyChanged interface implementation
    // has been skipped

    // ICommand
    private ICommand myCommand;

    public ICommand MyCommand
    {
        get { return myCommand; }
```

```
        set
        {
            If (myCommand != value)
            {
                myCommand = value;
                // notify ...
            }
        }
    }
}
```

Listing 12-11. *Binding the Button of Listing 12-10*

```
<Button Command="{Binding Path=MyCommand}">Click Here</Button>
```

Summary

I want to clarify a common misunderstanding I've seen in the NET communities in the past years, about using and working with the presentation patterns in general. A presentation pattern is adopted in order to loosely couple the UI logic from the presentation logic and to make the presentation part of the application more testable and flexible. It is not used to separate the domain from the UI; this is not the primary reason for adopting presentation patterns.

Presentations pattern such MVP and MVVM are only part of the UI; they don't represent the overall solution for UI architecture. With a presentation pattern, you should solve some specific aspects of the UI layer but this doesn't mean that you need a third-party framework or a personal set of facilities that will allow you to bootstrap the UI and orchestrate the navigation and the communication between the views, like we did in the TimeTracker application using Unity and the navigation pattern.

There is no single correct pattern to use, each one has pros and cons; and before choosing one instead of another, you should evaluate them and ask yourself questions like "Does my architecture need MVP?" or "Do I need to fully test the presentation surface of the application?" and so on. Also consider that it is not true that one presentation pattern is more complicated than another; they are simply different, and as with any other pattern, you need to try them out to understand and master them. Spend some time learning these patterns before making a final choice.

CHAPTER 13

■ ■ ■

WPF and Multithreading

With the computer hardware currently on the market and the powerful configurations you can buy for an acceptable price, you can have in your hands a robust machine that is able to execute millions of calculations per second. Unfortunately, having this kind of powerful calculator doesn't make an application faster by default, nor does it make an application's user interface faster or more responsive. If you plan to design an application to be responsive and to execute tons of operations in parallel, you need to write code that is able to do that instead of relying on expensive hardware.

Nowadays there are machines with multi-core processors (CPUs) that can execute parallel processes all at the same time. It used to be the case that processors only had a single core, which meant they could only execute a sequence of steps; they were not able to execute parallel operations. If you had to execute parallel processes, you had to write multithreaded code.

By multithreading I mean a system, program, or component that executes more than one process in parallel. The advantage of this is that software can execute instructions in parallel and often decrease the total time required to execute those instructions.

Of course, multi-core and multithreading are two terms that go together in computer science; if you program your software using multithreading but you have a machine with a single core, your code will share the resource of the core among all the parallel threads. If you have a multi-core processor, though, the performance of your "parallel" code should be faster.

To apply these concepts to WPF applications, one of the primary advantage of using a multithreading programming approach is to have a very responsive user interface, because any operation called by the UI will be executed in the background (which means on another thread) by the computer so that the thread involved in keeping the UI responsive (the UI thread) will not be occupied by the execution of the background call.

The .NET Framework offers different ways of running parallel code, and there are also different patterns to satisfy the requirements of a parallel programming approach. WPF provides a powerful and very easy mechanism for running parallel code that will keep the UI responsive without too much effort on the programming side.

In this chapter we'll take a look at some techniques and components that can be used with .NET to write parallel code and asynchronous operations. However, this is a huge topic and if you plan to learn about and program using parallel techniques, I recommend you follow up with a book that focuses more specifically on this topic, like Adam Freeman's *Pro .NET 4 Parallel Programming with C#* (Apress, 2010). I also suggest you examine the dedicated section of MSDN at `msdn.microsoft.com/library/ms173178.aspx`.

Writing Multithreading Code in .NET

In the first part of this chapter we'll look what solutions .NET 4 provides for writing and executing multithreaded operations. To execute the code, we will create a demo WPF 4 project with Visual Studio 2010, called "WPF.MultiThreading," which we'll use to execute the various examples. You can download the code from the Apress web site along with the code related to the TimeTracker application.

The Thread Object

When you turn on your PC and start to work in your operating system (OS), you start to execute parallel processes—applications—and each one is on a different thread. For example, if you have Visual Studio and Notepad open, you are executing two different processes in your OS, each on a different thread.

■ **Note** Windows, and operating systems in general, are able to multitask, meaning they are able to execute different processes at the same time. This ability gives users the impression that the OS is running different applications in parallel, which is not really true. The OS has an internal scheduler that is able to split the time needed by each process to be executed, by giving priority to one process instead of another. In this way, the OS can switch between executing a process to executing another one by giving a specific limit to the execution time.

When you write C# code, usually, you execute all the code within one single thread, so if you plan to execute three sequential steps, each step has to wait until the previous one is completed. This sequential execution can easily lock down the responsiveness of your UI when the same thread that is rendering the graphic interface is also in charge of executing commands in background. In such situations, it is really important to keep the UI responsive and to inform the user that a long-running task is executing and that the program has not simply crashed.

When you write an application with WPF, you may encounter three types of situations where you have to use multithreading:

- You want the UI to remain responsive while another thread is sending data to the UI.

- You have to execute a long-running task in the background and notify another thread when the process is completed.

- You are working with remote components like a WCF service or a .NET Remoting object that may lock the current thread while executing due to some latency in the response.

In these cases, you might consider moving the code that is locking down the application to a different thread and execute it in parallel.

Our demo WPF application creates a simple XAML `Window` that contains a `TextBox` and a `Button`; the button Click event is handled in the code-behind file. Listing 13-1 shows the XAML markup used to create it.

Listing 13-1. WPF Window That Runs Multiple Threads

```xml
<Window x:Class="ThreadClass.MainWindow"
        xmlns="http://schemas.microsoft.com/winfx/2006/xaml/presentation"
        xmlns:x="http://schemas.microsoft.com/winfx/2006/xaml"
        Title="MainWindow" Height="264" Width="345">
    <Grid>
        <Grid.ColumnDefinitions>
            <ColumnDefinition Width="10" />
            <ColumnDefinition Width="*" />
            <ColumnDefinition Width="10" />
        </Grid.ColumnDefinitions>
        <Grid.RowDefinitions>
            <RowDefinition Height="30" />
            <RowDefinition Height="*" />
            <RowDefinition Height="30" />
        </Grid.RowDefinitions>
        <TextBox Name="txtCurrentValue" Grid.Column="1" Grid.Row="1" />
        <Button Content="Run threads" Click="ButtonClick" Grid.Column="1" Grid.Row="2" />
    </Grid>
</Window>
```

In the code-behind there's a delegate that handles the Click button event. If you press F5 and run the application, you'll execute the sample code in a specific thread, the main thread of the application. Within this thread you can simply write some custom text in the **TextBox** and the UI will display the text. But, if you execute a long-running task during this operation or pause the current thread, the UI will be unresponsive.

The code in Listing 13-2 pauses the current thread for three seconds and then it writes "Hello World!" in the **TextBox**; during those three seconds the UI will be unresponsive.

Listing 13-2. Sample of a Long-Running Task Using the Thread.Sleep Method

```csharp
using System.Windows;
using System.Threading;
namespace ThreadClass
{
    /// <summary>
    /// Interaction logic for MainWindow.xaml
    /// </summary>
    public partial class MainWindow : Window
    {
        public MainWindow()
        {
            InitializeComponent();
        }
```

```
        private void ButtonClick(object sender, RoutedEventArgs e)
        {
            Thread.Sleep(3000);
            this.txtCurrentValue.Text = "Hello World!";
        }
    }
}
```

The only code that's new here is the Sleep method exposed by the Thread class; this method is used to pause the currently executing thread. By executing this code you are telling the operating system that you want to pause the current thread, which is also the thread that is rendering the user interface. For this reason, the UI becomes unresponsive.

You can, however, create a long-running task and execute it without locking down the UI; this is accomplished by creating a new Thread instance and associating the code of the long-running task to this thread object and then updating the UI when the operation is done (see Listing 13-3).

Listing 13-3. Long-Running Task Executed in a Different Thread

```
private void ButtonClick(object sender, RoutedEventArgs e)
{
    Thread thread =
        new Thread(() =>
        {
            Thread.Sleep(3000);
            txtCurrentValue.Text = "Hello World!";
        });
    thread.Start();
}
```

One of the ways of creating a new thread class is by passing in the constructor a delegate that represents the button. The application becomes responsive right away, but after 3 seconds you get an error saying the thread that is trying to access the TextBox object is not the same thread used by WPF to create the TextBox, as Figure 13-1 shows.

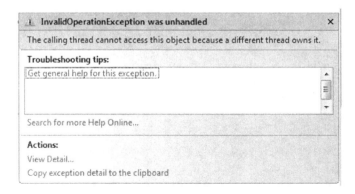

Figure 13-1. Exception thrown when the UI thread is not in sync

The first easy way to fix this problem is to call the `Dispatcher` class exposed by the WPF `TextBox`. This object, as you will see in the second part of the chapter, is in charge of dealing with concurrency and threading. The WPF dispatcher is able to handle messages by affinity and identify a message that is not coming from the same thread as the UI and dispatch it to the UI thread so that it can be handled properly.

Listing 13-4 modifies the way the thread is interacting with the `TextBox` so the UI will remain responsive while running the code in a different thread.

Listing 13-4. *Sample Using the WPF* `Dispatcher` *Object*

```
private void ButtonClick(object sender, RoutedEventArgs e)
{
    Thread thread =
        new Thread(() =>
        {
            Thread.Sleep(3000);
            txtCurrentValue.Dispatcher.Invoke(new Action(() => txtCurrentValue.Text =↵
 "Hello World!"));
        });
    thread.Start();
}
```

The `Dispatcher` object exposed by the `TextBox` class (and also by any other WPF component) has an `Invoke` method that can be used to dispatch a message (a delegate) to the correct UI thread, the one used by the `TextBox` that is calling the `Invoke` method. Most objects in WPF derive from `DispatcherObject`, which provides the basic constructs for dealing with concurrency and threading.

Now if you run the previous code, you should have a responsive UI and at the same time you should be able to print the "Hello World!" string in the `TextBox` after 3 seconds.

Interacting with the Thread class

The `Thread` class is a complex object exposed by a specific namespace: the `System.Threading` namespace, which provides facilities and components to work with multithreading. When you work with a multithreaded application, the most challenging tasks are when you need to synchronize the various threads, wait for a specific thread, or just need to kill a running thread.

As you saw in Listing 13-3, you can create and run a new thread simply by creating a new instance of the `Thread` class and then calling the `Start` method. The only way to stop a running thread is to call the `Abort` method, as shown in Listing 13-5.

Listing 13-5. *Starting and Stopping a Running Thread*

```
private void ButtonClick(object sender, RoutedEventArgs e)
{
    Thread thread =
        new Thread(() => txtCurrentValue.Dispatcher.Invoke(
            new Action(() =>
```

```
    {
        Thread.Sleep(3000);
        txtCurrentValue.Text = "Hello World!";
    })));
    thread.Start();
    thread.Abort();
}
```

In this case, after the code starts the thread it calls the **Abort** method, which will kill the execution and the thread so the **txtCurrentValue** TextBox will not be set using the action defined in the thread declaration.

In other cases, you might need to pause the thread for a while and then continue execution, like the Pause and Play commands on a CD player!

In order to pause and continue thread execution, the **Thread** class exposes two methods, **Suspend** and **Resume**, which can be used as shown in Listing 13-6.

Listing 13-6. *Pause and Continue a Thread*

```
private void ButtonClick(object sender, RoutedEventArgs e)
{
    Thread thread =
        new Thread(() => txtCurrentValue.Dispatcher.Invoke(
            new Action(() =>
                            {
                                Thread.Sleep(3000);
                                txtCurrentValue.Text += "01\r\n";
                            })));
    thread.Start();
    thread.Suspend();
    thread.Resume();
}
```

Remember that using methods like **Suspend** and **Resume** will pause and continue the calling thread and make the UI less responsive. Also, these two methods have been deprecated since .NET 2 and are used here just to introduce threading concepts.

If you plan to work with the **Thread** class, you should consider how you will keep multiple threads synchronized, how you will manage thread affinities, and how you will share resources among different threads.

Asynchronous Operations

The **Thread** object exposed by the **System.Threading** namespace is not the only object available in WPF to write code that keeps the UI responsive while it is executed in the background. In the previous section you saw that one solution for keeping the UI responsive is to execute the required code in a separate process by creating a new **Thread** object. You also saw that the use of the **Thread** object may bring additional hassles, like the need to architect a synchronization mechanism and additional thought about keeping the UI thread synchronized with the background thread. You may also have additional threads running in the background and each one may have the same issue of needing to be synchronized with the main thread.

Also, if you have to execute not one background process but let's say 100 of them, and you plan to execute each one in parallel by creating an additional thread, you can easily end up overtaxing the CPU, which can't handle so many parallel processes at the same time, and having the entire system unresponsive!

An alternative is to execute the long-running task or the code that is blocking the UI asynchronously. This means running the code without blocking the principle thread and advising the main thread of the completed execution using a callback method.

The .NET Framework by design allows you to call any method created using C# or VB.NET asynchronously, but in order to do that you need to provide a delegate to do it.

Suppose that the WPF `Window` created in Listing 13-1 is executing, from the `ButtonClick` event, a method that waits for 3 seconds and then writes something in the `TextBox`, as Listing 13-7 shows.

Listing 13-7. *Method That Updates the* `TextBox` *Content*

```
private void ButtonClick(object sender, RoutedEventArgs e)
{
    this.UpdateTextBox();
}

private void UpdateTextBox()
{
    Thread.Sleep(3000);
    this.txtCurrentValue.Text = "Hello World!";
}
```

If you run the demo application using this implementation, the UI will be locked down until the `TextBox` `Text` property is set to "Hello World!". What you have here is the same code introduced at the beginning of the chapter but refactored using a different approach. Now, what we need to do in order to keep the UI responsive while the `UpdateTextBox` is executing the remaining code is to call it asynchronously.

The asynchronous pattern in C# requires two methods, one called `BeginInvoke` that is used to initialize the async process, and one called `EndInvoke` that is called when the async process is completed. The `BeginInvoke` method has to return an `IAsyncResult` interface object that can be used to monitor the execution of the corresponding asynchronous method.

Listing 13-8 shows the implementation of this pattern using the Listing 13-7 sample code.

Listing 13-8. *Asynchronous Implementation Pattern in C#*

```
// step 01 create the async signature
private delegate string AsyncUpdateTextBox();
private AsyncUpdateTextBox async;

// step 02 create the callback and the method
private void UpdateCallback(IAsyncResult result)
{
    txtCurrentValue.Dispatcher.Invoke(
        new Action(()=>
```

```
    {
        txtCurrentValue.Text = async.EndInvoke(result);
    }));
}

private string UpdateTextBox()
{
    Thread.Sleep(3000);
    return "Hello World!";
}

// step 03 handle everything
private void ButtonClick(object sender, RoutedEventArgs e)
{
    async = new AsyncUpdateTextBox(UpdateTextBox);
    AsyncCallback callback = UpdateCallback;
    async.BeginInvoke(callback,null);
}
```

This listing performs four steps to make the method UpdateTextBox asynchronous:

1. It declares a delegate and an instance of this delegate, which needs to be global in order to be used in the EndInvoke method, to handle the async pattern implementation offered by the delegate object of .NET. In this case, the method takes no parameters and returns a string result.

2. It creates a delegate callback that will execute asynchronously when the delegate from step 1 has completed, and this will point to the UpdateTextBox method.

3. It orchestrates everything in the ButtonClick event.

4. At the end, EndInvoke is executed, which returns the value from the delegate when you pass in the correct IAsync object.

The ThreadPool Component

One of major problems of implementing the asynchronous pattern in C# is that you must provide the implementation of the BeginInvoke and EndInvoke methods; this forces you to make the callback public or at least internal because it will be probably shared across different classes, the calling and the called. You also have to remember to call the EndInvoke method in order to close the asynchronous process.

You can reduce the code used in the previous listing by using the asynchronous pattern implementation offered by the ThreadPool object, shown in Listing 13-9; this object sends the callback in the background and forgets it. …

Listing 13-9. *ThreadPool Object*

```
private void ButtonClick(object sender, RoutedEventArgs e)
{
    ThreadPool.QueueUserWorkItem(callback => UpdateTextBox());
}
```

```
private void UpdateTextBox()
{
    Thread.Sleep(3000);
    txtCurrentValue.Dispatcher.Invoke(
        new Action(() =>
        {
            txtCurrentValue.Text = "Hello World!";
        }));
}
```

The `ThreadPool` component offers an alternative approach, which can execute asynchronous code in a "call and forget" manner. It means you can use this component to fire a method and then forget about it. You are guaranteed that `ThreadPool` will pool the method and execute it as soon as it has a free thread available to handle it. When the method is done, the `EndInvoke` method will be called and executed by the `ThreadPool` object, giving you the power of firing and forgetting the asynchronous code!

■ **Note** You may wonder, after reading this section, what the difference is between creating your own thread and running asynchronous calls (in a new thread) using the `ThreadPool`. The `ThreadPool` is able to handle the resources of your machine and does not overload the CPU as you might do by simply creating and firing parallel threads using the `Thread` object.

On the other hand, if you have a long-running task that should be controlled and monitored (pause, kill, monitor), or you have to create an asynchronous thread that will lock the program execution (not the UI but the logical execution), you may well find a better solution in using the `Thread` object, which offers a greater degree of control.

The Task Object

The last .NET 4 component for running multithreaded code is provided by the `System.Threading.Tasks` namespace, a new section of the `System.Threading` namespace introduced by .NET 4. At first, the Task Parallel Library was an experimental project conducted by Microsoft Research, a special department of Microsoft that experiments with new technologies and patterns. With the release of .NET 4, Microsoft decided to include the Task Parallel Library in the core of the NET 4.

The main difference between using the `Thread` object and the `Task` object available in the `System.Threading.Tasks` namespace is that the `Task` object is controlled by the `ThreadPool` object, so the concurrency and the overall use of resources result in a better product. The `Task` object also allows you to:

- Schedule a task's execution.

- Chain together child and parent tasks, resulting in a sort of parallel workflow.

- Handle exceptions and propagate them to the parent and child tasks.

If you want to create a task and run it, you can use the static object `TaskFactory` exposed in the `System.Threading.Tasks` namespace, or you can create a new instance of the `Task` object and then start it, as shown in Listing 13-10.

Listing 13-10. *Creating a New Task and Starting It*

```
private void ButtonClick(object sender, RoutedEventArgs e)
{
    Task task = new Task(UpdateTextBox);
    task.Start();
}

private void UpdateTextBox()
{
    Thread.Sleep(3000);
    txtCurrentValue.Dispatcher.Invoke(
        new Action(() =>
        {
            txtCurrentValue.Text = "Hello World!";
        }));
}
```

Because the Task constructor requires an action object, instead of creating a separate delegate for the action and then associating it to the parameter of the Task constructor, you can easily create a delegate on the fly by using a lambda expression (see Listing 13-11).

Listing 13-11. *Task Object Using Lamba and an Anonymous Delegate*

```
private void ButtonClick(object sender, RoutedEventArgs e)
{
    Task task = new Task(() =>
    {
        Thread.Sleep(3000);
        txtCurrentValue.Dispatcher.Invoke(
            new Action(() =>
            {
                txtCurrentValue.Text = "Hello World!";
            }));
    });
    task.Start();
}
```

The Task object and the Task Parallel Library offer a number of additional methods and facilities that you can use to better control your asynchronous code, as shown in Listing 13-12. For example, you can execute additional code when the asynchronous code has completed, and you can also specify code to be executed if an exception is raised, using the fluent interface language approach.

Listing 13-12. *Additional Methods Available on the Task Object*

```
private void ButtonClick(object sender, RoutedEventArgs e)
{
    new Task(() =>
    {
        Thread.Sleep(3000);
```

```
        txtCurrentValue.Dispatcher.Invoke(
            new Action(() =>
            {
                txtCurrentValue.Text = "Hello World!";
            }));
    })
    .ContinueWith((parm) =>
    {
        txtCurrentValue.Dispatcher.Invoke(
            new Action(() =>
            {
                txtCurrentValue.Text += "\r\nCompleted!";
            }));
    })
    .Start();
}
```

This listing creates a new Task, then specifies the code to be executed asynchronously and the code to be executed at the end (using the ContinueWith method), and finally it starts the code. The ContinueWith method allows you to pass in the previous Task so that you can work with it if you need to.

The Task Parallel Library is a new component of .NET 4, and though it is very powerful, it is easy to use. If you want to learn more about it, MSDN has a Parallel Computing section available at msdn.microsoft.com/en-us/concurrency/. For a deeper look at the Task object and the Parallel Framework, see msdn.microsoft.com/en-us/library/dd460693.aspx.

The Background Worker Component

The .NET Framework (since version 2) exposes a component called BackgroundWorker in the System.ComponentModel namespace that is in charge of running and controlling asynchronous code without locking the user interface. Its purpose is specific to this role and it should only be used in a WPF or Windows Forms application.

The concept of the BackgroundWorker component is pretty straightforward; it exposes events and methods you can use to run a specific set of commands asynchronously and get updates and feedback from them without locking the UI.

In order to add a new BackgroundWorker component to your WPF window, you have to create one in the code-behind file. Design support for this component in Visual Studio is enabled only with the Windows Forms technology.

Listing 13-13 shows how to declare a new BackgroundWorker component in a WPF window.

Listing 13-13. *Creating a BackgroundWorker Component*

```
using System;
using System.ComponentModel;
using System.Threading;
using System.Windows;

namespace ThreadClass
{
    public partial class MainWindow : Window
    {
```

```
    private BackgroundWorker worker;

    public MainWindow()
    {
        InitializeComponent();
        worker = new BackgroundWorker();
    }
}
```

Now that you've created a new instance of the worker, you have to associate an event handler to the DoWork event exposed by the component; this code will be called by the worker when you execute the RunWorkerAsync method of the BackgroundWorker component. See Listing 13-14.

Listing 13-14. *Handling the DoWork Event*

```
public MainWindow()
{
    InitializeComponent();
    worker = new BackgroundWorker();
    worker.DoWork += WorkerDoWork;
}

private void WorkerDoWork(object sender, DoWorkEventArgs e)
{
    Thread.Sleep(3000);
    txtCurrentValue.Dispatcher.Invoke(
        new Action(() =>
        {
            txtCurrentValue.Text = "Hello World!";
        }));
}
```

In this case, in the constructor of the Window component the code creates a new instance of the private field worker and then associates an event handler to handle the work to be executed. In the WorkerDoWork method you still have to use the WPF dispatcher to update the TextBox because this code will be executed by the worker in a different thread that will not be able to sync the message with the UI thread automatically.

Finally, you need to associate the ButtonClick event to the RunWorkerAsync method exposed by the worker as shown in Listing 13-15.

Listing 13-15. *Calling the RunWorkerAsync Method*

```
private void ButtonClick(object sender, RoutedEventArgs e)
{
    worker.RunWorkerAsync();
}
```

If you run the application by pressing F5 in Visual Studio, you'll see that the Button's Click event will execute the WorkerDoWork method without locking the UI and after 3 seconds the TextBox Text property will be updated with the "Hello World!" string.

The event handler for the `DoWork` event carries with it a `RoutedEventArgs` argument type that can be used to carry parameters in the method. For example, you can call `RunWorkerAsync` by passing in a custom string and read the string in the `DoWork` event handler as the `Argument` property of `DoWorkEventArgs`, as in Listing 13-16.

Listing 13-16. *Passing Parameters in the BackgroundWorker*

```
// reading the parameter in the DoWork event handler method
txtCurrentValue.Dispatcher.Invoke(
    new Action(() =>
    {
        txtCurrentValue.Text = e.Argument.ToString();
    }));

// passing the parameter value from the RunWorkerAsync method
worker.RunWorkerAsync("Hello World!");
```

Finally, the `BackgroundWorker` also allows you to interact with it. For example, you may need to send notifications back to the UI while you are executing the long-running task. In this case, the `BackgroundWorker` exposes some events you can use to track the execution process of the worker:

- `RunWorkerCompleted` is raised when all the code in the `DoWork` event handler is successfully executed.

- `RunWorkerCompletedEventArgs` provides data for the `MethodNameCompleted` event.

- `ProgressChanged` is raised every time the `ReportProgress` method is called in the worker; this event carries with it the progress "amount" as an `int` value that is passed using the `ProgressChangedEventArgs` argument.

If you need to cancel a process that is running asynchronously using this component, you have to call the `CancelAsync` method exposed by the `BackgroundWorker` instance.

Summary

This chapter provides a brief overview of the different techniques that can be used to run asynchronous code in a WPF application using C#. The .NET Framework supplies a complete set of components and facilities, available in the `System.Threading` namespace, that can be used to create parallel code and asynchronous operations and to monitor them.

The first component you saw was the `Thread` object, a powerful object used to create new threads that will run as isolated parallel processes. Before using this object to run parallel code, you'll need to consider some major architectural issues, like thread synchronization and thread resources sharing.

Another way of running code that doesn't block the main process of the application is to use the asynchronous pattern offered by the .NET Framework delegate object. Any delegate in C# can be called asynchronously using the `BeginInvoke` and `EndInvoke` methods exposed by the delegate object. With this approach, any code will run asynchronously in a separate thread without blocking the current UI and will call a callback method when the asynchronous execution is completed.

An easier way to execute async code is to use the `ThreadPool` object, a component exposed in the `System.Threading` namespace that can be used to "call and forget" parallel code. Unfortunately, this component is easier to use but provides less control, so it shouldn't be used for complex solutions.

You also had a look at the new `Task` that is part of the Parallel Library section of the `System.Threading.Tasks` namespace introduced in .NET 4, and you saw a new thread object handler called `Task` that allows you to write multithreaded code with the same control as the `Thread` object but with a more understandable syntax and easier management provided by the `ThreadPool` component.

Finally, you saw that the `BackgroundWorker` component can be used in WPF and it is the easiest way to run asynchronous code in a WPF window, without the need to use any other more complicated multithreading approach.

CHAPTER 14

■■■

Interacting with WCF

During the development of the TimeTracker application, you have seen how to create a layered WPF application and how to separate the code into different components and layers. Keep in mind, though, that you still have to:

- expose all the components to the client computer.

- redistribute the components every time you release a new version.

In Chapter 11, you saw how easy the process of redistributing updated components can be, but in the end you still have to ensure that every client is using the latest version, and you are still "exposing" the components to the client side.

You also need to consider the distribution of the domain layer (or any other of TimeTracker's layers), in a different application. Let's say that the abstract data layer you built for TimeTracker is to be reused by a new WPF application; now you have two different applications that need to be redistributed every time you modify the DAL assembly, because it is shared between them.

An alternative way of redistributing components is to use Service-Oriented Architecture (SOA). In the SOA world, communication between services is accomplished using XML messages that are sent and received by the client and the server. Using XML messages encoded with a standard communication protocol such as Simple Object Access Protocol (SOAP), you can redistribute your components not only to various WPF applications but also to other technology platforms like Java.

The basic players in SOA are:

- An **endpoint,** the entry point to access the architecture.

- One or more **services** that expose methods for the client to use.

- **Messages** that are exchanged between the client and the server (sometimes also known as host and consumer).

In early 2000, Microsoft, along with IBM and some other companies, introduced a web technology known as *web services* that has been adopted in the web community. This technology, still alive, is used to distribute messages throughout the Web using the SOAP communication protocol. The big difference with this approach is that web services interact with the Web programmatically, in contrast to the old approach that typically involved a user at a terminal.

In 2006, with version 3.0 of the .NET Framework, Microsoft introduced Windows Communication Foundation (WCF), a new web technology more powerful than the standard web services. This technology is a framework for building service-oriented applications, and it is an entire set of services for creating SOA applications.

In this chapter we are going to explore this technology, first with an overview of how it works and then we'll see how easy it can be used to transform the TimeTracker WPF application into a distributed service application.

Introduction to WCF

Windows Communication Foundation (WCF) is hosted on Internet Information Services (IIS) and it uses the SOAP protocol (among other protocols that we won't look at in this chapter) to distribute messages between the endpoints.

WCF can be used for different purposes. It can be used to send and receive simple data or a complex graph represented by an XML structure; it can be used to enable live communications among various clients, or it can be used simply to share a business layer without the typical distribution problems because it doesn't require a redistribution process like the typical .NET assembly (.dll) requires.

WCF out of the box offers the following features:

- **Service orientation:** WCF lets you create service-oriented applications that offer an easy way to implement loosely coupled services that can be used by different technologies and platforms.

- **Multiple messages patterns:** With WCF you can send and receive messages in different ways. For example, you may have a service that sends and receives messages or a service that just receives messages and processes them.

- **Standard metadata:** WCF is designed to use common communication metadata standards beyond those used by the .NET Framework; WCF supports WSDL, XML, and WS-policy, which can also be used by non- .NET technologies.

- **Data contracts:** WCF provides a method of encapsulating into serializable contract objects the information exchanged between the messages and the services.

- **REST support:** With WCF, you can create plain XML messages that aren't wrapped in a SOAP envelope that can be accessed from any type of device.

WCF is not only a technology for implementing SOAP or plain XML messages. In .NET there are other technologies, like Windows Workflow Foundation (WWF or WF) or BizTalk or Windows Azure AppFabric that rely on this powerful SOA tool. In this chapter you'll see how to integrate Entity Framework and WPF with WCF, but you may also want to look at how WCF works in conjunction with:

- **Windows Workflow Foundation**

  msdn.microsoft.com/library/bb266709.aspx

- **BizTalk**

  msdn.microsoft.com/library/bb973215.aspx

- **Windows Azure AppFabric**

  www.microsoft.com/windowsazure/AppFabric/Overview/default.aspx

Brief Overview of WCF Architecture

WCF is a complex framework that would take a whole book[1] to explain fully. but let's take a quick look at the WCF architecture and see how the lifecycle of a WCF project is structured.

The Endpoint

A WCF service is composed of one or more *endpoints*. An endpoint is a sort of port used to expose the *service* or the *client* to the external world. Clients and services can expose one or more endpoints to enable one-way or duplex communication.

Figure 14-1 shows the structure of an endpoint and the components that constitute every part of the endpoint.

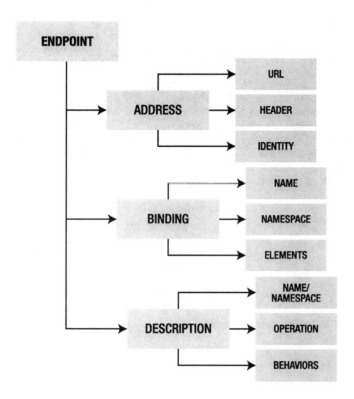

Figure 14-1. *WCF endpoint structure*

---

[1] See, for example, Nishith Pathak, *Pro WCF 4: Practical Microsoft SOA Implementation* (Apress, 2011) or Aaran Hamilton-Pearce, *Expert WCF 4: Maximizing Windows Communication Foundation* (Apress, 2011)

An endpoint consists of three components:

- **The address** of an endpoint is usually a physical network address or a URI object. In complex scenarios, the address carries additional information stored in the headers and in the identity.

- **The binding** identifies the service metadata type. In the binding element you specify how the data will be transported to the external world (TCP, HTTP, etc.) and how the communication for that specific binding will be orchestrated.

- **The description** is handled by the `ContractDescription` class, in which you describe the service operations and the service messages. With the behaviors collection you can extend the service structure and behavior by overriding the default settings.

The Service and the Client

The service, in order to be visible, has to be exposed by an endpoint, which describes the way the messages will be sent and the way the service will behave. Of course, an endpoint needs a *host*, something that can make the endpoint visible and accessible to the external world.

In the `ServiceDescription` class, you can describe the endpoints that will be used by the service and the service behaviors. This information can be manually added to a service using the `svcutil.exe` .NET utility or by changing the structure of the configuration file of the application that is hosting the WCF service. If you don't supply this information, the WCF runtime will do it with some default values.

In the same way, the `ChannelService` class is used to describe endpoints, behaviors, and types used and hosted by the client WCF component. The main difference is that a `Service` can host more than one endpoint channel while a `ChannelService` is able to expose only one endpoint that will be used for the communication.

You'll find more information about service and channels at `msdn.microsoft.com/library/ms729840.aspx`.

A Sample WCF Project

Now let's create a simple WCF application in order to better understand how to work with this technology.

Open Visual Studio 2010 and select New Project ➤ Visual C# ➤ WCF. You'll see a dialog like the one in Figure 14-2.

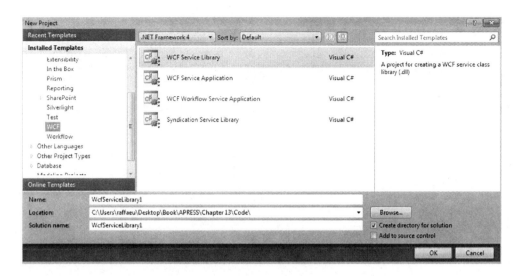

Figure 14-2. WCF project types in Visual Studio 2010

You can choose from four different project types:

- **WCF Service Library:** With this project type you can create an isolated assembly (.dll) that contains a set of WCF services that can be hosted in a WCF web application or in a Windows Service.

- **WCF Service Application:** This template creates a new ASP.NET web application that allows you to host and distribute WCF services within the project or in an external WCF service library project.

- **WCF Workflow Service Application:** With this project type you can create new WCF services that can interact with Window Workflow Foundation 4 (WF 4).

- **Syndication Service Library:** This template creates services to host syndication feeds in standard formats like RSS, ATOM, and so on.

In the dialog box, select the second option, WCF Service Application. Name the project SampleApplication and press OK. Visual Studio will create a new ASP.NET web site to host, by default, WCF services.

Take a look at the project structure that the WCF application template creates; you'll see three files in the root folder:

- `IService1.cs` represents the `ServiceContract` information used by WCF to host the service.

- `Service1.svc` implements the `IService1` interface and contains the concrete implementation of the service contract interface.

- `Web.config` describes the endpoint and the behaviors available in this WCF web application.

The WCF Test Client Utility

Now, if you press F5, Visual Studio will build the project and open the browser pointing to the project's default service address, using a web address like http://localhost:1167/Service1.svc, which will show an information page used by WCF to describe the default behavior of a WCF service.

If your browser is not showing this page, you can change the behavior of the web application by right-clicking the WCF project and selecting Properties, then changing the settings as shown in Figure 14-3.

Figure 14-3. *Web settings for a WCF project*

If you press F5 again, you should see a new application called WCFTestClient, which is also available from the .NET by typing WCFTestClient.exe in the command prompt window. Within this WCF client application you can run and test your services without having to create a custom client application.

Figure 14-4 shows you how the WCFTestClient UI should appear after you run the SampleApplication project for the first time.

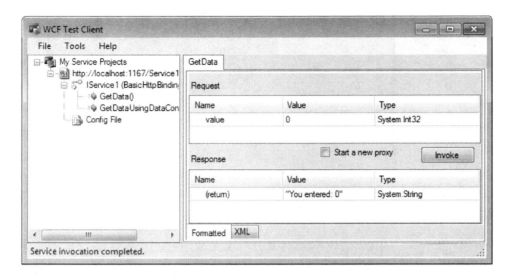

Figure 14-4. *The* `WCFTestClient.exe` *application running in a WCF project*

If you double-click one of the methods exposed by the default endpoint and available in the left-side treeview, the test client application will create a new tab on the right that allows you to invoke the method and see the results. For example, you can enter a number like 3 and the service will return the message "You entered: 3". You can use this UI to test the major parts of your services. Of course, you can't use this to test complex UI services where one method requires a complex `DataContract` as an input parameter, for example.

Customize the Sample Service

Now you have a service that runs and that exposes two default methods, so it's time to create your own service and try to expose something, for example a small object that includes some data.

To start, delete the existing `IService1.cs` and `Service1.svc` files from the current project; then select Add New Item from the project context menu and choose to create a new WCF Service from the Web section. Name the service `PersonService.svc` and press OK.

The configuration file has not been touched yet because with WCF 4 you can use the default configuration that Visual Studio provides, which allows us to run the service.

You should now have two new files in the root folder of your WCF application, one named `IPersonService.cs` and one named `PersonService.svc`. The first will contain the contracts (methods) you'll expose with WCF and the second will contain the concrete implementation of these contracts.

Before even starting to write and implement the service's methods, you need to create a new object that will be serialized (translated into an understandable XML message) by this service.

In the project root, create a new folder and call it Services, then create another root folder and call it DataContracts. Now move the `IPersonService.cs` and `PersonService.svc` files into the Services folder and add a new class called `PersonContract` to the DataContracts folder. The solution should look like the one in Figure 14-5.

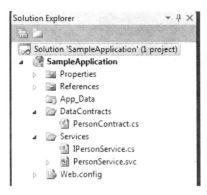

Figure 14-5. The SampleApplication project structure

Working with DataContracts

If you plan to share an object between the service and the client, like the PersonContract class, you need to explain to WCF how this object should be translated into an XML message and more precisely, how it should be serialized. For example, the PersonContract class may expose some properties and behaviors that can't be serialized while it may have some properties that must be shared between service and client.

Listing 14-1 shows the final PersonContract file.

Listing 14-1. The PersonContract Class

```csharp
using System.Runtime.Serialization;

namespace SampleApplication.DataContracts
{
    [DataContract]
    public class PersonContract
    {
        public int ID { get; set; }

        [DataMember]
        public string FirstName { get; set; }

        [DataMember]
        public string LastName { get; set; }

        public string ShowFullName()
        {
            return string.Format("{0} {1}", this.LastName, this.FirstName);
        }
    }
}
```

Listing 14-1 has a class called **PersonContract** that's decorated with a new attribute called [DataContract]; you use this attribute to inform WCF that the class can be shared between the service and the client and that it can be serialized in the default way. If you plan to add additional information to the serialization process, you can use one of the properties exposed by the data contract class, as in the code in Listing 14-2. In this case, the code tells WCF that when the **PersonContract** class is serialized in the client, the new class name should be **Person**, not **PersonContract**, and that the new namespace will be **SampleNamespace**.

Listing 14-2. Extended PersonContract Class

```
[DataContract(IsReference = false, Name = "Person", Namespace = "SampleNamespace")]
public class PersonContract
{
    [DataMember]
    public string FirstName { get; set; }
}
```

The code then decorates some properties using the [DataMember] attribute, which is used like the [DataContract] attribute to tell the WCF runtime to serialize this information. Also, if the ID property is marked with the public attribute, because it does not have the decoration to serialize it, when you share the PersonContract class, this property will not be visible in the serialized result. Moreover, the method ShowFullName will not be visible because WCF can serialize only properties and fields but not methods of any type, for obvious reasons. The IsReference attribute determines how objects are serialized. You can find information on the IsReference property at msdn.microsoft.com/en-us/library/system.runtime.serialization.datacontractattribute.isreference.aspx as well as at msdn.microsoft.com/en-us/library/cc656708.aspx

The [DataMember] attribute has some additional properties for customizing how the properties should look in the final result.

Take a look at msdn.microsoft.com/library/ms730035.aspx for more information about these and other customizations of the DataContract and DataMember attributes.

Add Methods to the Service

Now that you have an object you can share, you need to create a new method in the service that will be used to share this information from the service to the client. Open the **IPersonService.cs** interface file and change it as shown in Listing 14-3.

Listing 14-3. PersonService Modification

```
using System.ServiceModel;
using SampleApplication.DataContracts;

namespace SampleApplication.Services
{
    [ServiceContract]
    public interface IPersonService
    {
```

```
        [OperationContract]
        void AddPerson(PersonContract personContract);

        [OperationContract]
        bool HasPerson(PersonContract personContract);

        [OperationContract]
        PersonContract GetPerson(int id);
    }
}
```

Using the [ServiceContract] attribute, the code defines a new service that will be exposed by WCF. The attribute is used by WCF to understand and describe the service; in fact, this attribute also exposes additional properties that can be used to customize the way the service should look.

The [OperationContract] attribute is used to describe an operation that's available in the service and can be called by the client; if the operation described needs a complex object like the PersonContract as an input parameter or returns one as a method result, this object has to be decorated with the DataContract attribute in order to be used by the WCF runtime. Simple types like int, Guid, string, etc. are all known entities in the various specifications so they don't need to be marked as a DataContract in order to be serialized with WCF.

Now, let's open the PersonContract.svc file. You need to implement the previous methods as well as to instantiate a private collection of PersonContract objects that will act as a repository for the sample application. See Listing 14-4.

Listing 14-4. *The PersonService.svc Customization*

```
using System;
using System.Collections.Generic;
using System.Linq;
using System.ServiceModel;
using SampleApplication.DataContracts;

namespace SampleApplication.Services
{
    [ServiceBehavior(InstanceContextMode = InstanceContextMode.Single)]
    public class PersonService : IPersonService
    {
        private readonly List<PersonContract> persons = new List<PersonContract>();

        #region Implementation of IPersonService

        public void AddPerson(PersonContract personContract)
        {
            persons.Add(personContract);
        }

        public bool HasPerson(PersonContract personContract)
        {
            return persons.Contains(personContract);
        }
```

```
public PersonContract GetPerson(int id)
{
    return persons.Where(person => person.ID == id).FirstOrDefault();
}

#endregion
    }
}
```

The only thing in this code that you haven't seen before is the behavior attribute used in the class declaration to describe the behavior of this service's implementation. In this case you want, the first time the service is called, the WCF service runtime to handle one and only one instance of this class for all the sessions that call it. In this way, the collection of persons will be able to handle all persons in a single container.

■ **Note** Of course the code is trivial. The idea is just to show you how to handle a single collection of persons in one place. In a production environment you'll never have a singleton WCF service that will never dispose of its resources! In the Singleton pattern, the service instance is always alive and the resources used by the instance are never disposed. In terms of performance, memory, and resources, this can be a very bad approach that I do not recommend.

Now, before you can run this service, you need to change the web project properties you modified in the initial project setup by specifying the new path for the `PersonSevice.svc` service class. After that you can press F5 and you should be able to run and test these three new methods in the `WCFTestClient` utility. You can run the `WcfTestClient.exe` utility and edit the complex type from there.

Customize the Way the Service Will Behave

If you have ever worked with a .NET web application, like ASP.NET or ASP Web Services, you may have already noticed that the WCF application structure is very much like a normal ASP.NET web application. Of course, the differences are big in terms of technology, but there's still a configuration file called `Web.config` that you can use to customize the behavior and structure of the service.

But, if you don't already know the correct XML structure of an endpoint, a service contract, and a behavior, this step can be very painful!

No worries. If you plan to modify something in a WCF application, you can simply right-click on the project file in the Solution Explorer panel and select **Edit WCF Configuration**. Or, you can open the .NET command prompt and start `svcconfigeditor.exe`, or call it from the Visual Studio 2010 Tools menu by selecting the WCF Service Configuration Editor option.

Open the appropriate `Web.config` file in this utility and you should be able to access all the features of WCF that can be configured. Figure 14-6 shows the main windows of the utility used to customize the service by creating new endpoints using different channels (TCP, WS, etc.) or by adding new behaviors.

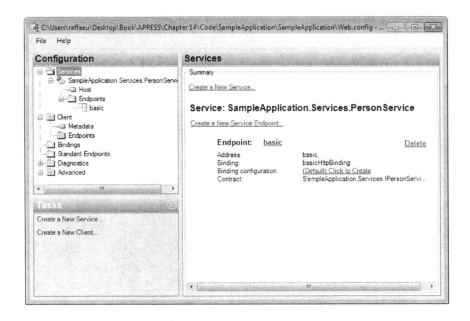

Figure 14-6. *Customizing a WCF service*

As soon as you are done with the changes, just select the Save command and close the file and you will see, right away, the changes in the `Web.config` file. This method can be also a useful way for you to learn how the WCF `ServiceContract` attributes are persisted in the `Web.config` file.

Test the Sample Service

You created the service and executed it by pressing F5. The `WCFTestClient` application starts up and you can call the sample methods exposed by the service, but this doesn't mean you've really tested the service.

To be sure that the WCF application is working as expected, create a new project of type `Test` in the same solution and call it `SampleApplication.Fixtures`. In this unit test project, you can verify that the project can be hosted and called as expected.

Delete the existing `UnitTest1.cs` file, add a new basic unit test object, and call it `PersonServiceFixture`. You'll use this unit test to verify that the endpoint works correctly and that the WCF service is hosted properly on IIS.

First you need to deploy the service to an IIS location as you did for the reporting service application in Chapter 10 and for the ClickOnce deployment in Chapter 11. You can do this by clicking on the `Properties` context menu of the WCF sample application project file, then clicking on the Web tab and choosing to run the project on a specific IIS server. You can also just deploy the project using the deploy context menu every time the project is ready to be deployed. In this case, let's keep the project on the local IIS and use the Web tab of the Visual Studio properties page. Remember that if you are running Windows 7 or Windows Vista on your development machine, you must also install the IIS 6 compatibility component and the IIS 6 management console using the Windows Control Panel. Note that if you're running Windows 7, you have to run Visual Studio with administrator privileges in order to be able to deploy a WCF application on the local IIS. You can do that by right-clicking the VS icon and selecting Run as Administrator.

You can test that everything has been successfully installed by selecting the Create Virtual Directory command on your Visual Studio web panel page and be sure that the SampleApplication is running on the local IIS by pressing F5 (see Figure 14-7). You shouldn't see the port number in the URL anymore.

Figure 14-7. SampleApplication running under local IIS

Figure 14-7 shows that the SampleApplication is now running on the local IIS as the port number has been removed from the localhost path.

Add Service Reference

You tell the Test project that it will work with the sample WCF application by adding a service reference to it. This step can be accomplished by right-clicking the Test project and choosing Add Service Reference. This brings up a dialog like the one shown in Figure 14-8, where you can search for and identify WCF services.

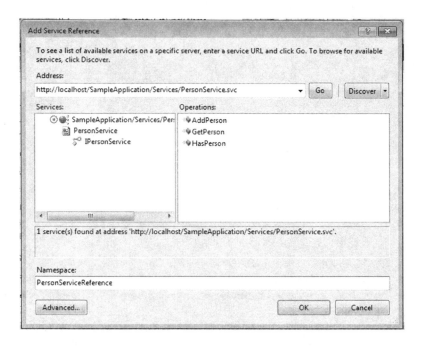

Figure 14-8. *The Add Service Reference window*

This dialog lets you add or discover WCF services available on your current network. If you don't find the service you need, you can manually add a URL in the Address TextBox and specify the .svc service path. You also have to provide the namespace that will be used in the client project and then press OK. When you do, Visual Studio will create all the necessary code for instantiating the proxies WCF needs to run the service locally. This information will be retrieved from the .svc service object by reading the attributes DataContract and ServiceContract used previously to create the sample service.

Test the Endpoint

Let's write a sample test method that will try to open the currently configured endpoint and verify that everything is active and working.

Listing 14-5 shows the test method used to verify that the WCF service is working properly.

Listing 14-5. *Test the WCF Service Connection*

```
using System.ServiceModel;
using Microsoft.VisualStudio.TestTools.UnitTesting;
using SampleApplication.Fixtures.PersonServiceReference;
```

```
namespace SampleApplication.Fixtures
{
    [TestClass]
    public class PersonServiceFixture
    {
        [TestMethod]
        public void AssertThatTheServiceCanRun()
        {
            PersonServiceClient client = new PersonServiceClient();
            client.Open();
            Assert.IsNotNull(client);
            Assert.IsTrue(client.State == CommunicationState.Opened);
            client.Close();
            Assert.IsTrue(client.State == CommunicationState.Closed);
        }
    }
}
```

This listing creates a new instance of the `PersonServiceClient` object, which is a proxy that Visual Studio creates when you add the service reference. Next the code tries to open the default channel using the default endpoint that Visual Studio created in the `app.config` file when you added the service reference to the test project. You want to test that the endpoint can be created, then that the endpoint can be opened and closed, and finally that the methods exposed can be used.

You should test each method and be sure that the result is what you're expecting. For example, the method in Listing 14-6 will test that the service is correctly adding a new `PersonContract` object.

Listing 14-6. *Test the AddPerson Method*

```
[TestMethod]
public void AssertThatCanAddANewPerson()
{
    using (PersonServiceClient client = new PersonServiceClient())
    {
        client.Open();
        Person person = new Person {FirstName = "Raffaele", LastName = "Garofalo"};
        client.AddPerson(person);
        bool result = client.HasPerson(person);
        Assert.IsTrue(result);
    }
}
```

In this case, the test will fail because in this trivial code you need to implement custom `Equals` and `GetHashCode` methods in the `PersonContract` object; otherwise the code will look for a different reference type object and it will always return false.

You can also consider testing all the other methods in order to be sure that the client application is getting the correct results from the WCF service methods.

Conclusion and Considerations

In this first part of this chapter you saw how WCF works, how it can be configured, and how it can be tested and used in a client application. The topic is complex and it really deserves an entire book to itself. So if your plan is to move your WPF application into the SOA world, I recommend you read one or both of the books mentioned in the footnote earlier in this chapter.

An additional consideration is about the domain you'll host using WCF. If you plan to work with WCF, you have to make your domain "serializable." This process is pretty straightforward if you are working with Entity Framework, as it makes the entity serializable. But you may still encounter some architectural issues in serializing your domain model; for example, some of the business logic code may not be easy to translate into XML.

The debate about serializing or not serializing the domain model has been exercising the SOA community for a while. According to the purist approach, you should have two different domains, one exposed in the client and one in the server. This approach should be used because the domain should contain the application business logic and, as I already said, in NET you can't serialize a method so you can't serialize the business logic.

Integrate WCF into the TimeTracker Application

Now it's time to open the TimeTracker Visual Studio solution and integrate the WCF technology into it. The main role of this technology in TimeTracker will be to add further availability to the TimeTracker domain. You will distribute the domain over the network using WCF and Data Services, a new component in NET 4 and Visual Studio 2010 that works with WCF technology.

Open the TimeTracker application and add to the solution a new WCF web application project with the name APRESS.TimeTracker.ServiceLayer, then configure the service to run on your local IIS using the same process as in the first part of this chapter. Call the application folder in IIS TimeTrackerService.

Now delete the default IService1.cs and Service.svc files and add a new WCF Data Service file; name it TimeTrackerDataService.svc and press OK.

The next step is to add a reference to the Entity Framework project in the WCF web application. You can do that by right-clicking the WCF web application and selecting the Add Service Reference menu item, then choosing the Business Layer project from the Projects tab.

WCF Data Service

The WCF Data Service is an extension of WCF that allows you to expose your data using the oData protocol, a protocol used to transform operations exposed by WCF into a representational state transfer (REST). You can think of a WCF data service as an alternative to the classic Repository object, exposed by a SOAP service.

The advantage of using the WCF data service is that the same operation, for example a GetAppointments method, can be used by both a WPF application and a simple web browser. An additional advantage is the ability to share the "code" of the data layer, the domain model, and the business logic in one single, big repository.

Of course a technology like the WCF data service comes with a significant risk of exposing critical information over the Web, and for this reason the WCF data service allows you to fully control access to only some specific items of the domain model.

To create a new WCF data service you need to modify the .svc service you created using the WCF data service template, as in Listing 14-7.

Listing 14-7. Using the WCF Data Service to Expose Appointments

```
using System.Data.Services;
using System.Data.Services.Common;
using APRESS.TimeTracking.BusinessLayer;

namespace APRESS.TimeTracker.ServiceLayer
{
    public class TimeTrackerDataService : DataService<TimeTrackerModelContainer>
    {
        public static void InitializeService(DataServiceConfiguration config)
        {
            config.UseVerboseErrors = true;
            config.DataServiceBehavior.MaxProtocolVersion = DataServiceProtocolVersion.V2;
            config.SetEntitySetAccessRule(
                "Employees",
                EntitySetRights.AllRead | EntitySetRights.AllWrite);
            config.SetEntitySetAccessRule(
                "Customers",
                EntitySetRights.AllRead | EntitySetRights.AllWrite);
        }
    }
}
```

The first thing to notice in the listing is the generics object `DataService<T>`, where the generics `T` object has to be of type entity container. This tells the data service object that the `TimeTrackerModelContainer` entity container will be used to host the corresponding domain model with the WCF data service.

Next the listing implements the code in the `InitializeService` method, which is called every time you start the WCF data service. This method receives, as an input parameter, the current configuration that can be used to customize the way the WCF service will act.

For example, the previous code specifies to WCF that you want a verbose log if an error occur and that you want to make only the `Employee` and the `Customer` entity collections visible, with read and write access.

Now, in order to have this service work properly, you need to add the Entity Framework connection string tag inside the `Web.config` file as you did in the `app.config` file for the WPF application. Listing 14-8 shows the `Web.config` file modified for the entity framework configuration.

Listing 14-8. `Web.config` Connection String Configuration

```
<?xml version="1.0"?>
<configuration>
  <connectionStrings>
    <add name="TimeTrackerModelContainer" connectionString="metadata=res:↩
//*/TimeTrackerModel.csdl|res://*/TimeTrackerModel.ssdl|res:↩
//*/TimeTrackerModel.msl;provider=System.Data.SqlClient;provider connection string=↩
&quot;Data Source=.\SQLEXPRESS;Initial Catalog=TimeTrackerDatabase;Integrated↩
 Security=True;MultipleActiveResultSets=True&quot;" providerName="System.Data.EntityClient"
/>
  </connectionStrings>
```

```
  <system.web>
    <compilation debug="true" targetFramework="4.0" />
  </system.web>
  <system.serviceModel>
    <behaviors>
      <serviceBehaviors>
        <behavior>
          <serviceMetadata httpGetEnabled="true" />
          <serviceDebug includeExceptionDetailInFaults="true" />
        </behavior>
      </serviceBehaviors>
    </behaviors>
    <serviceHostingEnvironment multipleSiteBindingsEnabled="true"↵
 aspNetCompatibilityEnabled="true" />
  </system.serviceModel>
  <system.webServer>
    <modules runAllManagedModulesForAllRequests="true" />
  </system.webServer>
</configuration>
```

Now you can open your web browser and navigate to the oData service created earlier using `http://localhost/TimeTrackerService/timetrackerdataservice.svc`. You should see an empty web page with the name of the current entity set hosted by the data service, which includes `Employees` and `Customers`.

Navigate the Data Using oData Queries

The data hosted by an oData service can be navigated using the oData syntax. For example, if you want to navigate the list of current employees you can type this address in your web browser:

`http://localhost/TimeTrackerService/timetrackerdataservice.svc/Employees`

while if you plan to retrieve the information for the employee with an ID equal to 8 you can type this address:

`http://localhost/TimeTrackerService/timetrackerdataservice.svc/Employees(8)`

If in the method exposed in the Listing 14-7 you add additional entities, like `Role`, `Address`, `Appointment`, and so on, you can filter the information using oData so that with the following code you can, for example, retrieve all the roles associated with a specific employee:

`http://localhost/TimeTrackerService/timetrackerdataservice.svc/Employees(8)/Roles`

and so on.

With oData, you can also query the data as if you were using LINQ. Let's say, for example, that you want to retrieve all the `Roles` with the `ID` greater than 20, you can write this `oData` URL:

`http://localhost/TimeTrackerService/timetrackerdataservice.svc/Roles?$filter=Id gt 20`

The syntax for using the oData query engine is to add the `?$filter` keyword after the URL.

If you want a better look at how the oData syntax works, you'll find a useful page at `msdn.microsoft.com/library/dd728283.aspx`. The page explains how to create simple queries using classic keywords that you can also use with LINQ or T-SQL to query the data directly from the entity framework container.

Integrate the WCF Data Service in WPF

Now I want to show you how you can integrate the WCF Data Service in an existing application, like TimeTracker, so you can remove all the dependencies from the data layer and business layer components and make your application more loosely coupled from the business logic.

The first step is to add a reference in the WPF project to the WCF data service just created. To do so, you need to add a new service reference to the TimeTracker application and point to the specific `.svc` service as Figure 14-9 shows.

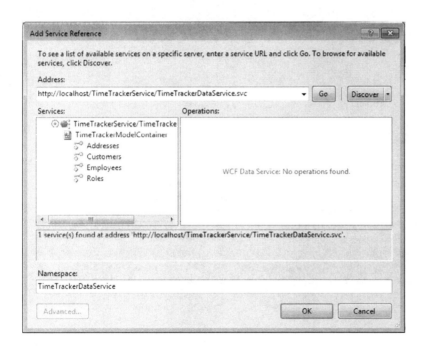

Figure 14-9. *Service reference dialog for the WCF data service*

Now that you've added the reference to the WCF data service, you can have full access (depending on the read and write security permissions you previously set up for the entities) to the domain model from the WCF service. That said, you may wonder now how you can access the entities from WCF instead of accessing them from the business layer.

The syntax is very close to what you just saw because the WCF data service also lets you use LINQ syntax to query the entities. But in the ViewModel, instead of using the repository object, you'll use the WCF service.

Open the `EmployeeListViewModel` and change the method used to search the employees as shown in Listing 14-9.

Listing 14-9. Search the Employees Using WCF oData Service

```
private void SearchEmployees()
{
    Uri svcUri = new Uri("http://localhost/TimeTrackerService/timetrackerdataservice.svc");
    Context context = new Context(svcUri);
    var result =
        (from e in context.Employees
        where e.FullName.FirstName.Contains(SearchCriteria)
        || e.FullName.LastName.Contains(SearchCriteria)
        select e).ToList();
    //List<Employee> result = repository.SearchEmployees(SearchCriteria);
    if (result == null || result.Count == 0)
    {
        dialogService.ShowAlert("No Employees found.", "There are no Employees using the↵
    following criteria.");
        return;
    }
    Collection.Clear();
    foreach (Employee employee in result)
    {
        Collection.Add(new EmployeeDetailsViewModel(employee, container));
    }
}
```

With this approach you first create a new URI object that contains the full path to the `.svc` data service file; then you can create a new instance of the data service context object and use it in the same way you'd use a classic Entity Framework data context object. Note that the point of this code is simply to show you how the `ObjectContext` can be used. In a real application, however, you'd hide the service path in a configuration variable to make the application more "configurable."

This example associates the current data service context object with the alias `Context`; this step can be accomplished by using the following statement at the beginning of the view model class file:
`using Context = APRESS.TimeTracker.TimeTrackerDataService.TimeTrackerModelContainer;`

In this way with few lines of code you switched the application from using the data layer created previously to using a global WCF service layer.

WCF Security

In this chapter you saw how you can distribute information over the network using WCF, and you saw how powerful but at the same time dangerous it can be if you expose the wrong component over the network using SOA. If you expose the wrong component, unwanted access to your SOA service may cause damage to your internal infrastructure. For example, an intruder accessing your TimeTracker WCF Data Service could cause a loss of the database data!

In this chapter, as already pointed out, we can't analyze WCF in depth . But it is essential to say something about security and how you can create a secure service structure using WCF. Please use this section as an overview of how the WCF security mechanism works, but remember that if you plan to work with WCF, you'll have to explore this powerful technology in a lot more depth! You can find additional resources related to the implementation of security in WCF at `msdn.microsoft.com/library/ms734736.aspx`.

In WCF, you can handle security in different ways. For example you can:

- Secure the endpoint that is exposing the service methods by introducing an authentication process in order to share the data only with authenticated users.

- Verify the integrity of the message in order to be sure that the message has not been "hacked" during its transmission.

- Encrypt the messages or transmit them through a secure channel (HTTPS) using a certificate so that the sender and the receiver will be the only ones able to translate and exchange the message.

- Provide authorization mechanisms for the code so that it can't be used for attacks by artful "black hats."

Security Requirements

Before even starting to tackle the security aspects of a WCF service, you need to understand what the requirements of your application are in terms of security and how you want to handle them. For example, an intranet WCF service that will never be exposed outside the company network can generally be deployed with a less complex security implementation than a service exposed over the World Wide Web. After all, if the service exists only "inside" the company network, it will be more difficult for someone outside the network to access the service and use it in a harmful way.

When you tackle security in WCF, you should divide your application requirements into three different aspects:

- *Authentication:* You need to analyze how you want to authenticate the users and the external components that will access your service. For example, you may consider authenticating the sender and receiver so that nobody "in the middle" of the transmission path will be able to see and change messages.

- *Authorization:* You can specify what can be executed in the service and by the service, and what can't be done. This adds an additional layer of security in case the service is hacked.

- *Integrity:* you can use certificates to encrypt the content of your messages, creating a more secure structure.

Bindings

The second step in determining your security requirements is to understand where the messages will be transmitted in order to decide what type of endpoint you will use. For the Web, SOAP is preferred over HTTP due to its standardized structure. For an intranet application, I prefer to use TCP with binary endpoints as I've found this to be faster in terms of performance.

Each binding in WCF can be configured in one of the following ways:

- *None.* Turns security off.

- *Transport.* Uses transport security for mutual authentication and message protection.

- *Message.* Uses message security for mutual authentication and message protection.

- *Both.* Allows you to supply settings for transport and message-level security (only MSMQ supports this).

- *TransportWithMessageCredential.* Credentials are passed with the message, and message protection and server authentication are provided by the transport layer.

- *TransportCredentialOnly.* Client credentials are passed with the transport layer and no message protection is applied.

Each binding technique has its own mechanism for implementing the security option you've chosen and it is part of WCF to implement security in any of the possible binding combination.

Provide the Credentials

It's also important to consider how you plan to transport the security credentials from the client to the server. Depending on the type of security implementation you've decided on, and depending on the endpoint you want to use to expose the service, you may be able to use one of the following credentials types:

- None

- Windows

- UserName

- Certificate

- IssuedToken

Authenticate and Authorize the Code

The final step is to authenticate the user that is calling the service and be sure it is authorized to execute a specific step. For example, suppose you have a service that exposes a set of methods, one of which is used to delete data from a database. You want to be sure that the delete method can be executed only by an authenticated Windows user who's recognized by the remote SQL Server database as a user who can delete data.

Authentication in WCF can be obtained in three different ways, depending on how it has been configured:

- *Process Identity;* Service operations are executed under the process identity of the service host. For ASP.NET hosts, this is usually the ASP.NET account. For self-hosting, it may be a different service account. The process identity is the Windows account that governs what the service code can do at runtime when attempting to access protected resources such as the database, registry, or file system.

- *Token Authentication:* Runtime identities, security principals and authorization policies also play an important role in the WCF security story.

- *Security Principal:* If you are familiar with traditional .NET role-based security, you know that there is a security principal attached to each executing thread. That security principal holds the caller's identity, which may or may not be tied to a Windows account and its roles. Roles govern which operations can be executed by the authenticated user when traditional .NET role-based security is applied.

- *ServiceSecurityContext:* This provides runtime access to other relevant information about the security context for a service operation. The `ServiceSecurityContext` is a runtime type that includes identities, a set of claims, and authorization policies. This information can be used to apply a more fine-grained security strategy specifically for services.

Figure 14-10 illustrates how WCF processes a secure request by applying authentication and authorization on a specific identity.

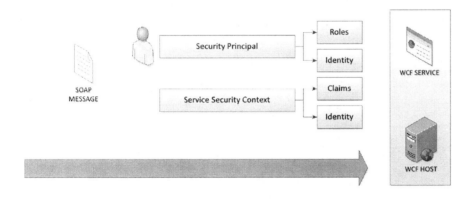

Figure 14-10. *Authentication and authorization in WCF*

Summary

In this final chapter you saw how to make the WPF TimeTracker application more loosely coupled by implementing a SOA approach, which was done, in our case, using Windows Communication Foundation.

WCF is a flexible web technology used to design distributed enterprise applications where the business logic and more generally a specific component or set of components need to be shared over the network to many clients and different applications.

The mechanism of WCF is complex and requires dedicated study, but the following statement summarizes the basics:

In WCF there are two major actors. One is a host that is in charge of exposing one or more services using one or more endpoints; the endpoint specifies how the data should be exposed by the service. The second actor is the client or receiver, a component or other piece of software able to open a dialog with the Host and call the methods exposed by the service.

In conclusion, you can use WCF instead of distributing the data layer and the business layer to the client, but if you plan to do that:

- You should always call the service using a multithreading approach (as you saw in Chapter 13) because there may be a substantial lag between the service call and the service answer.

- If you plan to host your data layer using a WCF service, consider including some security mechanism in order to prevent unauthorized access to and possibly modification of your data.

- Bear in mind that the business logic hosted by the domain model won't be available any more in the presentation layer, because it is now hidden by the WCF data layer.

Index

MaxHeight, 100

media integration layer (milcore), 13

messages, 289–290

metdata, 290

MethodNameCompleted event, 287

Microsoft Expression Blend, 1, 8, 21–22, 43–60

  animations, 51–53

  behaviors, 67–69

  creating mock-up and prototyping, 62–70

  design-time data, 57–58

  drawing, 48–51

    shapes and objects, 49–50

    text and text effects, 50–51

  dummy data in, 65

  hardware requirements, 43–44

  mockups, 59–60

  new features, 44

  New Project window, 46

  overview, 43–44

  SketchFlow, 59–60

  startup page, 45

  styling and template controls, 53–57

  workspace, 45–48

    panels, 46–48

    resizeable regions, 47

Microsoft Expression Studio, Ultimate version, 43

Microsoft Reporting Services. *See* SQL Server Reporting Services; reports

Microsoft Unity, 80

middle tier, 28

milcore, 13

mockups, 21, 59–60, 62–70

Model

  binding to ViewModel, 271

  in MVVM pattern, 269–271

Model Browser panel, 128

Model View Controller (MVC) pattern, 262

Model View Presenter (MVP) pattern, 191, 262

  Passive View, 263–268

  Supervising Controller, 266–267

  when to use, 268

Model View ViewModel (MVVM) pattern, 22, 26, 171, 191, 195, 261–262, 268–273

  exposing the commands, 272–273

  INotifyPropertyChanged interface, 269–271

modifying objects, 146–150

MouseDragElementBehavior, 67

MSDN Ultimate subscription, 43

MSTest, 209, 212–216

multi-core processors (CPUs), 275

multithreading, 275–288

  asynchronous operations, 280–282

  code, in .NET framework, 276–287

Q

queries, 114, 238–239

Query Designer window, 234–235

R

raster images, 48

.rdlc file extension, 227

.rdlc reports, 228

ReceiveWeakEvent method, 202

Rectangle control, 64

Rectangle-Sketch control, 64

red-green-refactor, 210, *See also* Test
Driven Development

references, 36–37, 39–41

region groups, 47

relationships, between entities, 128–134

RelayCommand, 196–198

ReportParameter array, 247

ReportProgress method, 287

reports, 227–249

creating dataset, 233–236

creating datasource, 232–233

designing, 236–237

detailed view, 237–240

displaying, in WPF view, 242–244

footer, editing, 236

header, editing, 236

introduction to, 227

loading

detailed view, 246–248

list view, 244–245

with parameters, 238–240

SQL Server Reporting Services (SSRS),
228–48

configuring, 228–231

creating dataset, 233–236

creating datasource, 232–233

creating reports, 231–232

designing report, 236–237

detailed view, 237–241

hosting, in a WPF control, 241–246

TimeTracker, 231–241

ReportViewer control, 227–228, 241–246

ReportViewModel, 246

Repository class, 117, 151

Repository object, 304

Repository pattern, 117–119, 121, 151–158

adding role, 152–153

additional methods, 157–158

deleting role, 153–154

GetAll roles, 155–156

GetById method, 156–157

IRepository interface, 151–152

updating role, 154–155

RepositoryBase class, 151

RepositoryBase object, 152

representational state transfer (REST), 304

RequerySuggested event, 200

resource dictionary, 2, 88–91, 167–168

Resource property, 14, 88

ResourceDictionary.xaml file, 97

resources, 87–88

REST support, in WCF, 290

Resume method, 280

RichTextBox, 50

Role domain entity, 122–127

Role entity, 128–130, 152

RoleRepository class, 152, 157

RoleRepositoryFixture test class, 152

RoleRespository delete method, 222

roles

    adding, 152–153

    deleting, 153–154

    GetAll method, 155–156

    GetById method, 156–157

    updating, 154–155

root elements, 2–3

RoutedCommand class, 177, 191–195, 204

RoutedCommand object, 272

RowDefinition property, 102

RunWorkerAsync method, 286

RunWorkerCompleted event, 287

RunWorkerCompletedEventArgs event, 287

■ S

sample data, 44, 57

Samples tab, Expression Blend, 45

SAP Crystal Reports, 227

SaveChanges() method, 140, 143

schedule controls, 108–109

SearchCommand, 205–206

SearchMethod, 205

security

    bindings, 309

    certificates, 252–253, 258

    ClickOnce, 252–253

    Code Access Security, 253–254

    credentials, 310

    TimeTracker application, 259

    WCF, 308–311

security principal, 311

SELECT statement, 240

self-closed elements, 3

self-reference relationships, 129

self-signed certificates, 252

separation of concerns concept, 27

sequential execution, of code, 276

[ServiceContract] attribute, 298

ServiceDescription class, 292

service-oriented applications, WCF and, 290

Service-Oriented Architecture (SOA), 28, 289

W

WCF. *See* Windows Communication Foundation (WCF)

WCF Data Service, 304–308

WCF Service Application, 293

WCF Service Library, 293

WCF Workflow Service Application, 293

weak event pattern, 202

WeakEvent, 202

WeakEventListener, 202–203

WeakEventManager object, 202–203

Web performances test, 216

web services, 289

WHERE SQL statement, 146

Window object, 2, 286

Window root element, 2

Windows Azure AppFabric, 290

Windows Communication Foundation (WCF), 28, 289–311

    adding methods to services, 297–299

    adding service references, 301, 302

    architecture, 291–292

    creating service, 295

    customizing services, 295–300

    DataContracts, 296–297

    Data Service, 304–308

    endpoints, 291–292

    features, 290

    hosting domain for, 304

    integrating into TimeTracker application, 304–308

    interacting with, 289–312

    introduction to, 289–292

    project types, 293

    sample project, 292–304

    security, 308–311

    service and clients, 292

    test client utility, 294–295

    testing endpoints, 302–303

    testing services, 300–301

    uses of, 290

    web settings for, 294

Windows Forms control, 14, 241–246

Windows Forms ReportViewer control, 228

Windows Presentation Foundation (WPF), 1

    architecture, 13–17

        assemblies and CLR, 13–14

        milcore, 13

        PresentationCore, 13

        PresentationFramework, 13

        technologies, 14–17

    integrating WCF Data Service in, 307–308

    introduction to, 8–23

    themes, 97

    tools, 17–23

        additional, 22–23

CPSIA information can be obtained at www.ICGtesting.com

230322LV00006B/23-24/P